What people are saying about …

The Fresh Life Series

"I'm touched and blessed by Lenya and Penny's heart for His kingdom."

Kay Arthur, Bible teacher and
author of many best-selling Bible studies

"What a great way for women to learn to study the Bible: interesting stories, thought-provoking questions, and a life-changing approach to applying Scripture. Lenya and Penny provide a great method so women can succeed and grow spiritually in a short period of time. Kudos!"

Franklin Graham, president and CEO of Billy Graham
Evangelistic Association and Samaritan's Purse

"Skip and Lenya Heitzig have been friends of my wife, Cathe, and I for more than twenty years. Lenya loves to study God's Word and teach it to women in a way that is both exciting and accessible. I trust her latest book will be a blessing to you."

Greg Laurie, pastor and evangelist of Harvest Ministries

"Lenya and Penny's love for the Lord and knowledge of His Word uniquely equips them to help other women discover the pathway to God through these in-depth Bible studies."

Kay Smith, wife of Chuck Smith (Calvary Chapel)

"The Fresh Life Series is an insightful and in-depth look at God's Word. Through these Bible studies Lenya Heitzig and Penny Rose lead women to deeper intimacy with God."

K. P. Yohannan, president of Gospel for Asia

"Lenya and Penny have created another wonderful Bible study series that invites participants to spend time in God's Word and then see the Word come to fruition in their lives. What a blessing! These studies are perfect for small groups or personal daily devotions."

Robin Lee Hatcher, women's event speaker
and award-winning author

Live Deeply

The Fresh Life Series

Live Deeply: A Study in the Parables of Jesus

Live Fearlessly: A Study in the Book of Joshua

Live Intimately: Lessons from the Upper Room

Live Relationally: Lessons from the Women of Genesis

A 20-MINUTES-A-DAY STUDY

Live Deeply

A Study in the Parables of Jesus

Lenya Heitzig & Penny Rose

transforming lives together

LIVE DEEPLY
Published by David C. Cook
4050 Lee Vance View
Colorado Springs, CO 80918 U.S.A.

David C. Cook Distribution Canada
55 Woodslee Avenue, Paris, Ontario, Canada N3L 3E5

David C. Cook U.K., Kingsway Communications
Eastbourne, East Sussex BN23 6NT, England

The Web site addresses recommended throughout this book are
offered as a resource to you. These Web sites are not intended
in any way to be or imply an endorsement on the part of
David C. Cook, nor do we vouch for their content.

Additional material provided by Christy Willis.

ISBN 978-1-4347-9986-9
eISBN 978-1-4347-0025-4

Published in association with William K. Jensen Literary Agency
119 Bampton Court, Eugene, OR 97404

The Team: Terry Behimer, Karen Lee-Thorp, Amy Kiechlin, Jaci
Schneider, Caitlyn York, Susan Vannaman, and Sarah Schultz
Cover/Interior Design: ThinkPen Design, Greg Jackson

Printed in the United States of America

First Edition 2009

1 2 3 4 5 6 7 8 9 10

032509

With Gratitude

One of our favorite parables is that of the Pearl of Great Price. Pearls are created when translucent, concentric layers develop around a small object. Jewelers will tell you that a pearl's iridescence grows when fine and frequent layers of nacre cause light to dance across the gem's surface.

The authors recognize that their contribution to this Bible study called *Live Deeply: A Study in the Parables of Jesus* is but a small grain of sand. We have been surrounded by radiant women who have enhanced this study, making it shine brighter. Like a string of pearls, each has added their priceless gift.

Thanks to Helen Davidson, Kristi DuBay, Cheryl Fowler, Anna Jones, Colette Lutz, Dianne Sanborn, Patti Snodgrass, and Christy Willis for their literary contributions.

Thanks to Melanie Brown, Chris Borszcz, Annette Hoffman, Kimber James, Ruth Kimsey, Jan Mumy, Judy Payne, and Kelly Visca for their godly influence.

Contents

Lesson Nine

Lesson Ten

Introduction

LIVE DEEPLY

From an early age children beg, "Tell me a story." Most of the time we respond by telling them a story that teaches a lesson. If a child is prone to fibbing, we might tell the story of *The Boy Who Cried Wolf.* If a young adolescent is going through that "awkward" stage, we might recount the story of the ugly ducking that turned into a lovely swan. The parables are the stories that Jesus told. Filled with encouragement, rebuke, or exhortation, they challenged His followers to understand that they were not of this world. He was the King of another kingdom, a spiritual kingdom, and therefore they must *Live Deeply.*

THE SETTINGS

The parables of Jesus depict various settings. Some deal with the agricultural world, as in the Sower; others, like the Prodigal Son, involve human relationships. Most are kingdom parables, often beginning with the phrase "the kingdom of heaven is like," and teach the reader how heavenly citizens must behave. The original setting is important because it holds the key to the interpretation of the parable.

The parables of Jesus focus largely on one central point. Therefore, the primary question a Bible student must ask is, "What is the main lesson being taught?" Too often we attempt to discover what each object represents, but not every detail in the parables contains deep meaning. For instance, the predominant principle in the Good Samaritan reveals who our neighbors are and that we must show them compassion. Our neighbor? Anyone in need. The reader would expect that the priest and Levite, devout religious men, would have treated the wounded outcast with compassion. Instead, a despised foreigner cared for the victim, a man not of his own nationality, race, or religion. The moral of the story? We are exhorted to "go and do likewise" (Luke 10:37). As you study the parables, be sure to carefully note the setting and context of the story.

Author: Jesus

Audience: Christ's followers

Theme: The kingdom of heaven

Timeline: Probably between AD 28 and 30

Setting: Various places from the Sea of Galilee to the region of Capernaum to the city of Jerusalem

Scripture: "And He said to them, 'To you it has been given to know the mystery of the kingdom of God; but to those who are outside, all things come in parables'" (Mark 4:11).

THE STORIES

Biblical parables are not simply stories. They are divinely inspired, living words from the mouth of God. Jesus used metaphors and similes, making comparisons from the natural world to relate truths about the spiritual world. *Vine's Expository Dictionary* tells us that *parable* literally means to lay by the side or place one thing beside another in order to compare. Thus, in a parable one thing is placed beside another to bring a truth to life. Jesus was a keen observer of human life and the natural world, so His parables truly hit home in the hearts of His followers.

He did not exaggerate as in myths, make up imaginary creatures as in fairy tales, or use unnatural imagery like the talking animals in fables. By using realistic images and characters from everyday life, Christ's earthly illustrations offer divine lessons that resonate to this day. Madeleine L'Engle said, "Jesus was God who told stories." Lay the stories beside your own life, and see what truth Jesus has in store for you.

THE SECRETS

Parables, because they drew from everyday life, had huge impact on the audience. However, not everyone understood their hidden meaning, including the disciples. Once, they asked Jesus to explain what the parable of the Wheat and the Tares meant. The Lord went on to interpret the story's true intent. We discover that the parables had the uncanny ability to reveal God's truth to one person while concealing it from another.

Jesus Himself explained why He spoke in parables by quoting from Isaiah 6:9–10: "Go, and tell this people: 'Keep on hearing, but do not understand; keep on seeing, but do not perceive. Make the heart of this people dull, and their ears heavy, and shut their eyes; lest they see with their eyes, and hear with their ears, and understand with their heart, and return and be healed.'" *Nelson's Bible Dictionary* says, "Like a double-edged sword, they cut two ways—enlightening those who sought the truth and blinding those who were disobedient." Parables are a litmus test! They reveal whether ears are opened or closed; whether your heart is soft or hard; whether you are a friend or foe, disciple or deceiver.

THE SAVIOR

The famous expositor G. Campbell Morgan said, "In a sense Jesus Himself is a parable through whom God has revealed Himself supremely through His Son. The Son therefore becomes the picture, the parable, which being known and investigated, God Himself is found!"[1]

What's more important than the parables? The Person who told them! A statement's impact doesn't merely come from what is said but *who* has said it. During the 1980s, financial investors believed that "when E. F. Hutton talks … people listen." Of course we'd take these stories more seriously than any others because Jesus is the truth. These stories aren't by Tolkien or Twain, Dr. Seuss or Dr. Spock, Aesop or Aristotle. They are God telling His stories.

May you live deeply,
Lenya Heitzig and Penny Rose

How to Get the Most Out of This Study

Would you describe your life as abundant or redundant? The secret to truly living rather than merely languishing is found in God's Word. We know that God reveals Himself through His Word. That's why doing a Bible study like this is so vital—because God's Word has the power to do His work in our lives. It is the catalyst that revives your heart, renews your mind, and restores your soul. That helps make life worth living!

This particular Bible study focuses on the parables of Jesus. We'll listen to the very words of Jesus, the Master Storyteller. He told short, simple stories based on true-to-life experiences to communicate spiritual truths. He wanted His followers to know who God is, what His kingdom is like, and how His subjects should live. The simplest definition of a parable is "an earthly story with a heavenly meaning." Since it's our Savior telling us these stories, we must take them to heart. Each parable demands a response on our part. They're a call to action, a solicitation to change, a lesson to be applied. The King of the kingdom demands allegiance. The Master of the household expects obedience. The Shepherd of our souls bids us follow. If you're ready, let's get started ...

Each week of the study is divided into five days for your personal time with God. There are five elements to each day's lesson. They are designed to help you fully "live" as you apply the truths you learn to your life:

1. Lift up ... Here we ask you to "Lift up" prayers to God, asking Him to give you spiritual insight for the day.

2. Look at ... This portion of the study asks you to "Look at" the Scripture text, using inductive questions. These questions help you to discover *What are the facts?* You'll learn the basic who-what-when-where-how aspects of the passage as well as some of the important background material.

3. Learn about ... The "Learn about" sidebars correlate to specific questions in order to help you understand *What does this text mean?* These sidebar elements offer cultural insight, linguistic definitions, and biblical commentary.

4. Live out … These questions and exercises are designed to help you investigate *How should this change my life?* Here you are challenged to personally apply the lessons you have learned as you "Live out" God's principles in a practical way. We encourage you to write out all of the answers to the questions in this study. You may want to write the answers to the personal application questions in a journal to ensure privacy. By writing your insights from God day by day, you'll have a record of your relationship with Him that you can look back on when you need a faith boost.

5. Listen to … We finish with inspiring quotes from authors, speakers, and writers. You'll be able to "Listen to" the wisdom they've gleaned in their lives and relate it to your own.

Live Deeply is ideal for discussion in a small-group setting as well as for individual study. The following suggestions will help you and your group get the most out of your study time:

PERSONAL CHECKLIST

- Be determined. Examine your daily schedule; then set aside a consistent time for this study.

- Be prepared. Gather the materials you'll need: a Bible, this workbook, a journal in which to write your thoughts, and a pen.

- Be inspired. Begin each day with prayer, asking the Holy Spirit to be your teacher and to illuminate your mind.

- Be complete. Read the suggested Bible passage, and finish the homework each day.

- Be persistent. Answer each question as fully as possible. If you're unable to answer a question, move forward to the next question or read the explanation in the "Learn about …" section, which may offer further insight.

- Be consistent. Don't get discouraged. If you miss a day, use the weekend to catch up.

- Be honest. When answering the "Live out …" questions, allow the Lord to search your heart and transform your life. Take time to reflect honestly about your feelings, experiences, sins, goals, and responses to God.

- Be blessed. Enjoy your daily study time as God speaks to you through His Word.

SMALL-GROUP CHECKLIST

- Be prayerful. Pray before you begin your time together.

- Be biblical. Keep all answers in line with God's Word; avoid personal opinion.

- Be confidential. Keep all sharing within your small group confidential.

- Be respectful. Listen without interrupting. Keep comments on track and to the point so that all can share.

- Be discreet. In some cases, you need not share more than absolutely necessary. Some things are between you and the Lord.

- Be kind. Reply to the comments of others lovingly and courteously.

- Be mindful. Remember your group members in prayer throughout the week.

SMALL-GROUP LEADER CHECKLIST

- Be prayerful. Pray that the Holy Spirit will "guide you into truth" so that your leadership will guide others.

- Be faithful. Prepare by reading the Bible passage and studying the lesson ahead of time, highlighting truths and applying them personally.

- Be prompt. Begin and end the study on time.

- Be thorough. For optimum benefit, allot one hour for small-group discussion. This should allow plenty of time to cover all of the questions and exercises for each lesson.

- Be selective. If you have less than an hour, you should carefully choose which questions you will address and summarize the edited information for your group. In this way, you can focus on the more thought-provoking questions. Be sure to grant enough time to address pertinent "Live out …" exercises, as this is where you and the other women will clearly see God at work in your lives.

- Be sensitive. Some of the "Live out …" exercises are very personal and may not be appropriate to discuss in a small group. If you sense this is the case, feel free to move to another question.

- Be flexible. If the questions in the study seem unclear, reword them for your group. Feel free to add your own questions to bring out the meaning of a verse.

- Be inclusive. Encourage each member to participate in the discussion. You may have to draw some out or tone some down so that all have the opportunity to participate.

- Be honest. Don't be afraid to admit that you don't have all the answers! When in doubt, encourage group members to take difficult questions to their church leadership for clarification.

- Be focused. Keep the discussion on tempo and on target. Learn to pace your small group so that you complete a lesson on time. When participants get sidetracked, redirect the discussion to the passage at hand.

- Be patient. Realize that not all people are at the same place spiritually or socially. Wait for the members of your group to answer the questions rather than jumping in and answering them yourself.

Root Determines Fruit

Matthew 13:1–23

Lenya adored Mrs. Johnson, her elementary school teacher, because she had the ability to bring *Chitty Chitty Bang Bang* to life. Lenya's sister would anxiously wait for her to arrive home to retell the story in every detail. Penny loved nothing more than spooky bedtime tales from her granddaddy. She'd lie awake at night, jumping at every sound, wondering whether the boogeyman was real. All our kids loved trips to the library for story hour.

Since ancient times, storytellers have enthralled audiences with tales both entertaining and instructive. In 300 BC, Aesop, the Greek storyteller, featured animals like the tortoise and the hare in his fables vividly illustrating how to solve problems. The Brothers Grimm gathered fairy tales like *Hansel and Gretel* in nineteenth-century Germany to teach children valuable moral lessons. Baby boomers were mesmerized when Walt Disney animated their favorite stories in amazing Technicolor.

However, throughout history no one has compared to Jesus Christ as a storyteller. Rather than telling fables or fairy tales, He told parables. A parable is a short, simple story designed to communicate a spiritual truth, religious principle, or moral lesson. It is a figure of speech in which truth is illustrated by a comparison or example drawn from everyday experiences. Warren Wiersbe simply says, "A parable is an earthly story with a heavenly meaning."[1] Throughout this study we'll learn from the stories Jesus told, comparing them to our lives and putting His eternal truths into practice.

Day 1: Matthew 13:1–3   **FLOATING PULPIT**

Day 2: Matthew 13:3–9   **FERTILE PARABLE**

Day 3: Matthew 13:10–13   **FEW PERCEIVE**

Day 4: Matthew 13:14–17   **FULFILLED PROPHECY**

Day 5: Matthew 13:18–23   **FOUR POSSIBILITIES**

DAY I
Floating Pulpit

LIFT UP ...

Lord, I love to gather with Your people and listen to Your Word. Help me to be a faithful hearer, not only listening to what You say but obeying Your commands. Thank You for being in our midst. Amen.

LOOK AT ...

Jesus proved Himself to be the promised King—the Messiah of Israel—through His impeccable birthright, powerful words, and supernatural deeds. Despite His amazing miracles and the many ways He fulfilled prophecy, the religious leaders rejected His lordship. Knowing the religious leaders had turned on Him, Jesus directed His attention to the common people. Matthew 13 tells how Jesus stepped onto a floating pulpit on the Sea of Galilee and spoke in parables to explain how the gospel—the good news of salvation—would inaugurate the kingdom of heaven on earth.

The parable of the Sower is one of seven parables Jesus taught to describe what His kingdom would look like as a result of the religious establishment's rejecting Him. This parable was a precursor to the Great Commission that Jesus would give His disciples after His death, burial, and resurrection: "Go into all the world and preach the gospel to every creature" (Mark 16:15). There is no evidence that the religious leaders stayed to listen to Jesus' simple stories. Yet after this teaching session, the resentment of the religious leaders only deepened.

READ MATTHEW 13:1–3.

On the same day Jesus went out of the house and sat by the sea. Matthew 13:1

1. Explain what Jesus did on this day in His ministry.

2. Matthew 13:1 is the continuation of a critical day in Jesus' ministry. Briefly scan Matthew 12; then answer the following questions to learn more about this "same day."

   a. What day of the week is referred to here?

   b. What miracles did Jesus perform on this day?

   c. Describe Jesus' encounters with the religious leaders.

   d. What did He teach about becoming a member of His family?

3. According to Mark 3:6, what did the Pharisees begin to do on this fateful day?

And great multitudes were gathered together to Him, so that He got into a boat and sat; and the whole multitude stood on the shore. Then He spoke many things to them in parables, saying: "Behold, a sower went out to sow."
Matthew 13:2–3

4. Explain why Jesus got into the boat.

5. How many people stayed to hear Jesus' message?

6. What method of teaching did Jesus use in speaking to the multitudes?

7. What types of things did He teach in parables?

Live out ...

8. Galilee was an important region to Jesus. Fill in the following table to learn more.

Scripture	Galilee's Significance
Matthew 4:18–21	
Matthew 17:22–23	
Matthew 26:31–32	
Luke 1:26–28	
Luke 2:39–40	
Acts 10:36–38	

9. We've learned that many people came to know Jesus in Galilee. Journal about the place where you encountered Jesus and how meeting Him affected your feelings about that location.

10. Jesus was "moved with compassion" for the multitudes that followed Him. Check the boxes below to indicate how you respond to the many people who are lost and looking for a shepherd.

- ❏ Eager to share the gospel
- ❏ Anxious to get away

- ❏ Frightened by their unruliness

- ❏ Impatient with their ignorance
- ❏ Concerned for their eternity

- ❏ Other
  _____

11. Journal a prayer asking God to supernaturally fill you with compassion for the multitudes that don't know Him.

Learn about ...

8 The Location

Galilee was important because Jesus was there. He walked its roads and sailed its seas. Eleven of His twelve disciples (Judas was the exception) hailed from Galilee. Capernaum of Galilee became His headquarters. Both Jews and Gentiles populated the area known as "Galilee of the Gentiles." From there, Jesus gladly spread His message to all.

10 The Motivation

While He felt contempt for religious hypocrites, Jesus felt only compassion and mercy for the multitudes. *Compassion* means sympathy or deep pity for another; the Greek term that Matthew uses literally means for your bowels to yearn. Compassion penetrates deep into one's inner being, prompting kindhearted actions. "The Lord is very compassionate and merciful" (James 5:11).

○ ○ ● ○ ○

The multitudes crowded around Jesus, so He turned a boat on the Sea of Galilee into a floating pulpit. In his book *Fully Human, Fully Alive*, John Powell tells about a friend vacationing in the Bahamas who was drawn to a noisy crowd gathered toward the end of a pier:

> Upon investigation he discovered that the object of all the attention was a young man making the last-minute preparations for a solo journey around the world in a homemade boat. Without exception everyone on the pier was vocally pessimistic. All were actively volunteering to tell the ambitious sailor all the things that could possibly go wrong. "The sun will broil you! … You won't have enough food! … That boat of yours won't withstand the waves in a storm! … You'll never make it!"
>
> When my friend heard all these discouraging warnings to the adventurous young man, he felt an irresistible desire to offer some optimism and encouragement. As the little craft began drifting away from the pier towards the horizon, my friend went to the end of the pier, waving both arms wildly like semaphores spelling confidence. He kept shouting: "Bon Voyage! You're really something! We're with you! We're proud of you!"[2]

If you had been there as the boat was leaving, which group on the pier would you have been among: the optimists, or the pessimists? More importantly, if you had been in the crowds along the Sea of Galilee, would you have joined the Pharisees seeking to harm Jesus or the crowd eagerly listening to the stories Jesus told?

LISTEN TO …

The best leaders … almost without exception and at every level, are master users of stories and symbols.

—*Tom Peters*

DAY 2

Fertile Parable

An elderly farmer who was terminally ill called his two sons to his bedside and said, "I've divided my farm in equal shares; I leave little cash. The bulk of my wealth is hidden not more than eighteen inches below the ground. But I've forgotten precisely where it lies." After his death, his two sons dug up every inch of ground to unearth the buried treasure. They failed to find it. But they thought they might as well sow a crop in the hope of a harvest. In autumn, they dug for the treasure again but with no better results. Since their fields were turned over more thoroughly than any others in the neighborhood, they reaped better harvests than anyone else. Year after year their search continued. Only when they had grown much older and wiser did they realize what their father had meant: Real treasure comes as a result of hard work.[3]

Jesus was an ordinary man. He came to earth as a hardworking carpenter, not a pampered king. Because He lived a simple life, He knew the power of simple stories. So His first tale was a parable about the most common occupation in the land—a farmer sowing seed. He understood that hidden truths could take root only in fertile hearts. Will you "humbly accept the word God has planted in your hearts, for it has the power to save your souls" (James 1:21 NLT)?

LIFT UP ...

God, please give me ears to hear and hands to serve that I may have a heart of peace. Amen.

LOOK AT ...

The multitudes had followed Jesus to the shores of the Sea of Galilee to hear Him teach in a new way: through parables based on their culture and the experiences of their daily lives. He began by teaching the parable of the Sower. Today, we see Him continue this fertile parable by teaching about some of the dangers that could befall the seed.

The multitudes could probably relate to this story, since Israel's society was primarily agricultural. Today, most of us are not farmers. Therefore it's important to try to put ourselves in the shoes of those who relied on planting seed to survive so we can understand

LEARN ABOUT ...

1 Farming

The Bible indicates that one of our basic roles is to "tend and keep" the land (Gen. 2:15). Humans have a God-given responsibility to be gardeners and farmers. Humanity's close relationship with the soil is indicated by the similarity between the Hebrew words for man (*adam*) and earth (*adamah*).

3 Fallow

The land where Jesus taught this parable was an area of limestone covered by dust from frequent volcanic eruptions. The areas where volcanic dirt settled heavily were particularly fertile. However, in some spots the soil was shallow and stony, gravelly with rocky protrusions and inhospitable to agriculture.

5 Fertile

In those days, an average yield for a farmer was usually less then tenfold—thirty and sixty were considered bountiful. It was considered supernatural to harvest a hundredfold, such as when "Isaac sowed in that land, and reaped in the same year a hundredfold; and the LORD blessed him" (Gen. 26:12).

the message Jesus was conveying. What would happen if the seed were whisked away, withered up, or choked out and rendered worthless?

READ MATTHEW 13:3–9.

Then He spoke many things to them in parables, saying: "Behold, a sower went out to sow. And as he sowed, some seed fell by the wayside; and the birds came and devoured them." Matthew 13:3–4

1. Recap what Jesus was doing, and describe the main character in this story.

2. Describe what happened to the first seed Jesus mentioned.

"Some fell on stony places, where they did not have much earth; and they immediately sprang up because they had no depth of earth. But when the sun was up they were scorched, and because they had no root they withered away." Matthew 13:5–6

3. Jesus next described some seed that fell on stony places.

   a. What was the problem with the soil here?

   b. What effect did this type of soil have on the seed?

   c. Why was this seed unable to flourish?

"And some fell among thorns, and the thorns sprang up and choked them. But others fell on good ground and yielded a crop: some a hundredfold, some sixty, some thirty. He who has ears to hear, let him hear!" Matthew 13:7–9

4. Describe how the thorny soil affected sown seed.

5. Explain what happened to the soil that fell on good ground.

6. In your own words, reword Jesus' call to listen to Him.

7. Why do you think He placed such an emphasis on hearing His words?

LIVE OUT ...

8. Not many people today are farmers, but some of us *are* gardeners. Journal about your experience sowing seeds. Have you gardened in hard, shallow, thorny, or fertile soil? How did tending the land link you to heaven? If you're not a gardener, journal about why it does or doesn't interest you.

9. Jesus urged us to have ears to hear. In Revelation, Jesus promised some amazing things to those with ears to hear. Fill in the following chart to discover Christ's promises. Circle the promises you are most delighted to receive.

SCRIPTURE	PROMISE TO THOSE WITH EARS TO HEAR
Revelation 2:7	
Revelation 2:11	
Revelation 2:17	
Revelation 2:26–29	
Revelation 3:5–6	
Revelation 3:12–13	
Revelation 3:21–22	

Tune your ears to wisdom, and concentrate on understanding. Cry out for insight, and ask for understanding. Search for them as you would for silver; seek them like hidden treasures. Proverbs 2:2–4 NLT

LEARN ABOUT ...

8 The Father

The Bible is resplendent with gardens. God planted the first one in Eden. Jesus spent His last evening in the garden of Gethsemane and was buried and rose again in the garden tomb. Jesus said, "My Father is the gardener" (John 15:1 NIV). Gardening can help you relate to the Master Gardener.

9 Figure Out

"To have ears to hear" means to perceive with the mind, to have in-depth understanding, and to know with a certainty. Spiritually, it means to perceive God's truths, understand how to apply them personally, and know Christ as Lord. If you have ears to hear, you will listen to and obey God's Word.

10. Journal a prayer rewording Proverbs 2:2–4. Ask God to give you ears to hear.

○ ○ ● ○ ○

True confessions: My (Lenya's) thumb is more brown than green. When I was growing up, my grandmother had a flower garden that drew admirers from all over the city. When Grandma passed away, my mother moved into her home and began tending the garden. A whole new generation of spectators still "ooh" and "ahh" as they pass by the colorful landscape.

When I finally became a home owner, I hoped that a "green thumb" was genetic. One spring morning my friend Patti stopped by with several flats of flowers. She hoped to inspire my latent gardening tendencies. With the utmost enthusiasm I planted the bright buds, then stood back with pride and said, "I do have gardening DNA!"

Unfortunately, after several weeks of neglect my unwatered pansies were no longer perky, my chrysanthemums had been crowded out by weeds, and my daisies were drooping from insufficient topsoil. I've discovered that gardening is much more than planting flowers—it requires time, patience, and lots of hard work.

This parable has revealed that the same seed sowed by the same sower produced varied results based upon the condition of the soil. For plants to flourish, they must take root in soil that is well prepared and carefully cultivated. As we continue this lesson, make sure your heart is fertile and ready to receive truth from God's Word.

LISTEN TO ...

The best thing to do with the Bible is to know it in the head, stow it in the heart, sow it in the world, and show it in the life.

—*Unknown*

DAY 3

Few Perceive

Few can perceive the answers to riddles. By definition, riddles are mind teasers that employ word tricks. Riddles exploit sneaky tricks that make a straightforward answer impossible. Once the riddle is solved, you slap your forehead and proclaim, "Of course—I should have known!"

Let's see if you can figure out the "GRY" puzzler: *Think of words ending in "GRY." Angry and hungry are two of them. There are only three words in the English language. What is the third word? The word is something that everyone uses every day. If you have listened carefully, I have already told you what it is.*

The first two sentences have nothing to do with the real riddle. They're meant to throw you off course—and it worked, didn't it? Reread the actual riddle, focusing on the third sentence, which holds the key phrase *the English language*. The third word in that phrase is simply *language*. Get it? *Language* is something "everyone uses every day"! Without that quirky twist, the puzzle would be just another trivia question.[4]

While riddles are not parables, they do have something in common—you must listen carefully to understand their true meaning. The disciples were puzzled about why Jesus taught in parables. He answered, "I speak to them in parables, because … hearing they do not hear, nor do they understand.… For the hearts of this people have grown dull" (Matt. 13:13, 15). Jesus knew there is a stark difference between hearers and listeners. Hearers don't necessarily believe. Believers listen with the intent to obey. Which are you?

LIFT UP ...

Lord, You are a mysterious and magnificent God. I am in awe that You have chosen to reveal Your secrets to a person like me. Help me to understand Your mysteries so I can walk in godliness. Amen.

LOOK AT ...

Jesus spoke about a farmer who sowed seed upon four different kinds of soil. Now we see the disciples' reaction to their Master's new style of teaching and learn that few could perceive the meaning behind Christ's words.

Jesus taught about the kingdom of heaven. No ordinary kingdom, it is the perfect kingdom designed by God since before time began. Sadly, sin interrupted God's reign on earth, so the kingdom of heaven (also known as the kingdom of God) was delayed in coming to its fullness on earth. But God had a plan. He waited patiently to inaugurate the kingdom of heaven with His Son, Jesus, as the King. Thus, the kingdom of heaven was worth waiting for. It is inaugurated in three phases. Phase one occurred when Jesus came to earth as the suffering Savior. Jesus said, "Repent, for the kingdom of heaven is *at hand*" (Matt. 4:17). Following Jesus' death, resurrection, and ascension, the kingdom became a spiritual kingdom where the Lord took residence in the hearts of all who believe. Jesus said, "The kingdom of God is *within* you" (Luke 17:21). But the King will come again and establish an earthly kingdom that will last forever—"The God of heaven will set up a kingdom which shall never be destroyed" (Dan. 2:44). The question is, are you a member of God's kingdom now? Ask yourself: Are you ready for Him to come and establish His kingdom when He will reign eternally?

READ MATTHEW 13:10–13.

And the disciples came and said to Him, "Why do You speak to them in parables?" He answered and said to them, "Because it has been given to you to know the mysteries of the kingdom of heaven, but to them it has not been given." Matthew 13:10–11

1. a. Rephrase the question the disciples asked Jesus.

    b. Why do you think they asked this?

2. In Jesus' reply, to whom does "them" refer? (See Mark 4:11 for added insight.)

3. What privilege was given to Christ's followers?

"For whoever has, to him more will be given, and he will have abundance; but whoever does not have, even what he has will be taken away from him. Therefore I speak to them in parables, because seeing they do not see, and hearing they do not hear, nor do they understand." Matthew 13:12–13

4. What did Jesus promise the "haves" in this passage?

5. What was His warning to the "have-nots"?

6. Following this warning, Jesus begins His next sentence with "Therefore." This key word marks the conclusion to a line of reasoning. With this in mind, reread the passage above; then use the words *hear, see, understand,* and *parables* to fill in the blanks, explaining why Jesus spoke to "them" in parables.

Therefore, many refused to listen to Jesus, so He spoke to them in

_____.

Though they were not blind, they chose not to _____.

Though they were not deaf, they chose not to _____.

Though they were not stupid, they refused to _____.

LEARN ABOUT ...

2 Us vs. Them

Israel's religious leaders and others had rejected Jesus as Messiah. Therefore, He turned His back on them and spoke in parables to reveal divine truth to His followers. Jesus realized it had become "us" versus "them." Jesus said, "He who is not with Me is against Me" (Matt. 12:30).

3 Concealed and Revealed

A *mystery* is God's hidden, eternal plan concealed for a while, then disclosed in His perfect timing. In the New Testament, a mystery is a secret revealed through the Holy Spirit to Christ's disciples. A mystery is not an unsolvable riddle, but a veiled truth that can be comprehended only by divine revelation.

4 More and More

Abundance means to have enough and some to spare and to excel or be better. Since Jesus is speaking of spiritual revelation, we discover that spiritual riches, more than material comforts, lead to a better, excellent, and abundant life. Jesus said, "I have come that they may have life, and that they may have it more abundantly" (John 10:10).

LEARN ABOUT ...

7 They Become Us

Rather than focusing on the gap between "us" and "them," God prefers that we invite "them" to become part of "us." He desires all of His creation to become His children: "Even so it is not the will of your Father who is in heaven that one of these little ones should perish" (Matt. 18:14).

---

8 One for All

One big mystery is, why does God love me? For some inexplicable reason, God loved me, even when I was unlovable. "God demonstrates his own love for us in this: While we were still sinners, Christ died for us" (Rom. 5:8 NIV). Before I was part of "us," I was one of "them."

LIVE OUT ...

7. Today we learned that in the kingdom of heaven Jesus makes a distinction between the believers and unbelievers, referring to those who fail to understand as "them." In the corresponding columns list some other contrasting titles used in Scripture for "believers" and "unbelievers."

Us	Them
Example: sheep	goats

8. a. Jesus promised to reveal the mysteries of the kingdom of heaven to His followers. Use a Bible concordance to discover some of the mysteries Jesus revealed. Look up "mystery" in your concordance and record the mysteries below. (You may have a concordance in the back of your Bible. You can also buy a concordance in book or CD-ROM format or use a Web site such as biblegateway.com.)

   b. If you do not completely understand these sacred secrets, ask God to give you wisdom.

9. a. Amazingly, Jesus promised to give even more to those who have already received His treasures. Place a + in the box beside the treasures you've already received and a − beside the riches you're still awaiting.

❒ "The riches of His goodness, forbearance, and longsuffering" (Rom. 2:4)

❒ "The riches of His glory" (Rom. 9:23)

❒ "The depth of the riches both of the wisdom and knowledge of God" (Rom. 11:33)

❒ "The exceeding riches of His grace in His kindness toward us" (Eph. 2:7)

❒ "All your need according to His riches in glory by Christ Jesus" (Phil. 4:19)

b. Now journal a prayer praising God for the riches you've been given and confidently asking Him to give you even more of His spiritual treasures.

○ ○ ● ○ ○

Just as a minority of people understands riddles, few perceive the truth about Jesus. Of the ten lepers healed by Jesus, only one returned to thank Him; of the religious leaders alive in Jesus' day, only Nicodemus and Joseph of Arimathea are named as followers of Christ. Jesus said, "Enter through the narrow gate. For wide is the gate and broad is the road that leads to destruction, and many enter through it. But small is the gate and narrow the road that leads to life, and only a few find it" (Matt. 7:13–14 NIV).

Modern Americans also have skewed perceptions of biblical truth. *U.S. Catholic Magazine* asked its readers what was beyond the grave:

One result: the old fire-and-brimstone idea of hell seems to be on its way out, being replaced by the idea of hell as an absence of God. Some theologians say this means people are becoming more concerned about doing good for its own sake—and less about doing good to avoid hell. As for heaven, it apparently is a great place for a picnic—a "sylvan setting where it never rains," and where you'll be reunited with departed members of your family. Who'll go there? Well, 83 percent of the magazine's readers expect to.[5]

Rather than giving complicated directions to heaven, Jesus offered Himself. He said, "I am the way" (John 14:6). This truth is so simple a child can understand it and so profound you can spend a lifetime exploring its depths.

LISTEN TO ...

God's love for poor sinners is very wonderful, but God's patience with ill-natured saints is a deeper mystery.

—*Henry Drummond*

DAY 4
Fulfilled Prophecy

Modern psychics and seers claim to see the future, predicting earthquakes, personal fortunes, and political upheavals. However, these prognostications rarely come to pass in the way, place, or time foretold. Let's face it, prophesying the future is as difficult as predicting the weather.

An old-timer claimed the ability to forecast the weather. A tourist driving through western Texas stopped at his gas station and noticed a piece of rope dangling from a sign labeled *Weather Forecaster*. "How can you forecast the weather with that piece of rope?" the tourist asked. "It's simple, son," drawled the attendant. "When the rope sways, it's windy; when it gets wet, it's raining; when it's frozen stiff, it's snowing; and when it's gone … tornado!"[6] Of course, this device didn't predict the weather; it simply reported the current conditions.

Biblical prophets were required to be 100 percent accurate or die: "The prophet who presumes to speak a word in My name, which I have not commanded him to speak … that prophet shall die" (Deut. 18:20). Today we see Jesus quote the prophet Isaiah, who predicted Christ's coming and rejection by Israel. As the product of a true prophet, Isaiah's words were fulfilled in God's perfect timing. Sadly, the Israelites rejected Isaiah's message and thereby foreshadowed their rejection of Messiah. Don't be left out in the cold when it comes to prophecy. Jesus fulfilled prophecy the first time He came to earth, and the prophets predict He's coming again soon.

LIFT UP …

Jesus, though I didn't see You when You walked on earth, I believe in You. Thank You that You died for my sins and rose again to sit in heaven. I can't wait to see You face-to-face. Amen.

LOOK AT …

We've seen that many people viewed the parables as mysteries that could not be solved. But for those who believed that Jesus was the promised Messiah, the parables unlocked the secrets to the kingdom of heaven on earth. Today, we'll discover that the lack of understanding fulfilled a key Old Testament prophecy.

LEARN ABOUT ...

1 Predictive

One role of a prophet was to predict the future. God also commissioned prophets as messengers of social and political reform. Their messages of righteousness and revival announced God's will and called His people to obedience.[7]

---

3 Comprehension

To understand means to put together mentally or perceive; it implies comprehension leading to belief. *To perceive* means to gaze earnestly, to inspect by experience and observation, using all of the senses. To understand and perceive is to know that you know. Do you know that you know Jesus is Messiah?

---

4 Insensitive

Dull heartedness can be translated to mean that the people's heart is fattened, implying sensuality and senselessness. When the heart is heavy with sin, the ears are dull to the Spirit. What weighs down your heart? As Hebrews encourages us, "Let us lay aside every weight, and the sin which so easily ensnares us" (Heb. 12:1).

Prophecy can be defined as prediction about the future and the end time. Prophecies were special messages from God revealing His divine will uttered through human spokespeople. Much of biblical prophecy speaks about the kingdom of God, giving particular information about the Messiah and His chosen people, Israel. It also foretells the destiny of the nations and their relationship to the kingdom of God. New Testament prophecy identifies Jesus as the King who spent much of His ministry describing His kingdom and its establishment, especially in the form of parables. Most prophecy speaks of undoing Satan's work and elaborates on the initial promise of Genesis 3:15, which announced that Christ, the seed of the woman, would crush the great Serpent, the Devil. Over three hundred prophecies in the Bible speak of Jesus Christ and events leading up to and including His first and second comings. As you study today's lesson, ask God to open your eyes and ears to His prophetic Word so that He might open your understanding. Prophecy is being fulfilled every day—don't let it escape your notice.

READ MATTHEW 13:14–17.

"And in them the prophecy of Isaiah is fulfilled, which says: 'Hearing you will hear and shall not understand, and seeing you will see and not perceive; for the hearts of this people have grown dull. Their ears are hard of hearing, and their eyes they have closed, lest they should see with their eyes and hear with their ears, lest they should understand with their hearts and turn, so that I should heal them.'" Matthew 13:14–15

1. Whose prophecy did the unbelieving Jews fulfill?

2. Though the people heard, what did they fail to do?

3. Though they saw, what did they fail to do?

4. a. Describe what had happened to their ears and eyes.

b. What was the underlying cause of this sensory deprivation?

5. Explain why Jesus desperately wanted the people to see, hear, and understand with their hearts.

"But blessed are your eyes for they see, and your ears for they hear; for assuredly, I say to you that many prophets and righteous men desired to see what you see, and did not see it, and to hear what you hear, and did not hear it." Matthew 13:16–17

6. What phrase did Jesus use to let His followers know how fortunate they were?

7. Explain why, according to Jesus, they should feel so blessed.

LIVE OUT ...

8. a. Because their hearts had grown dull, many people were unable to understand that Jesus was the Messiah. List some things that might cause your spiritual senses to grow dull.

   b. List some things that cause you to stay spiritually sharp.

9. By allowing His followers to come to divine knowledge of Him using their five senses, Jesus proved that He was Messiah. Fill in the following chart to discover which sense Jesus used to reveal Himself to His followers: taste, hearing, sight, touch, or smell.

SCRIPTURE	SENSE ENGAGED
Matthew 26:26–28	
Mark 9:2–3	
Luke 24:38–40	

LEARN ABOUT ...

6 Sensitive

Blessed can mean to make happy. A blessing is not a wish regarding the future or the description of a present condition. Rather, it is a special pronouncement on those the statement portrays—those who see and hear what the prophets have predicted. "Blessed is the man who fears the LORD" (Ps. 112:1).

8 Decisive

As the heart goes, so goes the person. Biblically, the heart refers to a person's character. It is the center of all emotions, good or evil. Thinking processes such as understanding, imagination, and remembrance occur in the heart. The heart controls the will, which makes godly or ungodly decisions.

9 Positive

Although your eyes have beheld God's creation and your ears have heard His Word, the best is yet to come! Paul told the church at Corinth that "eye has not seen, nor ear heard, nor have entered into the heart of man the things which God has prepared for those who love Him" (I Cor. 2:9).

Luke 24:44

John 12:3

10. Jesus wants *you* to use all of your senses to come to saving knowledge of Him as well. Using the openings below, journal about how Christ has engaged all of your senses.

I tasted God's goodness when …

I heard God's voice when …

I saw Christ when …

I touched my Savior when …

I smelled the fragrance of God when …

○ ○ ● ○ ○

Matthew Henry was right when he said, "There are none so blind as those who will not see." The religious leaders of Jesus' day claimed spiritual insight, yet Jesus called them "blind leaders of the blind" (Matt. 15:14). But of those groping for truth, Scripture says, "The people who sat in darkness have seen a great light" (Matt. 4:16). The paradox is that some who claim to see are spiritually blind, while those who have been spiritually sightless develop eyes to see.

A blind man stood at an intersection reading aloud from his Braille Bible. A gentleman stopped at the edge of the crowd to listen when the sightless man lost his place. Trying to find his place in Acts 4, the blind man kept repeating the last three words of the Scripture: "No other name … No other name …" The gentleman went away deeply moved. That one phrase haunted him. He had been searching for inner peace and was influenced by the few choice words. Before morning he had accepted Christ as his personal Savior. "I see now," he mused, "I thought my works could save me. But only Jesus saves. The Bible is true: 'There is no other name under heaven given among men by which we must be saved' (Acts 4:12)."[8] You could say that this was a case of the physically blind leading the spiritually blind.

LISTEN TO ...

To be blind is bad, but worse is it to have eyes and not to see.

—Helen Adams Keller

DAY 5

Four Possibilities

Fred inherited $10 million with the stipulation that he travel to either Chile or Brazil to accept. So he chose Brazil. Sadly, his Chilean inheritance would have been land rich in uranium, gold, and silver. In Brazil, he chose nuts over coffee. Too bad! The nut market tanked while coffee soared to over $1.30 a pound. Poor Fred lost everything and sold his watch to buy a ticket home. At the airport he faced two possibilities: New York or Boston. He chose Boston. Walking past the New York plane, he noticed it was a brand-new 747 loaded with chic people. Wouldn't you know it? The Boston plane was a 1928 Ford trimotor filled with crying children. Over the Andes, one of the engines fell off. Our man Fred made his way to the captain and said, "I'm jinxed. If you want to save your lives, give me a parachute and I'll jump." So Fred jumped. As he pulled the rip cord, the line snapped. Desperately, Fred cried out, "St. Francis, save me!" A hand from heaven reached down and seized Fred by the wrist, letting him dangle in midair. Then a voice asked, "St. Francis Xavier or St. Francis of Assisi?"[9]

Life is full of possibilities. Invariably these possibilities involve choices. In our parable, Jesus reveals that there are four possible outcomes concerning how the Word of God is received in the human heart. The choice is up to us.

LIFT UP ...

Lord, I so want to be a fruitful disciple. I know there are many choices involved in following You. Help me to make the right choices so that I might bear much fruit. Amen.

LOOK AT ...

We know that Jesus spoke in parables because the religious leaders had hardened their hearts toward Him. Since His followers recognized Him as Messiah, He continued to teach them in the "secret code" of the parables. Now we'll see how He explained to them the meaning behind the parable of the Sower and learn that there were four possible outcomes when the seed of God's Word is sown in the hearts of people.

It is interesting to note that in this parable (and others) the Word of God is compared to seed that can take root and grow. But, like real seed, it needs good soil to flourish. The soil in this parable is the hearts of people. Since God sees people as unique individuals capable of making free-will choices, whether the seed flourishes is often a matter of the will. But there are also other influences at work that can cause the seed harm. As you study this passage, take a soil sample of your heart, and make sure that your heart is in prime condition for God's Word to thrive.

LEARN ABOUT ...

1 The Wayside

"Wicked one" refers to Satan. Satan is the superhuman enemy of God, humanity, and good. Other titles include "the tempter" (I Thess. 3:5); "Beelzebub" (Matt. 12:24); "the ruler of this world" (John 12:31); "the god of this age" (2 Cor. 4:4); "Belial" (2 Cor. 6:15); and "the accuser of our brethren" (Rev. 12:10).

---

2 Stony Ground

Tribulation means to be pressed together, squeezed, or pinched. It sometimes speaks of the hardships that Christ's followers will suffer. Jesus said, "In the world you will have tribulation; but be of good cheer, I have overcome the world" (John 16:33).

READ MATTHEW 13:18–23.

"Therefore hear the parable of the sower: When anyone hears the word of the kingdom, and does not understand it, then the wicked one comes and snatches away *what was sown in his heart. This is he who received seed by the wayside."* Matthew 13:18–19

1. In the parable, Jesus told of the sower whose "seed fell by the wayside; and the birds came and devoured them."

   a. What does the seed represent? (See also Mark 4:14 and Luke 8:11.)

   b. Explain what the soil by the wayside represents and what happens to the seed (see also Mark 4:15 and Luke 8:12).

"But he who received the seed on stony places, this is he who hears the word and immediately receives it with joy; yet he has no root in himself, but endures only for a while. For when tribulation or persecution arises because of the word, immediately he stumbles." Matthew 13:20–21

2. Explain how the seed on stony places is initially received and why it does not flourish (see also Mark 4:16–17 and Luke 8:13).

"Now he who received seed among the thorns is he who hears the word, and the cares of this world and the deceitfulness of riches choke the word, and he becomes unfruitful." Matthew 13:22

3. Next Jesus addressed the seed that fell on thorny soil. Explain why the seed in this type of soil is unfruitful (see also Mark 4:18–19 and Luke 8:14).

"But he who received seed on the good ground is he who hears the word and understands it, who indeed bears fruit and produces: some a hundredfold, some sixty, some thirty." Matthew 13:23

4. Jesus finally discusses the good soil.

   a. What type of heart do those with good soil possess (see Luke 8:15)?

   b. How do they respond to the implanted word (see also Mark 4:20 and Luke 8:15)?

   c. What is the outward evidence of their inward faith (see also Mark 4:20 and Luke 8:15)?

5. Detail any additional insight you gain concerning the parable of the Sower from Mark's and Luke's accounts (Mark 4:1–20 and Luke 8:4–15). Why do you think they included or excluded some details?

LIVE OUT ...

6. We've learned that our hearts are susceptible to Satan's sabotage. Fill in the table below to learn some of his evil strategies.

SCRIPTURE   SATAN'S STRATEGY

2 Corinthians 11:3

2 Corinthians 11:14

2 Corinthians 12:7

1 Thessalonians 3:5

Revelation 12:10

LEARN ABOUT ...

7 The Way

God's Word can't thrive in hearts made barren by Satan's influence, life's trials, or greed for the world's goods. The way to till the ground is simple: Repent and receive. James exhorted people to "lay aside all filthiness and overflow of wickedness, and receive with meekness the implanted word, which is able to save your souls" (James 1:21).

7. There are four possible soil conditions for the seed of God's Word in our hearts. Briefly tell how you've experienced each of these conditions on your spiritual journey:

    a. Satan snatched away what God had planted:

    b. Stumbled on stony soil because of tribulation:

    c. Stuck in the trap of the deceitfulness of riches:

    d. Seed took root and produced fruit:

8. We've learned that those who faithfully hear will be fruitful. Read the list of the fruit of the Spirit in the passage below. Circle the fruit you have borne, and underline the fruit you want to cultivate.

The fruit of the Spirit is love, joy, peace, longsuffering, kindness, goodness, faithfulness, gentleness, self-control. Galatians 5:22–23

∘ ∘ ● ∘ ∘

An agricultural school in Iowa reported that producing one hundred bushels of corn from one acre of land required hours upon hours of the farmer's labor, 4,000,000 pounds of water, 6,800 pounds of oxygen,

5,200 pounds of carbon, 160 pounds of nitrogen, 125 pounds of potassium, 75 pounds of yellow sulfur, and other elements too numerous to list. In addition to these things, which no person can produce, the success of the farm also depends on rain and sunshine at the right time. The report concluded that only 5 percent of the produce of a farm can be attributed to human efforts.[10]

It's the same with spiritual fruit. Though as believers we may show some outward signs of holiness, it's only because the Holy One has taken up residence in our hearts. He is expending His energy to shape us into His image so that we can bear witness to others. Jesus said, "I am the vine, you are the branches. He who abides in Me, and I in him, bears much fruit; for without Me you can do nothing" (John 15:5). Simply put, the root of a tree determines the fruit of a tree—the branches have little or nothing to do with the process. The key is for the branches to stay connected to the root so they can hold the fruit.

LISTEN TO ...

The Christian should resemble a fruit tree, not a Christmas tree! For the gaudy decorations of a Christmas tree are only tied on, whereas fruit grows on a fruit tree.

—*John R. W. Stott*

LESSON TWO

Looks Can Be Deceiving
Matthew 13:24–43

A successful building contractor called a promising carpenter, John Smith, into his office one day and said, "John, you supervise the next house we build; order all the materials and oversee the job from the ground up."

John enthusiastically accepted the assignment. Before breaking ground he studied the blueprints, checking every measurement and specification. Then a deceptive thought crept into his mind: *If I'm really in charge, I could cut corners, use cheaper materials, and pocket the extra money. With a coat of paint, no one will ever know the difference.*

John set about his scheme, ordering second-grade lumber, inexpensive concrete, cheap wiring, and cutting every corner he could. Yet he reported the purchase of much better materials. When the home was completed with a fresh coat of paint, he invited the contractor to preview it.

"John," said the contractor, "you've done a magnificent job! Since you've been a faithful employee all these years, as a token of my appreciation I'm giving you this house you have built!"[1] The carpenter knew that looks could be deceiving, but in the end he was fooling only himself.

In this week's parable, we'll observe a different kind of misleading laborer. Rather than using shabby building materials, this worker substitutes harmful weeds for fruitful wheat. But God, who can be seen as both a Master Builder and a Master Gardener, knows the difference between the genuine and the counterfeit. He has a perfect plan to purify His fields of harmful weeds. Let's uncover the hidden truths found in the parable of the Wheat and the Tares.

Day 1: Matthew 13:24–26   **THE ENEMY'S INFILTRATION**
Day 2: Matthew 13:27–30   **THE OWNER'S REVELATION**
Day 3: Matthew 13:34–36   **THE PROPHETIC ILLUSTRATION**
Day 4: Matthew 13:37–39   **THE MASTER'S EXPLANATION**
Day 5: Matthew 13:40–43   **THE FINAL EXAMINATION**

DAY 1
The Enemy's Infiltration

LIFT UP ...

Dear Lord, thank You for planting me in Your kingdom. Remind me that, regardless of the Enemy's tactics, You have a purpose for planting me where You have. Amen.

LOOK AT ...

Last week, we studied the ways people respond to the Word of God in the parable of the Sower. This week, Jesus continues to use agricultural metaphors to reveal His truths about the kingdom of heaven.

This parable focuses on the kingdom of heaven. This does not mean that the parable is about heaven itself or about the kingdom when Christ comes again to reign as King of kings. This parable refers to the church age. The church age is the period of time between the first and second comings of Christ. It is an age of grace when Jesus rules over His subjects in a spiritual role. The kingdom of heaven is a voluntary kingdom: Jesus allows everyone the chance to accept or reject His rule. Some people profess to be Christians, and some absolutely reject Christ's rule. As with any true king and kingdom, there are those who stand in opposition. As you read this parable, examine your heart to make sure you are a true servant of Christ the King.

READ MATTHEW 13:24–26.

Another parable He put forth to them, saying: "The kingdom of heaven is like a man who sowed good seed in his field; but while men slept, his enemy came and sowed tares among the wheat and went his way. But when the grain had sprouted and produced a crop, then the tares also appeared. Matthew 13:24–26

Learn about ...

1 Put Forth

The Greek word for "put forth" is *parathithemi*, which means to present or deposit something of value. Jesus' parables were not simply appealing stories meant to entertain; they were spiritual nuggets of gold meant to change the heart.

2 Planted Faith

In Scripture, the phrase "kingdom of heaven" is used interchangeably with "kingdom of God" to describe God's supremacy over the world's affairs. The Jews believed only physical heirs of Abraham would inherit the kingdom. But Jesus taught that true children of the kingdom are those who put their faith in Him (see Matt. 8:10–12).

3 Planting Fakes

Tares are darnel weeds that closely resemble wheat but produce worthless fruit, taste bitter, and can even cause death if consumed. This seed was sometimes planted in an enemy's field out of revenge. The Romans made this practice illegal because of its devastating effects.

1. What phrase describes the manner in which Jesus presented this parable?

2. Describe what crops were planted in this parable and to what they were likened.

3. In your own words, describe what happened to the owner's field.

4. Explain how the enemy went undetected.

5. When and how was the enemy's plot discovered?

Live out ...

6. The Jews were expecting a Messiah who would reign over a political kingdom, but Jesus came the first time to reign in our hearts. Name some situations where you have difficulty submitting to His Lordship. (Examples: habits, schedule, marriage, parenting, finances, friendships, etc.)

7. Now journal a prayer to the King of kings, submitting your desires wholly to Him.

8. Most of us have been the victims of an enemy's plot. It's easy to become fearful or even vengeful when attacked. Fill in the following chart to discover how to respond.

Scripture	How to Respond to Enemies
Leviticus 19:17–18	
Psalm 31:13–15	
Proverbs 24:17–19	
Isaiah 41:10–11	

9. Rewrite the following verses into a prayer of repentance: "Forgive us our sins, as we have forgiven those who sin against us. And don't let us yield to temptation, but rescue us from the evil one" (Matt. 6:12–13 NLT).

○ ○ ● ○ ○

4 Prowling Fiend

The enemy in this parable acted while everyone was asleep. There is no time to sleep spiritually as believers. We need to "be self-controlled and alert. Your enemy the devil prowls around like a roaring lion looking for someone to devour" (I Peter 5:8 NIV).

7 Powerful Father

Jesus is both King of kings and Lord of lords. Lord denotes ownership and implies absolute control. It is used in reference to owners of slaves, kings ruling their subjects, or husbands as lords of the wives. It is applied to God as the owner and governor of the whole earth.

8 Pesky "Flower"

Daisy weed first appeared in a farmer's field in the 1930s when a neighbor with a grudge scattered the pesky seed throughout the field. The effects are still evident today.[2] Instead of sowing destructive seeds in others' lives, may we "be careful to lead a blameless life" (Ps. 101:2 NIV).

American intelligence agencies were compromised by a con man who mastered the art of deception. Larry Wu-Tai Chin seemed to be a meek and mild-mannered man, but in reality he was a master of deception.

Chin was born in Peking and became a naturalized American citizen. For almost thirty years he betrayed his adopted country. Working as a high-level translator and analyst for the CIA, Chin used his position to transfer classified documents to the People's Republic of China. Chin was so skilled at deception he even passed polygraph tests administered by government agencies. When asked why he turned traitor, Chin said he wanted to improve relations between the two countries.

Chin seemed emotionless when the jury sentenced him to life in prison. However, the meek mask he wore was only another layer of deception. Soon after his incarceration, the seemingly emotionless Larry Wu-Tai Chin, played his final trick by committing suicide.[3]

No one could tell from the outside what was happening on the inside of Larry Wu-Tai Chin. His coworkers believed he was a faithful analyst rather than a fraudulent spy; his captors thought he was subdued when he was suicidal. His looks truly were deceiving.

Warning! Don't be fooled by the Enemy of your soul—he's a master of disguise: "Satan himself transforms himself into an angel of light" (2 Cor. 11:14).

LISTEN TO ...

Anger is a weed; hate is the tree.

—*St. Augustine of Hippo*

DAY 2

The Owner's Revelation

Abraham Lincoln said, "You can fool some of the people all of the time, and all of the people some of the time, but you cannot fool all of the people all the time." But is it possible to ever fool an expert in his field?

The story is told of a group of students at Harvard who tried to fool the famous Professor Agassiz, the great nineteenth-century paleontologist, teacher, scientist, and lifelong opponent of Darwin's theory of evolution. The students took parts from several different bugs and skillfully combined them into a creation they were convinced would baffle their teacher. On the day they presented it to him for identification, he examined it carefully. As time passed, the students grew more confident they had duped this genius. Finally, Professor Agassiz straightened up and with great authority proclaimed, "I have identified it." Scarcely able to control their amusement, they asked him for the name of the species. With a straight face Agassiz replied, "It is a humbug."

In today's parable we meet an expert in a different field—a field of wheat. Unlike the farmer in the parable of the Sower, this expert agriculturalist owns the farm, has servants, and hires harvesters. Like Professor Agassiz, he is not fooled by a counterfeit. He can differentiate weed from wheat. More importantly, God is an authority in discerning true faith from phony profession. He can spot "humbugs" a mile away.

LIFT UP ...

Heavenly Father, Your wisdom is infinite. Teach me to seek Your wisdom before acting foolishly on my own. Amen.

LOOK AT ...

Jesus began this parable by comparing the kingdom of heaven to a man who sowed good seed in his own field while his enemy sowed destructive seed in the same field. Next we learn how the owner of the field responded.

The word *enemy* occurs more frequently in the Old Testament than in the New. The

Old Testament focused on the existence of the nation of Israel against the other countries of the ancient world. Before Israel could serve as the channel of God's grace to the world, its existence as a nation had to be securely established. The Israelites' enemies were regarded as God's enemies. The paradigm shifted after the Messiah was born. In the New Testament, enemies were primarily spiritual in nature. The greatest enemy of all is Satan. When you are engaged in conflict, remember what Jesus said: "Love your enemies, bless those who curse you, do good to those who hate you" (Matt. 5:44).

READ MATTHEW 13:27–30.

"So the servants of the owner came and said to him, 'Sir, did you not sow good seed in your field? How then does it have tares?' He said to them, 'An enemy has done this.' The servants said to him, 'Do you want us then to go and gather them up?' But he said, 'No, lest while you gather up the tares you also uproot the wheat with them. Let both grow together until the harvest, and at the time of harvest I will say to the reapers, "First gather together the tares and bind them in bundles to burn them, but gather the wheat into my barn."'" Matthew 13:27–30

1. Describe the problem and who discovered it.

2. How did the owner explain the presence of tares in his field?

3. What solution did the servants offer?

4. Explain why the owner rejected their solution.

5. Carefully examine the owner's solution.

   a. When did he plan to remove the tares?

LEARN ABOUT ...

I Good Seed

The good seed was wheat seed. It is the most important grain mentioned in the Bible. Wheat can be cultivated throughout most of the land of Israel. Tares are the bad seed that infiltrate the wheat fields, sometimes planted purposefully by saboteurs. James Montgomery Boice wrote, "Nothing good has ever come into the world without opposition, and that is especially true in spiritual matters."[4]

4 Bad Seed

Purposefully scattering bad seed in another's field was a vindictive act. It took tremendous effort to remove harmful tares. By the time darnel weed was recognizable, its root system was intertwined with the wheat. The insidious weed would remain in the soil, adversely affecting the crops for seasons to come.

5 Harvest Time

Harvest time for the southern parts of Palestine occurred during the middle of April, but in the northern mountainous sections, crops did not ripen until three weeks later or more. The harvest began with the barley (celebrated at the festival of Passover) and ended with the wheat (celebrated at the festival of Pentecost).

b. What two actions would be taken to separate the tares from the wheat?

c. Explain what would eventually be done with the tares and the wheat.

6. Based on what you've learned about tares, describe the wisdom in the owner's solution.

LIVE OUT ...

7. Rather than reacting to his enemy's plot, the owner wisely took action to protect his wheat. God's Word instructs us to take specific actions when an enemy attacks. Fill in the chart below with the action and a personal application.

SCRIPTURE	ACTION	PERSONAL APPLICATION
Exodus 23:4–5		
Matthew 5:44		
Mark 11:25		
Romans 12:17–19		

8. The darnel weed appeared to be healthy wheat until it matured. Then the servants recognized there was a problem. Describe a time when you allowed something that seemed harmless to become poisonous as it matured (example: an attitude, a behavior, a relationship, etc.).

9. When the owner realized there were unhealthy plants in his field, he wisely chose to identify the tares, bind them up, and burn them.

    a. Identify some harmful tares (sins) in your life.

    b. Describe the practical steps you'll take to bind them up (remove them).

    c. Ask God to burn the tares (forgive you). Describe how you'll divert the energy you've been using growing tares to grow in godly endeavors instead.

○ ○ ● ○ ○

LEARN ABOUT ...

9 Bundles

This parable teaches that the reapers will bundle the tares together at the harvest. Interestingly, the Bible talks about God bundling not only bad things but also precious things (see Song 1:13). Abigail approached King David and entreated him by saying, "The life of my lord shall be bound in the bundle of the living with the Lord your God" (1 Sam. 25:29).

The field owner made the best of what his enemy meant for evil, using tares for fuel. Often we react to an offense, missing priceless opportunities to see the glory of God amid evil. Joseph said, "God [will turn] into good what you meant for evil" (Gen. 50:20 TLB).

The story is told of a Chinese boy who wanted to study the trade of turning jade into jewelry. He traveled far to become the apprentice of a seasoned old jeweler. The old man handed the young man a precious piece of stone and told him not to let it go. The jeweler began to speak about life, death, love, hate, the sun, and everything that revolved around it. Finally, he took the stone and sent the boy back to his home. They repeated the process for two months, each time with a different piece of jade. The youth inwardly grew impatient but had been brought up too well to question his teacher. Finally, the old man put a smooth stone into the boy's hands. The boy said, "Master, that's not jade!" The teacher said, "You have passed the first lesson in working with jade."[5]

The sage teacher knew the wisdom of studying something real rather than concentrating on a copy. As an FBI chaplain, my (Lenya's) husband, Skip, reports that new FBI agents are trained to watch for counterfeit money by thoroughly studying genuine bills.

Likewise, Jesus told His followers that the way to recognize true believers was to become expert fruit inspectors. He said, "You will know them [false prophets] by their fruits" (Matt. 7:16). If a person is exhibiting the fruit of the Spirit, he or she comes from the right seed. But those who fail to practice what they preach may be imposters.

LISTEN TO ...

Of evil grain, no good seed can come.

—English Proverb

DAY 3

The Prophetic Illustration

Jesus spoke in parables more than anyone else in Scripture. The word *parable* is used thirty-five times in the Gospels, referring to the stories Jesus told. The word is utilized twice in the book of Hebrews, although it is translated "figurative" or "symbolic." But Jesus was not the only one to use compelling stories. Ezekiel knew their power and spoke them to rebuke the nation of Israel for its rebellion. To expose King David's adulterous affair with Bathsheba, Nathan the prophet employed a parable about a rich shepherd who robbed a poor citizen of his pet sheep. The Jewish rabbis often incorporated parabolic teachings because of their ability to provide unforgettable lessons.

Today we see Jesus quote another prophetic Scripture: "I will open my mouth in a parable (Ps. 78:2). *Nelson's Bible Dictionary* defines prophecy as predictions about the future and the end time, special messages from God uttered through human spokespeople. The focus of all prophetic truth is Jesus Christ. On the road to Emmaus, Jesus elaborated on *every* Old Testament prophecy regarding Himself to two of His disciples. "Beginning with Moses and all the Prophets, he explained to them what was said in *all* the Scriptures concerning himself" (Luke 24:27 NIV). Wouldn't you love to have a recording of that message? Undoubtedly, Jesus used Psalm 78:2 to partially explain His reasons for speaking in parables. Asaph the psalmist had predicted He would. Isn't it incredible to realize that as we study these parables we are witnesses of prophetic illustrations fulfilled?

LIFT UP ...

Lord, I'm so grateful for Your Word. Because You know all things, I can trust You to guide my life. Thank You for being faithful and true. Amen.

LOOK AT ...

We've learned about the devastating effects of darnel weeds and the caution required in removing them. Today we pause to ponder why Jesus began teaching in parables. The Lord's closest disciples noticed a change in His teaching methods and asked, "Why do You speak to them

in parables?" (Matt. 13:10). He gave them three reasons. First, we've seen that He spoke in parables to fulfill prophecy: "I will open my mouth in a parable; I will utter dark sayings of old" (Ps. 78:2).

Second, Jesus had "secrets" or things He had not previously shared with His disciples. These secrets were presented to the multitudes in parables and then explained to the disciples in private. The disciples were blessed with an understanding not shared by the leaders or the masses. Jesus told them, "Because it has been given to you to know the mysteries of the kingdom of heaven, but to them it has not been given" (Matt. 13:11).

Third, by speaking in parables, Jesus could conceal these "secrets" from those who refused to believe. Quoting Isaiah, He said, "Hearing you will hear and shall not understand, and seeing you will see and not perceive" (Matt. 13:14).[6] As you read today's lesson, ask God for unencumbered hearing and sight so that you may truly grasp the mystery, truth, and blessing found in these parables.

READ MATTHEW 13:34–36.

All these things Jesus spoke to the multitude in parables; and without a parable He did not speak to them, that it might be fulfilled which was spoken by the prophet, saying: "I will open My mouth in parables; I will utter things kept secret from the foundation of the world." Then Jesus sent the multitude away and went into the house. And His disciples came to Him, saying, "Explain to us the parable of the tares of the field." Matthew 13:34–36

1. a. To whom did Jesus speak in parables?

    b. Why are we reminded of this fact?

2. How often did Jesus speak in parables during this time in His ministry?

3. Explain how His use of parables proved He was Messiah.

4. Jesus fulfilled over three hundred prophecies during His life on earth. Twenty of these fulfilled prophecies are in the Psalms. Look up three or more of the following references to find the prophecies. Then try to find references in the New Testament for each prophecy's fulfillment: Psalm 2:7; 8:6; 16:10; 22:1, 7–8, 16, 18; 34:20; 35:19; 40:7–8; 41:9; 45:6; 68:18; 69:9, 21; 109:8; 110:1, 4; 118:22, 26.

OLD TESTAMENT PROPHECY   **NEW TESTAMENT FULFILLMENT**

5. What did Jesus do after He finished teaching the multitude in parables?

6. Describe what the disciples did and why you think they used this approach.

LIVE OUT ...

7. Psalm 78 was quoted in today's text as being prophetic of the Messiah's teaching style. Read verses 1–8 of this psalm.

    a. Explain how these verses persuade you to learn God's Word and teach it to others.

    b. How are you sharing the truth God reveals to you with the physical or spiritual children in your life?

8. The parables revealed "things kept secret from the foundation of the world." Look up the following verses to discover other things that happened at or before the foundation of the world.

LEARN ABOUT ...

5 Safe At Home

The house was probably owned by Simon Peter and located in Capernaum. It was large enough to accommodate his wife's mother and his brother Andrew. Jesus seems to have lived in this house during this time. It was through this house's roof that the paralytic was lowered (see Mark 2:1–12).

7 Shared Lesson

Before we can share God's Word, we must "give ear" to it (v. 1). This means to broaden out the ear with the hand and listen intently. Many people in Scripture called out to God, asking Him to "give ear" to their cry. When you listen to Him, He'll listen to you.

8 Secret Revealed

God's eternal plan, designed before the foundation of the world, was a mystery to be unveiled in His perfect time. This secret primarily referred to God's plan of salvation through Christ. It also refers to the salvation of Gentiles, the resurrection of believers, and the future salvation of Israel.

SCRIPTURE	WHAT ELSE HAPPENED?
Matthew 25:34	
John 17:24	
Ephesians 1:4	
1 Peter 1:18–20	

9. We saw that Jesus lived at Peter's house in Capernaum. Read John 14:23, and explain where Jesus is now at home and how He comes to dwell there.

10. If you have not invited Jesus to live at home in your heart, rewrite the following verse into a prayer responding to His: "I stand at the door and knock. If anyone hears My voice and opens the door, I will come in to him and dine with him, and he with Me" (Rev. 3:20).

o o ● o o

In an article on keeping secrets, Dr. Myrna Dartson, a psychologist in Dallas, offers a simple rule of thumb: "If you want a secret to remain a secret, keep it to yourself. If someone tells you something in confidence, assume that it's not meant to be shared with others." In the same article, Dr. Lauren Durant, a licensed clinical psychologist based in Durham, North Carolina, reveals that honesty is the best policy. She says, "If you're capable of doing it, you should be capable of disclosing it." However, Durant says sharing secrets with the right person can be advantageous: "The benefit is that it gives you closeness that you might not otherwise be able to accomplish."[7] Jesus told secrets to draw His disciples closer. He said, "I no longer call you slaves, because a master doesn't confide in his slaves. Now you are my friends, since I have told you everything the Father told me" (John 15:15 NLT).

Old Testament prophets alluded to the mystery of the three phases of the kingdom of heaven. But no one really understood that, between Christ's two appearances, there would be a period of time when good and evil would coexist on earth. As a good friend, Jesus explained this mystery to His disciples, but even they didn't completely comprehend this mystery until the Holy Spirit came to dwell in their hearts. Now the kingdom of heaven is a secret no more—it is a truth we are free to share with everyone we know, drawing others near to God.

LISTEN TO ...

Keep a secret and it is yours; tell it to God and it's prayer; tell it to people and it's gossip.

—*Anonymous*

DAY 4

The Master's Explanation

To *master* something means to become skilled or proficient and to gain a thorough understanding.[8] For instance, a skillful carpenter could be called a "master builder"; Alfred Hitchcock was known as the "master of suspense"; Jim Henson, creator of Kermit the Frog and Miss Piggy, was a "puppet master."

Mr. Ali Hassan proved himself to be master of Egyptian artifacts through a famous discovery. During 1977, millions of curiosity seekers flocked to museums throughout the United States to behold the treasures from King Tutankhamen's tomb. A story appeared shortly afterward in a Chicago newspaper. It seems that Ali Hassan, curator of the Egyptian Museum in Cairo, discovered that some of the jewels found in the tomb were not genuine—they were nothing but glass! The question was raised, how could this fact go undetected for so many years? Mr. Hassan explained, "We were blinded by the gold. One just assumes that real gold and real gems go hand-in-hand. This is a case where they don't."[9] Although other experts were fooled by all that glitters, Mr. Hassan detected the difference between genuine gems and glittering glass.

Shiny objects don't fool God either. He can tell the difference between "gold, silver, costly stones, wood, hay or straw" (1 Cor. 3:12 NIV). He is a discerner of the thoughts and intents of the human heart. Today we'll see that God knows the difference between "sons of the kingdom" and "sons of the wicked one." As Master of His domain, He gives an explanation concerning the parable of the Wheat and the Tares.

LIFT UP ...

Thank You, Holy Spirit, for enlightening my natural mind so I can understand the wonders of my God through His Holy Word. Amen.

LOOK AT ...

We see in today's lesson how faithful Jesus was to explain the parable of the Wheat and the Tares to His disciples. In these verses He equated each character in the story to his spiritual counterpart. Here we see a picture of good and evil existing side by side as the Lord, identified as the sower of good seed, looks on.

The owner of the field, the sower of the wheat, is Jesus Christ Himself. The picture painted of the sower is one of wisdom, patience, and compassion. He wisely recognized the bad seed as the influence of evil in the lives of His children. He patiently observed but never failed to nourish and protect His own. He compassionately waited to destroy any life until it was clear which would bear fruit and which would not. He wasn't willing to chance the destruction of the good simply to eliminate the bad. On the other hand, He wasn't willing to eliminate the bad without taking every opportunity to confirm that evil would not result in good. Though we may not understand it, Jesus allows evil to grow for a period of time. But good will be victorious. In God's perfect plan, we must patiently coexist with the bad in order to await the harvest of the ultimate good.

LEARN ABOUT ...

1 Son of Man

Son of Man is used in the Old and New Testament to refer to the Messiah. Jesus used this title for Himself over eighty times. *Son of Man* conveys Christ's humanity and His ability to reach out to both Jews and Gentiles. "The Son of Man is Lord" (Matt. 12:8).

---

3 Portraits of People

The Bible teaches that there are only two types of people in the world: those who belong to God and those who belong to Satan. Jesus said, "He who is not with Me is against Me, and he who does not gather with Me scatters abroad" (Matt. 12:30).

READ MATTHEW 13:37–39.

He answered and said to them: "He who sows the good seed is the Son of Man. The field is the world, the good seeds are the sons of the kingdom, but the tares are the sons of the wicked one. The enemy who sowed them is the devil, the harvest is the end of the age, and the reapers are the angels."
Matthew 13:37–39

1. On Day 1, we learned that the owner of the field in this parable sowed good seed in his own field. According to Jesus, who did this man represent?

2. Explain what the field represents.

3. Describe the types of people planted in the world.

4. Read 1 John 3:10–12; then describe the differences between the children of God and the children of the Devil.

5. While the Son of Man sowed good seed in His field, who sowed the tares?

6. What does the harvest represent?

7. Who will remove the sons of the wicked one at the end of the age?

LIVE OUT ...

8. Today we discovered that the field—the world—in this parable belongs to Jesus Christ. However, not all who live in the world are His children.

   a. Why do you think God plants His children in a field where He knows the Enemy will plant counterfeit believers?

   b. How will you commit to becoming a stronger wheat plant—someone God uses to transform "sons of the wicked one" into "sons of the kingdom"?

   ❏ Spend time in prayer for _____

   ❏ Refuse to go along with the crowd

   ❏ Be prepared to share the truth of the gospel

   ❏ Other _____

9. As we saw in the parable of the Sower, one of the Devil's tactics is to snatch away the good seed of God's Word from the wayside. A second tactic is demonstrated in this week's parable: to secretly infiltrate the wheat field with counterfeit wheat.

a. According to 2 Corinthians 11:13–15, who could this counterfeit wheat represent?

b. Compare their fate to the fate of the tares in our parable.

10. Assisting in the separation of evil from good at the end of the age is only one of the angels' jobs. Look up the following verses to discover additional activities of angels.

SCRIPTURE	ACTIVITIES OF ANGELS
Psalm 91:11	
Psalm 103:20–21	
Hebrews 1:14	
Revelation 22:8–9	

LEARN ABOUT ...

10 Fallen Angels

In contrast to God's angels, there are also fallen angels, who chose to follow Satan into rebellion: "He was cast to the earth, and his angels were cast out with him" (Rev. 12:9). Their activities include opposing God's angels and His people, corrupting the truth, and performing lying signs and wonders.

○ ○ ● ○ ○

I (Penny) am not a gardener. But I researched master gardeners and learned that they share three characteristics: They're hands on, willing to lend a hand, and hands off. And God is truly the Master Gardener. He's hands on, willing to dig in the dirt of our lives and plant new hearts and new habits. He's also willing to lend a hand—He even sent the Holy Spirit to be our Helper. But He can also be hands off. As the true Master Gardener, He has the patience to wait and see what grows in the soil of our hearts.

While I'm no gardener, my husband, Kerry, is: He enjoys planting flowers, pruning bushes, and even pulling weeds. In his mind's eye, there's always potential for new growth. Not long ago, I walked by a little sprout peeking up in our yard and plucked it out. Kerry came outside and said, "Did you pull up that shoot growing in the corner? I've been watching it for three years to see what it would turn into." Oops—I had weeded out what needed to be watched and watered with love.[11]

Aren't you glad God was hands off and graciously waited for you to turn into wheat rather than a tare in His garden? Pray for His supernatural gardening ability to transform the unbelievers around you into those who are rooted in the faith.

LISTEN TO ...

When there is pruning, the gardener is nearby.

—Unknown

DAY 5
The Final Examination

New York City flaunts its extravagance from the stock exchange on Wall Street to the department stores lining Fifth Avenue. Trend-setting fashionistas adorn themselves with heels by Manolo Blahnik and handbags by Louis Vuitton. And many of us find ourselves fighting our own insecurities based on what Madison Avenue tells us is hip and cool. If looks could kill, judging a person's worth based on outward appearance can be deadly.

But many people know a little secret that confuses such quick judgments—camouflage. Tucked away on a side alley in Soho are street vendors selling fake Louis Vuitton handbags that will fool the most discriminating sophisticate. Complete with dust covers, tags, and certificates of authenticity, there are purses that masterfully copy Louis Vuitton's logo on vinyl with leather trim. It would take a real expert to discern the knockoff from the real McCoy.

Judging by externals is not easy or wise. The parable of the Wheat and the Tares reminds us that sometimes it's impossible for us to tell the difference between genuine faith and a facade. That's why God prudently tells the harvesters not to touch the harvest until the end of the age. That's when He will send His angels to judge between true and false—righteous and religious. This parable is an explanation of Jesus' comment "Judge not, that you be not judged" (Matt. 7:1). Judgment is a heavenly, not a human, function. In the final examination, God alone will be the judge.

LIFT UP ...

Heavenly Father, give me Your heart for those who are lost. Remind me to pray and boldly speak to those You are drawing to Yourself. Amen.

LOOK AT ...

Yesterday we learned the true identity of the characters portrayed in the parable of the Wheat and the Tares. Today we experience the reality of the judgment to come at the end of this age. At that time God will send His angels to gather together those whose names are not found written in the Book of Life. On this day there will be no confusion or

LEARN ABOUT ...

2 Fire

Fire is frequently used to portray God's judgment. Jesus spoke of hellfire as "the fire that shall never be quenched" (Mark 9:45). Revelation 21:8 describes "the lake which burns with fire and brimstone" as "the second death."

---

3 Offend

"Offend" is translated from the Greek word *skandalon*, which means to ensnare or entrap. Jesus said this about causing others to sin: "Woe to the world because of offenses! For offenses must come, but woe to that man by whom the offense comes!" (Matt. 18:7).

negotiation, no begging or bargaining. The Book of Life will contain the accurate record of all who have been saved through the sacrifice of Jesus Christ. No one will argue with the righteousness of the judgments made.

Scholars disagree on the specific details surrounding the Book of Life—but on the outcome they all agree. Unbelievers' names will not be found in the Book of Life, and they will be forever separated from God, condemned to the lake of fire (see Rev. 20:15). Those who believe will have their names listed in the Book of Life. These will spend eternity with the Lord (see John 5:24). It must be one way or the other; there is no middle ground.

Search your heart! Do you believe? Are you saved? Be sure, today, that your name is written in the Lamb's Book of Life!

READ MATTHEW 13:40–43.

"Therefore as the tares are gathered and burned in the fire, so it will be at the end of this age. The Son of Man will send out His angels, and they will gather out of His kingdom all things that offend, and those who practice lawlessness, and will cast them into the furnace of fire. There will be wailing and gnashing of teeth. Then the righteous will shine forth as the sun in the kingdom of their Father. He who has ears to hear, let him hear!" Matthew 13:40–43

1. Based on what you've learned about the meaning of this parable, what will happen at the end of the age?

2. According to Revelation 20:15, who will meet this horrible fate?

3. What kinds of "tares" will be removed by the angels at the Son of Man's command?

4. Use the Scriptures above to fill in the blanks. Offensive and lawless ones will be gathered *"out of _____"* and cast *"into _____."*

5. What descriptive phrases did Jesus use to depict the atmosphere in the furnace of fire?

6. What word picture did Jesus use to describe the future of the righteous (Matt. 13:43)?

7. Compare the final destination of the wheat in this parable with that of the righteous. (See also Matt. 13:30.)

8. How do you know Jesus believed this parable was profoundly important?

Live out ...

9. In this parable we see God's patience in allowing tares and wheat to grow together until the latest possible hour: "The Lord ... is longsuffering toward us, not willing that any should perish but that all should come to repentance" (2 Peter 3:9). Journal about God's long-suffering toward you. How did He patiently wait for you to respond? Is He still waiting?

10. This parable warns that the lawless will be cast into the "furnace of fire," or hell. Answer the following questions to discover how to avoid this fate.

    a. Revelation 21:7 promises, "He who overcomes shall inherit all things, and I will be his God and he shall be My son." Read Revelation 12:10–11, and explain how to be an overcomer.

    b. Make a list of the loved ones in your life who have not yet overcome. Keep this list in your Bible, and regularly ask God "to open their eyes and turn them from darkness to light, and

Learn about ...

5 Entrap

"Wailing and gnashing of teeth" is used exclusively by Jesus to describe the anguish of eternal separation from God's presence. Those rejecting Christ's offer of salvation will not be found in the Book of Life. A vastly different experience awaits the true believer, for "in Your presence is fullness of joy" (Ps. 16:11).

9 Everlasting

Even though the "everlasting fire [was] prepared for the devil and his angels" (Matt. 25:41), many humans will meet their destiny there. Those who live for this life face two deaths: physical and spiritual. Those who are born twice (physically and spiritually) die only once (physically) and then enter into everlasting life.[12]

10 Gehenna

The word translated "hell"—*Gehenna*—was the name of Jerusalem's garbage dump. It held the filth of the city, including animals' and criminals' dead bodies. The waste burned continuously. Wild dogs howled and gnashed their teeth, fighting over the rubbish. Because God is holy, no garbage will be allowed in His heavenly kingdom.

from the power of Satan to God, so that they may receive forgiveness of sins and a place among those who are sanctified by faith" (Acts 26:18 NIV).

11. Jesus promised the righteous would shine forth like the sun. According to 2 Corinthians 5:21, explain how we become righteous.

○ ○ ● ○ ○

More than anything in the world, a goat wanted to be a lion. He thought, *If I can walk like a lion, talk like a lion, and go where a lion goes, then I'll be a lion.* Day after day he practiced stalking through the jungle and swishing his stubby little tail majestically. Then he tried to transform his pitiful little bleat into the awesome roar of the king of beasts. He worked and worked on it. Finally, he convinced himself that he looked and sounded like a lion. "Now," he said, "all I have to do is go where lions go." So one day about lunchtime he marched into lion territory. You can imagine what happened. It turned out very baaaad for him.

Like the poor goat, sometimes people think that because they've learned to walk, talk, and act like Christians, they really are. However, in the final examination, God will separate the sheep from the goats and the tares from the wheat. Thankfully, unlike plants that are destined to remain wheat or weeds, God is able to transform "sons of the wicked one" into "sons of the kingdom." All He needs is an ear that will hear His still small voice and a heart that will bend to His gentle hand.

LISTEN TO ...

The devil wrestles with God, and the field of battle is the human heart.

—*Fyodor Dostoyevsky*

LESSON THREE

What Goes Around Comes Around

Matthew 18:21–35

The modern Hebrew language is clear and colorful. However, it's not necessarily forgiving. One favorite phrase is *Magiyah Lo*. It literally means "To him it should be received." In English we'd say, "What goes around comes around" or "You deserve it." *Magiyah Lo* can be used when a snotty politician gets his comeuppance or when a wealthy cheapskate gets caught by the IRS. It must be stated with a certain smugness. When uttered, it might make the person speaking feel better, but it won't make the situation better.[1]

Unfortunately, modern and ancient human beings aren't very forgiving. Secretly, we rather enjoy seeing others get what they deserve. We've all driven past cars stopped by the highway patrol and said, "They deserved it!" But the other side of the coin is that as imperfect human beings, we don't want to get what *we* deserve. How many times have you broken the speed limit and gratefully driven away without a ticket?

Thankfully, God's standard for forgiveness is different from ours. He says, "For as the heavens are higher than the earth, so are My ways higher than your ways, and My thoughts than your thoughts" (Isa. 55:9). This truth was lived out in Jesus Christ, who uttered something beautifully gracious: "Father, forgive them, for they do not know what they do" (Luke 23:34).

This week we'll study the parable of the Unforgiving Servant and discover that forgiveness doesn't come naturally, but it can be acquired supernaturally.

Day 1: Matthew 18:21–22   **QUESTIONING THE LIMITS**
Day 2: Matthew 18:23–27   **RELEASING THE DEBTOR**
Day 3: Matthew 18:28–30   **REQUIRING JUSTICE**
Day 4: Matthew 18:31–33   **CAUSING GRIEF**
Day 5: Matthew 18:34–35   **REAPING THE CONSEQUENCES**

DAY I
Questioning the Limits

LIFT UP ...

Lord, thank You for forgiving me completely and unconditionally. Help me to forgive others in the same manner that You have forgiven me. Amen.

LOOK AT ...

Many things had happened since Jesus last spoke to the multitudes in parables. The Pharisees continued to test Him. John the Baptist had been beheaded. Jesus had fed the five thousand and walked on water. He had predicted His death and resurrection and was transfigured on a mountaintop in the presence of Peter, James, and John. He had healed the sick and miraculously paid His taxes. In this week's parable, Jesus departed from speaking of the kingdom of God generally to addressing an individual spiritual matter: personal forgiveness.

For generations, the Pharisees and Sadducees had interpreted the laws of Moses by emphasizing a works-based religion rather than one focused on faith in God. Their teachings had become legalistic and burdensome. Jesus' teachings must have been so refreshing to the simple people who were often treated as lower-class citizens by the religious leadership of the day. Today we see Jesus teach about the true meaning of forgiveness, beginning when Peter questioned the limits of forgiveness. This week, ask yourself if have the faith to simply forgive.

READ MATTHEW 18:21–22.

Then Peter came to Him and said, "Lord, how often shall my brother sin against me, and I forgive him? Up to seven times?" Jesus said to him, "I do not say to you, up to seven times, but up to seventy times seven." Matthew 18:21–22

LEARN ABOUT ...

3 Brotherhood

Brother can describe many relationships: blood kin, a fellow citizen, a disciple or follower, a person sharing the same faith, a colleague, people united in affection. Jesus described His brothers clearly: "Whoever does the will of My Father in heaven is My brother" (Matt. 12:50).

4 Forgiveness

Peter took it for granted that forgiveness was a given. However, he did question how often he should forgive a perpetual offender. He probably thought he was being generous by offering to forgive seven times, since traditional rabbinic teachings required people to forgive an offender only three times. He doubled it and added one.

6 Completeness

The numbers seven and ten are used in Scripture to symbolize completeness. Jesus did some math— 7 x 10 x 7 or "seventy times seven"—to convey that forgiveness should be complete and infinite. Since He forgives us completely, we are to forgive others without limits. Peter learned this well, writing, "love will cover a multitude of sins" (1 Peter 4:8).

1. What was the first part of Peter's question to Jesus?

2. Read Matthew 18:15–17 for context, and explain what prompted Peter's query.

3. What term of endearment did Peter use to describe who he should forgive? In modern vernacular what does this term encompass?

4. How far was Peter theoretically willing to extend forgiveness?

5. What limit did Jesus *not* place on forgiveness?

6. Explain the upward boundaries of forgiveness according to Jesus.

LIVE OUT ...

7. A willingness to forgive is an essential characteristic for Christ's brethren.

   a. Write the name of a family member or brother or sister in Christ you have a hard time forgiving.

   b. Describe how this situation has affected you spiritually, emotionally, and physically.

   c. Journal a prayer asking God to help you forgive the person you named "up to seventy times seven."

8. Today we explored forgiveness without limits. Describe how you have personally experienced God's boundless forgiveness in your own life.

9. Christ's forgiveness wasn't limited to His brothers (those who believed).

    a. Explain who you think Jesus was asking His Father to forgive in Luke 23:34.

    b. According to Romans 5:10, what were we in relation to God before He forgave us?

    c. In order to mirror His example, who else do you think we should forgive? Why and under what circumstances? (Use your Bible concordance to find Scripture to back up your answers.)

○ ○ ● ○ ○

Shortly after World War II, a church invited two prominent Christian women to attend a conference: Mrs. Eumura from Japan and Mrs. Llano from the Philippines. It was evident that their relationship was strained. The Filipino was resentful, remembering the atrocities the Japanese had inflicted upon her family members during the war. One night, she went to her room, feeling guilty about her attitude toward a sister in Christ. Suddenly there was a knock on the door. When she opened it, she saw Mrs. Eumura standing there. "I sense tension between us," she said. "I wonder if it is related to the recent war between our countries. If so, will you forgive my people for the terrible crimes they committed?" The women embraced, then knelt together and prayed.

Though Mrs. Eumura had not personally warred against Mrs. Llano's family, she took it upon herself to humbly ask for forgiveness for the pain Mrs. Llano's family had endured. God gave Mrs. Llano the grace to forgive, and the animosity was supernaturally healed.[2]

How beautiful for former enemies to become close friends through the power of forgiveness. Even more beautiful was the bond these

LEARN ABOUT ...

7 Pardoned

To forgive is to put aside or release from debt; to pardon despite slights, shortcomings, and errors. God's forgiveness is based upon a price paid in blood for sin. Our forgiveness is based on forgiveness received from God for sin. We forgive because He forgave: "forgiving one another, even as God in Christ forgave you" (Eph. 4:32).

9 Obedience

Jeremiah 17:9 says, "The heart is deceitful above all things, and desperately wicked." Our willingness to forgive should not be based on feelings, but on obedience to God's Word: "Forgiving one another ... even as Christ forgave you, so you also must do" (Col. 3:13). Forgiveness is a divine command, the Sovereign's direction.

spiritual sisters shared in the Lord. Paul explained the mysterious family relationship available to all God's children: "For you are all children of God through faith in Christ Jesus. And all who have been united with Christ in baptism have put on the character of Christ, like putting on new clothes" (Gal. 3:26–27 NLT). To become like Christ, we must learn to forgive like Christ—seventy times seven.

LISTEN TO ...

As we practice the work of forgiveness we discover more and more that forgiveness and healing are one.

—Agnes Sanford

DAY 2
Releasing the Debtor

In Snellville, Georgia, a startling tale of an unneighborly neighbor unfolded. For years, Earl Lazenby had carried the mail to the home with overgrown plants and a National Rifle Association sticker on the front door. William Crutchfield was always friendly to his letter carrier, visiting with Lazenby as they shopped at their local store. But Lazenby didn't know that Crutchfield was desperate. You might say he was ready to go postal! Crutchfield had seen Olympic bomber Eric Rudolph head to prison and envied his fate. He wanted the pressure from deep debt off him. So in July 2005, Crutchfield decided to shoot the only federal employee he knew—his friendly postman—so he could be in federal prison receiving medical care rather than on the streets. After the shooting, he drove to the police station and said, "I just shot the letter carrier." Lazenby lived but would never be able to digest food or produce insulin by himself.[3]

Today in the parable of the Unforgiving Servant, we meet a man much like Crutchfield. He threw himself on the mercy of the court but was unwilling to show mercy to others.

LIFT UP ...

Thank You, Lord, for having compassion on me and setting me free from sin and death. Help me to walk in the Spirit so that I can be merciful as well. Amen.

LOOK AT ...

Yesterday Christ taught how forgiveness toward fellow believers should be complete and unlimited. Believers can rest in the knowledge that we can impart forgiveness to others based on the mercy and faithfulness Christ has extended to us. We need to grasp on to this mercy and cling to His faithfulness when we find it difficult to forgive the wounds that others have inflicted on us. Perhaps if we remembered the gravity of our own sin, we would be more willing to forgive. If we saw ourselves through Christ's pure and perfect eyes, we would understand the debt we owe to Him for dying on our behalf and paying the price for our sin.

Today, as you read the parable of the Unforgiving Servant and learn through Christ's

LEARN ABOUT ...

2 Accounting

To settle accounts means to come together and compute or to reckon a debt that is owed and resolve it. It was not atypical for kings to audit their books to determine the faithfulness of their servants and stewards. God will do this with us: "So then each of us shall give account of himself to God" (Rom. 14:12).

3 Uncountable

John MacArthur said, "Just as 'seventy times seven' represents a limitless number of times, ten thousand talents represents a limitless amount of money."[4] Ten thousand was the largest numerical term in the Greek language and gives us our English word *myriad*. It literally meant innumerably many. This was a vast, uncountable debt.

4 Crouching

The English phrase "fell down" does not adequately describe the servant's response. The Greek word is *proskuneo*, which literally means to fawn or crouch. The implication is that he prostrated himself like a dog, begging for mercy. The promise to "pay you all" was absurd ... his debt was so enormous as to be unpayable.

storytelling about the immense debt we owe because of our sin, remember that there is no amount of money that can pay the debt you owe to Christ.

READ MATTHEW 18:23–27.

"Therefore the kingdom of heaven is like a certain king who wanted to settle accounts with his servants. And when he had begun to settle accounts, one was brought to him who owed him ten thousand talents. But as he was not able to pay, his master commanded that he be sold, with his wife and children and all that he had, and that payment be made. The servant therefore fell down before him, saying, 'Master, have patience with me, and I will pay you all.' Then the master of that servant was moved with compassion, released him, and forgave him the debt." Matthew 18:23–27

1. To whom did Jesus compare the kingdom of heaven?

2. Explain what the king decided to do and with whom.

3. Let's learn more about one particular servant.

   a. Describe this servant's debt and his capacity to pay.

   b. Explain the master's ruling and its effect on the servant.

4. Describe the servant's physical response and verbal requests.

5. What deep feeling did the master have for the servant? Where else have you seen this in the Gospels?

6. In your own words describe how the master treated his servant.

7. Based on your knowledge of the parables, who do you think the master and servant represent?

LIVE OUT ...

8. a. The servant was brought before the king to settle his account. What do you learn from the following verses about our future day of accounting?

   2 Corinthians 5:10

   Hebrews 4:13

   b. Journal your thoughts about standing before God to give a reckoning for your actions. Are you fearful or hopeful about that day?

9. a. In one sense, the servant's debt symbolizes the infinite debt we owe God for our sin. What does Psalm 38:4 reveal about our sin?

   b. According to Romans 6:23, what is the punishment for our sin?

   c. According to Acts 8:22, what must we do to be forgiven?

10. The king in the parable exercised both patience and compassion in forgiving the servant's debt. Match the Scripture references with the truths about God's forgiveness and the way He shows patience and compassion toward us.

LEARN ABOUT ...

8 Reckoning

Believers will not experience judgment for sin because Christ died for them on the cross. However, believers will be evaluated at Christ's judgment seat for reward or loss of reward: "If anyone's work which he has built on it endures, he will receive a reward. If anyone's work is burned, he will suffer loss" (1 Cor. 3:14–15).

9 Repentance

Only the Bible teaches that God forgives sin. Biblically, two conditions must be met for God to extend forgiveness: (1) A life must be taken as a substitute for that of the sinner since "without shedding of blood there is no remission" (Heb. 9:22); (2) the sinner must accept Christ's sacrifice in a spirit of repentance and faith.

Psalm 103:12	He does not condemn.
Isaiah 43:25	Freely offers justification from sin.
Romans 3:24	He blots out sin.
Romans 8:1	He forgives sin.
1 John 1:9	He removes sin.

○ ○ ● ○ ○

Bill Carey won't be retiring anytime soon. The president and owner of a small business in Wichita, Kansas, got the first clue his retirement would be postponed when his trusted bookkeeper stepped out for the weekend in January 1999. Checking to see if a bill had been paid, Carey discovered that the bookkeeper—a single mother who was like family to him—had written two company checks totaling $10,000 to pay her MasterCard and Visa bills. To cover her tracks, she had forged Carey's signature and recorded the checks as payments to company suppliers. When he confronted her, Carey says, she broke down, begged forgiveness, and claimed it was the first time she'd ever done it. But an FBI investigation revealed otherwise. In the end, she pleaded guilty to embezzling $250,000 over five years. Carey thinks the actual amount is closer to $500,000.... Embezzlement, it turns out, knows no bounds.... "It's corporate America's dirty little secret," adds Martin Biegelman, a certified fraud examiner.... "The question is not will I be victimized, it's when and for how much?"[5]

The servant in this parable had probably embezzled from his master. How amazing that the master was willing to forgive when he saw the servant fall at his feet. So, too, as sinful humans, we are completely bankrupt and have robbed God of His glory by our errant actions. How wonderful that all He asks is for us to bow down in humility and seek forgiveness. He will graciously forgive our debt.

LISTEN TO ...

As mercy is God's goodness confronting human misery and guilt, so grace is his goodness directed toward human debt and demerit.

—*A. W. Tozer*

DAY 3

Requiring Justice

Aesop, like Jesus, was a storyteller whose tales always carried strong moral lessons. His story "The Woodman and the Serpent" is one of his lesser-known stories, but it resonates with one of the truths found in the parable of the Unforgiving Servant. Let's read the timeless tale:

> One wintry day a Woodman was tramping home from his work when he saw something black lying on the snow. When he came closer, he saw it was a Serpent to all appearances dead. But he took it up and put it in his bosom to warm while he hurried home. As soon as he got indoors he put the Serpent down on the hearth before the fire. The children watched it and saw it slowly come to life again. Then one of them stooped down to stroke it, but the Serpent raised its head and put out its fangs and was about to sting the child to death. So the Woodman seized his axe, and with one stroke cut the Serpent in two. "Ah," said he, "no gratitude from the wicked."[6]

Today, we see the how the servant who had been forgiven a great debt acted like a snake in his treatment of a fellow servant. He required justice from a fellow human being when he had received mercy from his master. The moral is clear: When we are offered mercy and forgiveness, we ought to extend mercy and forgiveness to others.

LIFT UP ...

Lord, You have forgiven me so much. Mold me into one who is willing to forgive others as I have been forgiven. Amen.

LOOK AT ...

Our parable has shown us a man forgiven a tremendous debt by a compassionate master. Now we see how the servant who was forgiven treated another who owed him a petty debt.

Throughout His ministry, Jesus emphasized the importance of showing forgiveness

LEARN ABOUT ...

1 Small Change

The silver denarius was a Roman coin, probably equal to a laborer's daily wage. It was used for paying taxes to the Roman emperor, whose image it carried. One hundred denarii could have been repaid in a short time; 10,000 talents was a king's ransom, impossible to repay.

3 Small-Mindedness

While the servant had the legal right to request the debt be repaid, he did not have the moral right to assault the man. A Latin saying explains, *Summum jus summa injuria*—Push a claim to an extremity, and it becomes a wrong. It is possible to demand your rights to the point of being wrong.

6 Mean Spirit

"Would not" implies a conscious decision made by the unforgiving servant. In contrast to the king, he chose unforgiveness and cast the fellow servant into the prison he had been sentenced to. Because the debtor could not work to repay the debt while in prison, the unforgiving servant's actions were plainly vengeful and mean-spirited.

to the least and the lost. It has been said that harboring unforgiveness is like drinking poison and waiting for the other person to die. On the other hand, mercy is a godly characteristic highly valued highly by God. The Jewish people knew that mercy is one of God's characteristics. For instance, He established the Year of Jubilee to free debtors and to allow those who had lost their inherited land to reclaim it. God shows great mercy and forbearance. Should we do any less?

READ MATTHEW 18:28–30.

"But that servant went out and found one of his fellow servants who owed him a hundred denarii; and he laid hands on him and took him by the throat, saying, 'Pay me what you owe!' So his fellow servant fell down at his feet and begged him, saying, 'Have patience with me, and I will pay you all.' And he would not, but went and threw him into prison till he should pay the debt." Matthew 18:28–30

1. Describe who the servant sought after receiving his pardon and why he sought him.

2. Based on your knowledge of the parables, who do the two servants represent?

3. Describe the physical action the servant took against his debtor.

4. Reread Matthew 18:26. Compare the two servants' responses to the repayment demands.

5. What realistic promise did this debtor make?

6. Contrast the way the servant treated his debtor with the way he had been treated.

LIVE OUT ...

7. If the first servant's debt to the king is a picture of what we owe to God, then the debt one servant owes to another symbolizes what we owe to fellow believers we have hurt in some way.

   a. Read Luke 17:3–4. When a believer has been wronged, what should be done?

   b. Where do you think the unforgiving servant in the parable went wrong?

8. Read Galatians 6:1, and explain in what spirit restoration should take place.

9. The first servant's unforgiveness led to a physical reaction—he laid hands on and tried to choke the debtor. How has unforgiveness impacted your life?

❏ Physical: Outbursts of anger, throwing, yelling, hitting, other:

❏ Emotional: Depression, grief, fatigue, other:

❏ Spiritual: Feeling distant from God, unanswered prayer, other:

10. Journal about a time you let anger get the best of you. Ask God to make you more like Him: "The LORD is gracious and full of compassion, slow to anger and great in mercy" (Ps. 145:8).

∘ ∘ ● ∘ ∘

Perhaps the unforgiving servant was so embarrassed at his encounter with his master that he decided to let off steam by seeking his fellow servant. Perhaps he wanted to "show" the master that he would repay him, so he

LEARN ABOUT ...

7 Responsibility

Where forgiveness is concerned, the ball is always in our court. If someone sins against us, we should offer forgiveness. "If you ... remember that your brother has something against you ... be reconciled to your brother" (Matt. 5:23–24). Sinner or sinned against, the believer is responsible for seeking reconciliation.

8 Restoration

The goal in addressing wrongs among the brethren is to bring about restoration, not to seek revenge or retaliation: "See that no one renders evil for evil to anyone, but always pursue what is good both for yourselves and for all" (1 Thess. 5:15).

went after everyone who owed him money. Whatever the case, the unforgiving servant acted out in vengeance and anger.

Anger can make us bitter, withdrawn, negative. It can cripple or destroy friendships or other relationships. Anger is destructive, and unless you learn to control it, it will control you. Some suggestions for controlling your anger include the following:

1. Do something to "let off steam" without hurting someone, such as hitting your pillow, doing some physical exercise, or simply taking a deep breath and counting to ten.

2. Try to laugh at little irritations instead of letting them frustrate you.

3. Find out what really made you mad. Look beneath the surface for the root problem.

4. Write an angry letter to the person or situation that got you upset. Be totally honest about your feelings; then tear up the letter.

5. Confront the person you're mad at—but only after you've calmed down—and do it gently without blaming or getting emotional.

6. Learn to forgive.

7. Channel your anger into constructive action. For example, if world hunger makes you angry, volunteer to work at a soup kitchen on weekends.

8. If you find that you consistently can't handle your anger in appropriate ways, get help from a professional counselor.[7]

LISTEN TO ...

If you are suffering from a bad man's injustice, forgive him lest there be two bad men.

—*Augustine of Hippo*

DAY 4

Causing Grief

My (Penny's) kids were stair stepped two years apart, so they served as one another's playmates … and often one another's worst enemies. Sometimes my daughters, Erin and Ryan, would gang up on my son, Kristian, and tell me what naughty things he'd done. Sometimes the older two would take on baby sis, Ryan. She'd hurry in to tattle on her big brother and sister.

One time, Kristian bit Erin when they were playing a game. They had been learning about forgiveness, so this was a good time for Kristian to put his Sunday school lessons into practice. His little face was so serious as he got out a piece of paper and pencil and sat down at his miniature desk. He wrote a note: "Dear Erin, Please forgive me." He even drew a happy face on the note to show that he meant business. Erin took one look at the note, grabbed a pencil, and wrote, "I do not forgive you."

That's when I stepped in. I said to Erin, "Kristian asked for forgiveness. Jesus says we must forgive people." She stubbornly shook her head *no*. So I put her in time-out to think about it. After a few minutes I went to her and asked, "Do you forgive Kristian?" She shook her head *no*. So she was sent to bed for the night. All of us learned a hard lesson: Unforgiveness causes grief to the one who sins and to the one sinned against. But it also causes grief to those caught in the middle.

LIFT UP …

Jesus, it breaks my heart that my unforgiveness causes others sorrow. You have bought me, and I belong to You. Please give me the desire to obey You even when it's difficult. Amen.

LOOK AT …

We've seen that forgiving others not only releases a personal burden but also makes us more like Christ. On the other hand, a lack of forgiveness can bring a great deal of grief to us, others, and God. Paul insists, "Do not grieve the Holy Spirit of God" (Eph. 4:30). Today we see how those who worked alongside the debtor were moved at how their friend was

LEARN ABOUT ...

2 Fellow Servants

"The sins and sufferings of our fellow servants should be a matter of grief and trouble to us. It is sad that any of our brethren should either make themselves beast of prey, by cruelty and barbarity; or be made beasts of slavery, by ... those who have power over them."[9]

---

4 Wicked Servant

Wicked means degenerate, diseased, or derelict; full of mischief and malice. Scripture teaches that "the heart is deceitful above all things, and desperately wicked" (Jer. 17:9). The servant had deceived his master into thinking he was truly repentant.

---

6 Unforgiving Servant

Since the master had forgiven the servant's debt, the servant was honor-bound to show the same compassion he had received. Unfortunately, he did not live up to the master's code of honor: "Whatever you want men to do to you, do also to them" (Matt. 7:12).

treated. What about you? Do you look at injustice in the world and turn a blind eye? Or do you cry out to the Lord and ask Him to make things right? You can trust that God is not simply a God of mercy; He is a God of justice. Though God was merciful to the unforgiving servant, the servant was unmoved. R. C. Trench said, "The guilt which he is charged with is, not that, needing mercy he refused to show it, but that, *having received mercy*, he remains unmerciful still."[8]

READ MATTHEW 18: 31–33.

"So when his fellow servants saw what had been done, they were very grieved, and came and told their master all that had been done. Then his master, after he had called him, said to him, 'You wicked servant! I forgave you all that debt because you begged me. Should you not also have had compassion on your fellow servant, just as I had pity on you?'" Matthew 18:31–33

1. Describe how the other servants responded when they saw the incident.

2. Who do you think the fellow servants represent in this parable?

3. What immediate action did the master take?

4. How did the master describe the servant?

5. What reason did the master give for initially forgiving the servant?

6. Describe how the master expected the one forgiven to treat his fellow servant and why.

LIVE OUT ...

7. Today we read how people took action when they saw one of their own being persecuted.

   a. Because there are persecuted Christians all around the world, what actions can you take today on their behalf?

   - ❐ Make myself more aware of the persecuted church in other countries
   - ❐ Pray regularly for the persecuted church
   - ❐ Give funds or materials to help the persecuted church
   - ❐ Other

   b. The least we can do is the best we can do, and that is to take our grief to the King in prayer. Take action by journaling a prayer for those suffering for their faith.

8. Who do you know or have you heard about who is suffering persecution or ill-treatment because of their faith? Journal a prayer interceding to the King of kings on behalf of their sufferings.

9. As believers we are bound to forgive others because we have been forgiven.

   a. Fill in the chart to discover some other things we are honor-bound to do.

SCRIPTURE	WHAT TO BIND
Proverbs 3:3	
Proverbs 7:2–3	
Romans 7:2	

LEARN ABOUT ...

7 Persecuted Servants

Unfortunately, many of us are ignorant of the persecution of believers in other countries. Here are some basic facts: Since the death of Jesus 2000 years ago, 43 million Christians have been martyred (over 50 percent in the last century alone). Two hundred million face persecution each day. Every day three hundred Christians are killed for their faith.[10]

2 Thessalonians 2:13

b. Which of the above are you failing to do?

c. What actions will you take to change things?

· · ● ○ ○

The neighbors of a Cambodian Christian named Ta Hum bribed a surveyor to alter a property line so that they could claim half an acre of his land. His first response was anger. Determined that they would not get any of his trees or banana plants, he went out one night with a machete to cut down everything valuable. But he couldn't carry out his plan, for he knew that Christ would not approve of his behavior. He asked the Lord to forgive him and to help him turn the other cheek. The next morning he went to his neighbors and said, "You have taken my land. I'll give you my house, too, if you want it. I will go to Ba Xuyen and help the pastor there spread the gospel of Jesus." Ta Hum's surprising reaction quickly became the talk of the village. The chief was so impressed that he decided to look into the matter. After learning the truth, he declared that the property belonged to Ta Hum and that anyone who caused him further trouble would go to jail.[11]

Ta Hum learned the truth found today in the parable of the Unforgiving Servant: Those who see injustice can bring it to the Master, trusting Him to make it right. Paul wrote that the church has a responsibility to watch out for one another: "The members should have the same care for one another. And if one member suffers, all the members suffer with it" (1 Cor. 12:25–26).

LISTEN TO ...

We go to Calvary to learn how we may be forgiven, and to learn how to forgive others, to intercede on their behalf, to join the noble band of intercessors.

—S. J. Reid

DAY 5

Reaping the Consequences

I (Lenya) remember rolling my eyes as Dad said, "This is going to hurt me a lot more than it's going to hurt you," just before spanking my bottom. But now that I have a son, I believe it's one of the truest statements he ever made. No parent enjoys disciplining. I dreaded putting Nathan in time-out, swatting his hand, washing out his mouth, spanking his bottom, or revoking his privileges. However, all of these tactics aided in setting safe boundaries (don't play in the street) or served as consequences when the boundaries were broken (like shooting a friend with his BB gun). Reaping consequences encouraged Nathan to avoid inappropriate behavior, kept him safe from harm, and lovingly taught him to be a mature, godly man.

Our heavenly Father watches over us with paternal love and care so we can grow up spiritually. As the perfect Father, He forgives us, encourages us, and disciplines us. We should find comfort in the knowledge that "as you endure this divine discipline, remember that God is treating you as his own children" (Heb. 12:7 NLT). Scripture encourages us to accept and learn from God's chastening, knowing it is for our own good. The writer of Hebrews reminds us, "Our earthly fathers disciplined us for a few years, doing the best they knew how. But God's discipline is always good for us, so that we might share in his holiness" (Heb. 12:10 NLT). I'm convinced that when God disciplines me, it hurts Him a whole lot more than it hurts me. But it helps me to grow up.

LIFT UP ...

Heavenly Father, because You are both merciful and just, I can put my trust in You. Thank You. Amen.

LOOK AT ...

Yesterday we learned how our unforgiveness affects others, especially our brothers and sisters in Christ. We learned that God takes it seriously when servants who have been forgiven refuse to forgive others. Today we see the consequences of unforgiveness.

LEARN ABOUT ...

1 Indignation

The anger spoken of here is the displeasure and indignation arising from the discovery of offense against the law. God's anger, symbolized by the master's response, is that which stands opposed to humanity's disobedience, obstinacy, and sin. Anger is not evil in itself, since "God is angry with the wicked every day" (Ps. 7:11).

3 Trespasses

The Greek word translated as "trespasses" speaks of a false step or a blunder. Used ethically, it speaks of deviating from what is right and true. To commit a trespass means to violate a law, civil or moral. This may relate to a person, a community, the state, or an action against God.

5 Will to Forgive

In this passage, the word *heart* is not only synonymous with the word *mind*—the center of desires, feelings, and passion—but also involves the will. Forgiveness is not a feeling but a decision: "You have tested my heart.... I have purposed that my mouth shall not transgress" (Ps. 17:3).

Commentators disagree regarding the meaning of the unforgiving servant's fate. Some believe that the unforgiving servant represents one who does not belong in God's household and thus deserves eternal judgment. Others hold that this teaching does not speak of eternal consequences but of the discipline under which God places His children who fall short of His standards. The Bible tells us, "For whom the LORD loves He chastens, and scourges every son whom He receives" (Heb. 12:6). Regardless of the interpretation, we should all take this parable to heart. When we refuse to forgive, we are the one who suffers most horribly.

READ MATTHEW 18:34–35.

"And his master was angry, and delivered him to the torturers until he should pay all that was due to him. So My heavenly Father also will do to you if each of you, from his heart, does not forgive his brother his trespasses." Matthew 18:34–35

1. What emotion did the master feel for the servant?

2. To whom did the master deliver him?

3. Explain what had to happen before the unforgiving servant would be released and how long you think this would take.

4. Explain what lesson Jesus wants us to learn from this parable.

5. From where should forgiveness spring?

6. We have seen that the unforgiving servant experienced forgiveness but did not have a forgiving spirit. What are some results of having an unforgiving spirit? Have you ever experienced this?

LIVE OUT ...

7. Unforgiveness between believers does not require us to pay the ultimate penalty for sin—eternal separation from God. In the following chart, use these phrases to discover the possible consequences of sin in a believer's life: grieve Holy Spirit; loss of fellowship; loss of reward; corruption.

SCRIPTURE	CONSEQUENCE OF SIN FOR BELIEVERS
1 Corinthians 3:1–3	
1 Corinthians 3:13–15	
Galatians 6:8	
Ephesians 4:30–32	

8. According to Revelation 3:19, what should we do when we experience the Lord's divine discipline?

9. Though the consequences of unforgiveness seem harsh, we can take comfort that when we forgive, our heavenly Father will be both merciful and just. The Lord said, "It is mine to avenge; I will repay" (Deut. 32:35 NIV). Based on what you've learned this week, journal about why you think it's better to trust your heavenly Father to bear the burden of justice when people sin against you than to carry the burden yourself.

○ ○ ● ○ ○

Corrie ten Boom was imprisoned in a German concentration camp during World War II, and she suffered much under one of the German guards. Years later she met him at a meeting in postwar Germany. After the meeting, he approached her and asked her to forgive him.

For a brief moment she recalled the suffering of her imprisonment at his hands. He didn't deserve it, but she forgave him. She writes in *Tramp for the Lord,* "Forgiveness is the key which unlocks the door of resentment and the handcuffs of hatred. It breaks the chains of bitterness and the shackles of selfishness." Corrie offered forgiveness to her persecutor. Instead of allowing unforgiveness toward a man to grow into hatred toward a nation or disdain of an entire gender, she allowed forgiveness to unshackle her heart.[13] Have you been liberated from all forms of unforgiveness, from prejudice to self-pity?

Robert Muller (former assistant secretary general of the UN) developed a suggested plan: "Sunday—forgive yourself; Monday—forgive your family; Tuesday—forgive your friends and associates; Wednesday—forgive across economic lines within your own nation; Thursday—forgive across cultural lines within your own nation; Friday—forgive across political lines within your own nation; Saturday—forgive other nations."[14] This week, by the grace of God and in light of His great mercy toward you, won't you please forgive those who have sinned against you?

LISTEN TO ...

He that demands mercy, and shows none, ruins the bridge over which he himself is to pass.

—*Thomas Adams*

All's Fair in God's Love and Word

Matthew 20:1–16

Growing up, my (Lenya's) older sister accused me of being Daddy's darling. But I chided that she was Mother's much beloved. If Dad gave me a compliment and she didn't receive one, she wrinkled her nose at me. If Mom allowed her a "big girl" curfew while I went to bed early, I rolled my eyes at her. Each Christmas morning after piling our packages into designated stacks, we tallied them to ensure equality. When shopping for school clothes, we cautiously calculated whether we had acquired the identical amount of outfits. For our parents, there was no way to win this tug-of-war. Although they assured us that all was fair in a loving home, we just couldn't see it that way.

Do you ever feel that God plays favorites? Have you ever accused Him of being unfair? Sibling rivalry exists not only with earthly offspring but also with our heavenly Father's children. God's kids compare and contrast their lot in life, their looks in the mirror, or the loot in their bank account. Paul said, "But they, measuring themselves by themselves, and comparing themselves among themselves, are not wise" (2 Cor. 10:12).

Today's parable teaches us that comparing leads to complaining that God's love is lop-sided. The truth is, life isn't always fair. However, God is always just. Viewing circumstances from an earthly perspective makes life appear off-kilter. But God promises that in eternity the scales of justice will be perfectly balanced. This week in the parable of the Laborers, we'll discover that all's fair in God's love and Word.

Day 1: Matthew 20:1–2	**HIRING HELPERS**
Day 2: Matthew 20:3–7	**SEEKING SERVANTS**
Day 3: Matthew 20:8–10	**LOATHSOME LABORERS**
Day 4: Matthew 20:11–12	**WEARY WORKERS**
Day 5: Matthew 20:13–16	**LAVISH LANDOWNER**

DAY 1
Hiring Helpers

LIFT UP ...

Thank You, Lord, for supplying everything I need. Help me to trust in Your provision. Amen.

LOOK AT ...

Last week we learned in the parable of the Unforgiving Servant about the vertical forgiveness God offers people and the horizontal forgiveness believers should offer one another. This week's parable examines the great biblical mystery about the gospel dispensation "first for the Jew, then for the Gentile" (Rom. 1:16 NIV). Although the Jews were God's original chosen people, their temporary rejection opened the way for the Gentiles to become coheirs, inheriting the very same promises. Paul revealed that this caused the Jews to envy the late-coming Gentiles: "But through their fall, to provoke them to jealousy, salvation has come to the Gentiles" (Rom. 11:11). Matthew Henry says that this parable shows "that the Jews should be first called into the vineyard, and many of them should come at the call; but, at length, the gospel should be preached to the Gentiles, and they should receive it, and be admitted to equal privileges and advantages with the Jews ... which the Jews, even those of them that believed, would be very much disgusted at, but without reason."[1]

We can find a secondary lesson comparing man's system of compensation to God's offer of unmerited favor. All of us suffer from jealousy in one form or another. We wonder why God blesses someone who doesn't seem as spiritual as we are. We envy those who get more although they have done less. How do you measure up to the lessons of this parable?

READ MATTHEW 20:1–2.

"For the kingdom of heaven is like a landowner who went out early in the morning to hire laborers for his vineyard. Now when he had agreed with the laborers for a denarius a day, he sent them into his vineyard." Matthew 20:1–2

LEARN ABOUT ...

1 Contrary Kingdom

God's kingdom is an upside-down kingdom where the first are last, the weak are strong, and the poor are rich. Jesus uses the parable of the Laborers to amplify that those who are great in their own eyes may end up last, while those who go unnoticed take first place.

---

3 Crops

When the time came for the landowner to harvest his crop, the harvest would need to be finished in one day to prevent it from spoiling or being devastated by rain. The regular servants would begin harvesting at six in the morning while the landowner went to hire additional workers in nearby villages.

---

4 Contract

To agree means to be harmonious or in accord like musical instruments or a symphony. By coming to an agreement, the laborers and landlord entered into a mutually acceptable, binding contract. "If a man ... swears an oath to bind himself by some agreement, he shall not break his word" (Num. 30:2).

1. a. Read Matthew 19:27–30. Describe what Peter believed the disciples had sacrificed to follow Jesus (v. 27).

   b. What pointed question did Peter therefore ask Jesus (v. 27)?

   c. Describe the rewards Jesus promised those who follow Him and what it might cost them (vv. 28–29).

   d. What key lesson did Jesus want the disciples to learn (v. 30)?

2. To whom did Jesus compare the kingdom of heaven in 20:1?

3. Recount what this individual did.

4. What wage did the landowner and laborers agree upon?

5. What happened after this agreement was made?

6. Based on past lessons, who do you think the landowner represents?

LIVE OUT ...

7. a. Peter said he and the other disciples had "left all" to follow Jesus. What have you left or given up to follow Him?

   ❏ Friendships ❏ Unhealthy habits ❏ Conveniences
   ❏ Income ❏ Family relationships ❏ Other: _____

   b. Journal a prayer asking God to help you leave all that hinders you from following Him.

8. The landowner and the laborers made a verbal contract: one denarius for a day's work. A contract is similar to a covenant. Look

up the following verses and record the covenants God made with various people.

SCRIPTURE	GOD'S COVENANT	PERSON(S)
Genesis 9:8–11		
Genesis 15:18		
Genesis 17:2–6		
Hebrews 9:13–15		

9. After agreeing upon a wage, the landowner sent the laborers into the vineyard.

a. Where has God sent you to work for Him?

b. How has He rewarded you for your work?

One of the many truths revealed in this week's parable is that God cares much more about *why* we're serving than *how much* we're serving.

You know, Lord, how I serve You	But how would I react, I wonder,
With great emotional fervor	If You pointed to a basin of water
In the limelight.	And asked me to wash the calloused feet
You know how eagerly I speak for You	Of a bent and wrinkled old woman
At the women's club.	Day after day
You know how I effervesce	Month after month
When I promote a fellowship group.	In a room where nobody saw
You know my genuine enthusiasm	And nobody knew.[2]
At a Bible study.	

o o ● o o

We shouldn't serve God because we seek a reward but because we love Him. Nothing we could do is worthy of receiving recompense.

LEARN ABOUT …

7 Compensation

Peter did not understand that it is impossible to outgive God. He believed he had given up everything. In reality, when you give to God, He promises to give back more than you can imagine: "Give, and it will be given to you: good measure, pressed down, shaken together, and running over" (Luke 6:38).

8 Covenant

A covenant is an agreement that involves promises on the part of two groups or people. The concept of covenant between God and His people is fundamental to understanding the Bible. The most important covenant God made was the new covenant that promised salvation through Jesus' atoning death on the cross.

Fortunately, God doesn't give us what we deserve—He gives us far better than we deserve. Only Jesus knew Peter's motive for asking the question, "Therefore what shall we have?" But we should serve with the attitude Paul described: "Whatever you do, do it heartily, as to the Lord and not to men, knowing that from the Lord you will receive the reward of the inheritance; for you serve the Lord Christ" (Col. 3:23–24).

LISTEN TO ...

God sat in silence while the sins of the world were placed upon his Son. Was it right? No. Was it fair? No. Was it love? Yes. In a world of injustice, God once and for all tipped the scales in the favor of hope.

—*Max L. Lucado*

DAY 2

Seeking Servants

A little book called *Expectation Corner* tells of a king who prepared a city for his poor subjects. Not far away he constructed a large storehouse containing everything they needed if they sent him their requests. He had only one condition: They must constantly be on the lookout for his messengers coming with their requested gifts. The petitioners must be found ready and waiting to receive their supplies. One faithless subject, full of disbelief in the king's goodness, never watched for the delivery. One day he was taken to the king's storehouse. To his amazement, he saw scores of packages addressed to him. The messengers had come to his door, but because he was not watching and waiting, the king's gifts never satisfied his needs.[3]

The old saying is true: *Good things come to those who wait.* The workers in this parable who waited to be hired until the very end of the day are to be commended. They weren't discouraged; they stuck it out until the last possible hour. And they were rewarded richly for their patience. In addition, we can contrast them to those who were hired first. The first in line demanded a contract before accepting work; the second trusted the owner to give them what was right.

LIFT UP ...

Father, thank You for choosing and seeking me to bear fruit for You. Amen.

LOOK AT ...

Yesterday we saw the landowner hire laborers for a denarius a day. Now we see the landowner seeking additional workers for his vineyard. With each new batch of workers, the landowner wisely enlisted laborers who were not fatigued so they could bring fresh energy for the task at hand. Their enthusiasm ensured that the harvest would be gathered by the end of the day. The excitement of new recruits often inspires the regulars to persevere. Each new shift probably elicited hope in the previous workers.

There's nothing like a helping hand to lift your spirits. Have you ever been in the middle of a big project when a friend or loved one stopped by to offer support? Perhaps your new neighbors helped unload the moving truck. Or your women's study group

LEARN ABOUT ...

3 Returned

The third, sixth, ninth, and eleventh hours refer to 9:00 a.m., 12:00 noon, 3:00 p.m., and 5:00 p.m., respectively. The landowner needed additional workers to complete the harvest in his vineyard. Therefore, he returned to the marketplace several times in one day.

4 Remained

The word *idle* means not working or unemployed. It can also imply being lazy or useless. But these men, instead of returning home when they weren't hired early in the day, remained in the marketplace, hoping to find even one hour of work or possibly a job for the following day.

delivered meals after a painful surgery. Instead of competing with or complaining against new members to the team, we should celebrate their arrival. Paul wrote, "I am glad about the coming of Stephanas, Fortunatus, and Achaicus, for what was lacking on your part they supplied. For they refreshed my spirit and yours. Therefore acknowledge such men" (1 Cor. 16:17–18).

READ MATTHEW 20:3–7.

"And he went out about the third hour and saw others standing idle in the marketplace, and said to them, 'You also go into the vineyard, and whatever is right I will give you.' So they went. Again he went out about the sixth and the ninth hour, and did likewise. And about the eleventh hour he went out and found others standing idle, and said to them, 'Why have you been standing here idle all day?' They said to him, 'Because no one hired us.' He said to them, 'You also go into the vineyard, and whatever is right you will receive.'" Matthew 20:3–7

1. When did the landowner return to the marketplace, and what did he see?

2. The landowner told the workers to go into the vineyard.

   a. What did he promise them?

   b. How did they respond?

3. How many additional times did the landowner return to the marketplace for workers?

4. What did the landowner ask those he encountered at the eleventh hour?

5. How did the laborers respond to the question?

6. What did the landowner promise when he hired these laborers?

LIVE OUT ...

7. The laborers in this parable waited in the marketplace, seeking opportunities to work. But there are ways we can prepare ourselves to work for Him. Complete the chart to discover how to prepare for God's work.

SCRIPTURE	WAYS TO PREPARE FOR GOD'S WORK
1 Thessalonians 5:17	
2 Timothy 2:15	
2 Timothy 2:20–22	
James 1:22	
1 Peter 3:15	

8. Perhaps you want to work for God, but you don't know where to start. Maybe you are running on empty and weary from working. Journal a prayer seeking God's direction and trusting that He "is able to make all grace abound to you, so that in all things at all times, having all that you need, you will abound in every good work" (2 Cor. 9:8–9 NIV).

9. Using the word LABOR as an acrostic, describe some ways you can be a faithful laborer for God.

L (Love others)

A

B

O

R

LEARN ABOUT ...

6 Relied

Right means equitable or fair. The laborers were eager to work and didn't negotiate a specific wage.[4] Perhaps the landowner—like God—had a reputation for being more than fair: "O LORD ... your faithfulness reaches beyond the clouds. Your righteousness is like the mighty mountains, your justice like the ocean depths" (Ps. 36:5–6 NLT).

7 Ready

To wait in the biblical sense means to gather, to watch, or to expect. It is never passive; it is active. Such waiting is never wasted, but productive. David tells us, "Wait on the LORD; be of good courage, and He shall strengthen your heart; wait, I say, on the LORD!" (Ps. 27:14).

8 Rewarded

As God's laborers, we don't need to negotiate a wage. We work because it's a privilege to be part of what He's doing in the world. Paul encourages, "Be steadfast, immovable, always abounding in the work of the Lord, knowing that your labor is not in vain" (I Cor. 15:58).

○ ○ ● ○ ○

There was a missionary who did not receive her monthly check. She was seriously ill and because of no money had to live on oatmeal and canned milk. She received her check thirty days later. On furlough, she mentioned this incident to a doctor. She described the intestinal digestive trouble she had been having, and the doctor said, "If your check had arrived on time and you had been eating your current diet, you would now be dead, because the best treatment for your illness was a thirty-day oatmeal diet." The missionary was forced to wait upon the Lord, and she received a reward for her patience. Only through faith and patience do we obtain God's promises.[5]

God is never late; He is always right on time. The difficulty is that we try to force Him onto our earthly timetable instead of adjusting to His heavenly schedule. If you are in a season of idleness, do not lose heart. Jesus, like the landowner, seeks servants to bring in the harvest (see Matt. 9:37–38). He has chosen us to bear fruit—fruit that will remain. He never stops searching for faithful laborers who are willing to diligently serve Him. It's never too late to begin working for Him, and the wages He promises are immeasurable: "He who reaps receives wages, and gathers fruit for eternal life, that both he who sows and he who reaps may rejoice together" (John 4:36).

LISTEN TO ...

Simply wait upon him. So doing, we shall be directed, supplied, protected, corrected, and rewarded.

—Vance Havner

DAY 3

Loathsome Laborers

I (Penny) admit that I grew up slightly spoiled. My dad and mom were more privileged than poverty-stricken. We were fortunate enough to have a cleaning woman come in to do the deep cleaning. The only things I was responsible for were making sure my room was straightened up and putting my laundry away so Lucy could come in and change the sheets, dust, and vacuum my room. Oh, how naive I was!

When I got married, I expected life to go on as it always had. After Kerry and I returned from our honeymoon, we began to set up house. I said, "Who will we get to clean house for us?" Kerry looked at me and shook his head. "Honey, we don't have the money for a housekeeper. *You're* responsible for the cleaning." I couldn't believe it—I would have to clean the toilets! My expectations of married life took a nosedive.

Amazingly, I didn't mind cleaning the house … even the toilets. It gave me a sense of accomplishment to leave a room sparkling and disinfected. Don't get me wrong—I wouldn't mind having a housekeeper. But I've learned not to expect the privileges other people have.

In hindsight, I realize that God wanted to teach me about using money wisely. He wanted me to learn to live within my means. And He wanted me to learn to honor my husband. Those lessons cleaned up my heart and helped me to change my expectations from earthly treasures to heavenly rewards.

LIFT UP …

Thank You, Father, for Your awesome grace. Help me to give others the same love, mercy, and grace You have given to me. Amen.

LOOK AT …

We've seen that the landowner went out seeking servants to work in his vineyard. Now we see the workday end and the landowner call the laborers in to receive their wages. Each received a denarius, which represented a full day's wages. This was the average wage

LEARN ABOUT ...

1 Sunset

Biblically, it was a violation of Levitical law to hold laborers' wages overnight. The law stated, "The wages of him who is hired shall not remain with you all night until morning" (Lev. 19:13). The landowner's business practices reflected his obedience to God's Word.

2 Steward

"Steward" is translated from the Greek word *epitropos* and describes one to whose care something is committed, a domestic manager or guardian. A good steward is faithful and trustworthy. "As each one has received a gift, minister it to one another, as good stewards of the manifold grace of God" (I Peter 4:10).

for soldiers and laborers. It is interesting to note the order in which the workers were paid—from the last to the first. Compensating them in this sequence introduced suspense and anticipation. Those hired first made the mistake of changing their expectations. Although they had previously negotiated a fair contract, they began to expect more. Unfulfilled expectations often get us into trouble. Since our dad mowed the lawn, we expect our husbands to do the same. Because their mothers did the mending, our husbands expect us to darn and knit. Have you ever expected one thing and then gotten another? How did it make you feel? Place yourself in the position of these workers. You probably would respond much the same. What lessons can you learn from them?

READ MATTHEW 20:8–10.

"So when evening had come, the owner of the vineyard said to his steward, 'Call the laborers and give them their wages, beginning with the last to the first.' And when those came who were hired about the eleventh hour, they each received a denarius. But when the first came, they supposed that they would receive more; and they likewise received each a denarius." Matthew 20:8–10

1. When did the landowner prepare to pay the laborers?

2. Who was responsible for calling the laborers and giving them their wages?

3. In what order were the workers called?

4. a. Why do you think the landowner used the system of "last to the first"?

   b. How do you think the laborers felt about this system?

5. How much did those hired at the eleventh hour receive?

6. a. In your own words describe the expectations of the first laborers.

   b. Do you think this was reasonable or not? Why?

7. a. What wage did the first laborers actually receive?

   b. How would you expect them to respond? Why?

LIVE OUT ...

8. The landowner trusted his steward with his finances. God asks us to be stewards and watch over things as well.

   a. Describe some things God has given you stewardship over (such as a house or employees).

   b. Would you describe yourself as a faithful steward? Why or why not?

9. God proved Himself to be generous to the laborers in His field. Use your Bible concordance to find other Scriptures that reflect this character trait of God. Record the Scriptures, and share them with your small group.

10. The first laborers supposed they would receive more wages than agreed upon. Journal about a time when you expected something from God but His response was completely different than you anticipated. What did you learn about God and about yourself from this experience?

LEARN ABOUT ...

7 Supposed

To suppose means to assume, to be of the opinion, or to think that something is true. The first laborers assumed their wages would be significantly more when they saw the last group of laborers receive a whole denarius. But the landowner chose to bless all equally. "My people shall be satisfied with My goodness, says the LORD" (Jer. 31:14).

8 Stewardship

For Christians, stewardship is the privilege and responsibility of working through the church and using the gifts and talents God has bestowed upon us. God has entrusted all Christians to become His stewards. As Paul said, "God has given me this sacred trust" (1 Cor. 9:17 NLT).

9 Suspense

By paying the eleventh-hour workers first, those who had worked more hours were able to witness the landowner's gracious generosity. This is a picture of God's character: "I will be gracious to whom I will be gracious, and I will have compassion on whom I will have compassion" (Ex. 33:19).

○ ○ ● ○ ○

Little Freddie was telling his mother everything as he discussed his new teacher. "She's mean, but she's fair," he said. "What do you mean by that?" asked his mother. "She's mean to everyone," he replied.[6]

The landowner in our parable was generous and good to *all* who labored in his fields. He paid those who were hired at the end the same as those who came at the first. Of course, the landowner can be seen as a picture of God, who distributes rewards based on His grace and sovereignty rather than on our greed or service. God does not give to us because He owes us something but because He loves us. The writer of Hebrews tells us, "Without faith it is impossible to please Him, for he who comes to God must believe that He is, and that *He is a rewarder of those who diligently seek Him*" (Heb. 11:6). God gives good gifts to all of His children without prejudice.

LISTEN TO ...

Conflicting expectations are like a tight shoe. They begin with a pinch, but if left unattended, they soon become painfully tender to the slightest touch.

—*Richard P. Hansen*

DAY 4
Weary Workers

Do you know that many members of the Tate family belong to your church? There is old man Dic Tate, who wants to run everything, while Uncle Ro Tate tries to change everything. Their sister Agi Tate stirs up plenty of trouble, with help from her husband, Irri Tate.

Whenever new projects are suggested, Hesi Tate and his wife, Vege Tate, want to wait until next year. Then there is Aunt Imi Tate, who wants the church to be like all the others. Devas Tate provides the voice of doom, while Poten Tate wants to be a big shot.

But not all members of the family are bad. Brother Facili Tate is quite helpful in church matters. And a delightful, happy member of the family is Miss Felici Tate. Cousins Cogi Tate and Medi Tate always think things over and lend helpful, steady hands. And of course there is the black sheep of the family, Ampu Tate, who has completely cut himself off from the church.[7]

Today in the parable of the Laborers, we see that the first laborers in the field were much like sister Agi Tate, willing to stir up trouble because they didn't receive the earnings they felt they were due. As we see how disrespectful this type of behavior really is, let's purpose in our hearts to become like the helpful members of the Tate family rather than the harmful family members.

LIFT UP ...

Dear Lord, I can always trust You to be fair. Forgive me for being discontent. Help me to remember that Your plans for me are perfect. Amen.

LOOK AT ...

Yesterday we saw the attitude of the laborers who were hired first. Now we see them grumble to the landowner. Giving a whole day's wages to those who only worked one-tenth as much as those first hired teaches us that God distributes rewards based on grace, not works. It's hard for humans to grasp grace. We struggle with the concept of unmerited favor because it takes us out of the equation. If there is truly nothing we can do to earn God's

LEARN ABOUT ...

1 Complained

"Complained" is translated from *gogguso*, a word describing the actual sound made when murmuring or muttering.[8] The laborers' discontent was audibly apparent. But Scripture tells us, "Do not grumble against one another, brethren, lest you be condemned" (James 5:9).

2 Carried

"Burden" refers to heavy labor. In Israel, September's harvesttime could be extremely warm in the afternoon. These men had indeed worked during the heat of the day. However, the landowner's expectations were not unreasonable, just as Christ tells us, "For My yoke is easy and My burden is light" (Matt. 11:30).

3 Compensated

Equal means alike in quantity, quality, and dignity.[9] Rather than being happy for those who received a generous wage, the grumbling laborers became dissatisfied with their wages. However, as followers of Christ, we are told to "let each esteem others better than himself.... look out not only for [your] own interests, but also for the interests of others" (Phil. 2:3–4).

love or forgiveness, we feel useless. Mistakenly we believe that there is something we can do to gain God's acceptance. Perhaps we can pray longer or harder to gain His approval. What if we tithe 20 instead of 10 percent? Would God be more likely to bless us? But these premises are simply not true. God does not love us because we are lovely but because He is loving. Once we accept grace for ourselves, we will be more gracious with others. How can we complain as others reap the same benefits we have enjoyed through no merit of our own?

READ MATTHEW 20:11–12.

"And when they had received it, they complained against the landowner, saying, 'These last men have worked only one hour, and you made them equal to us who have borne the burden and the heat of the day.'" Matthew 20:11–12

1. Describe how the laborers responded to the landowner upon receiving their pay.

2. Explain why the laborers complained against the landowner.

3. Why do you think these laborers were unhappy with a wage they originally considered fair?

4. Who do you think the laborers represent in this parable and why?

5. According to Revelation 15:3, is it possible for God to be unfair? Why or why not?

LIVE OUT ...

6. Just as the laborers complained against the landowner, the Jewish religious leaders complained against Jesus. With this in mind, look up the following Scriptures and record (1) complaints made against Jesus and (2) Jesus' response.

SCRIPTURE	COMPLAINT	RESPONSE
Matthew 21:15–16		
Luke 5:30–32		
Luke 19:37–40		
John 6:41–43		

7. Describe a time when you compared yourself with another then complained against God either orally or silently.

8. a. The laborers who were hired first in this parable had an attitude problem. Check the boxes that indicate what sinful attitude(s) cause you to grumble and complain.

   ❑ Pride   ❑ Jealousy

   ❑ Discontent   ❑ Unbelief

   ❑ Anger   ❑ Other: _____

   b. Journal a prayer of confession to God. Ask Him to help you obey Philippians 2:14–15: "Do all things without complaining and disputing, that you may become blameless and harmless, children of God without fault in the midst of a crooked and perverse generation, among whom you shine as lights in the world."

LEARN ABOUT ...

6 Conceit

Just as the first group expected to receive more than the last group of laborers, the religious leaders believed they were worth more than the common people. However, "the LORD does not see as man sees; for man looks at the outward appearance, but the LORD looks at the heart" (1 Sam. 16:7).

7 Compared

Comparisons are unwise. There will always be somebody who has more or less than you. Those with more can make you feel envious, while those with less can make you feel superior. When Peter compared himself to John, Jesus rebuked him, "What is that to you? You follow Me" (John 21:22).

○ ○ ● ○ ○

By the age of twenty-one, C. H. Spurgeon was the most popular preacher in nineteenth-century London. He preached to thousands at Exeter Hall and the Surrey Music Hall. When the Metropolitan Tabernacle was built, thousands gathered every Sunday for over thirty years to hear his lively sermons. Acquainted with grumbling congregants, Spurgeon wrote this:

> A heavy wagon was being dragged along a country lane by a team of oxen. The axles groaned and creaked terribly, when the oxen turning around thus addressed the wheels, "Hey there, why do you make so much noise? We bear all the labor, and we—not you—ought to cry out!" Those complain first in our churches who have the least to do. The gift of grumbling is largely dispensed among those who have no other talents, or who keep what they have wrapped up in a napkin.[10]

The early laborers grumbled at receiving the same wage as those who came to work later. Similarly, many Jews who heard the gospel message first were jealous "that the Gentiles should be fellow heirs … and partakers of His promise in Christ through the gospel" (Eph. 3:6). This parable also holds a warning for believers today. When we compare our spiritual gifts, blessings, or opportunities for service with those of other Christians, we run the risk of becoming complainers.

LISTEN TO ...

What are the thoughts of the canvas on which a masterpiece is being painted? "I am being soiled, brutally treated and concealed from view." Thus men grumble at their destiny, however fair.

—Jean Cocteau

DAY 5
Lavish Landowner

The United Methodist church in Swan Quarter, North Carolina, was literally moved by the hand of God. In 1874 the church members approached a wealthy landowner, hoping to buy the perfect piece of land upon which to plant their church. However, the owner of the lot, Sam Sadler, refused to sell. The congregation accepted the gift of another lot from James W. Hayes and soon began to worship there. That's when things got interesting.

On September 16, 1876, the church started to hold its dedication ceremony when a storm began to brew. The tide rose so high and the wind blew so hard that the church was transplanted to the exact location the people had originally chosen. Mr. Sadler immediately began to secure the title for the church. The people changed the name from Methodist Episcopal Church South to Providence United Methodist Church.[11]

Although Mr. Sadler, the landowner in North Carolina, was not originally generous in his negotiations with the church, an act of God changed his heart. In the end, the church didn't have to pay for the land at all. Instead, it was freely given to them as an act of grace. The landowner finally did the right thing.

In the parable of the Laborers, we see that God, the perfect landowner, will always do the right thing, even if it means shifting things around. When we leave negotiations to Him, He'll give us better than we deserve. It may surprise some to discover that "the last will be first, and the first last" (Matt. 20:16).

LIFT UP ...

Where would I be, Lord, without Your abundant mercy? Thank You for lavishing goodness, forgiveness, and mercy on me each day. Amen.

LOOK AT ...

Yesterday we heard the laborers grumble because they felt they had been treated unfairly. Today we gain insight into the landowner's generosity as he wisely responded to their complaints. The contrast in their attitudes is meant to illustrate the stark difference between

1 Laborers

The laborer was a *hetairos*—a friend as well as comrade. The other word for friend is *philos*—a beloved friend. The laborers were "friends" for personal gain. A true friend is one who loves to give, not get, for "greater love has no one than this, than to lay down one's life for his friends" (John 15:13).

4 Landowner

The landowner could have paid in proportion to the hours worked. Instead, he generously gave everyone a whole denarius. God's grace doesn't circulate in percentages. Rather, "from the fullness of his grace we have all received one blessing after another" (John 1:16 NIV).[12]

5 Look Inside

In Scripture, an evil eye represents envy, jealousy, and covetousness. Thus, the landowner's questions exposed the envy in the laborers' hearts. Jesus said, "Out of the heart of men, proceed evil thoughts" (Mark 7:21).

God's goodness and our greed. The grumbling workers displayed envy, and the landowner described them as having "an evil eye." It's true that those who envy have "I" trouble. We become consumed with I, me, and mine. The eye, like the heart, provides the gateway for sin. Remember when King Saul heard the women elevate David in their victory song? "'Saul has slain his thousands, and David his ten thousands.' Then Saul was very angry, and the saying displeased him" (1 Sam. 18:7–8). An evil eye becomes green with envy at the prosperity of others and eventually desires to see them harmed. How do you respond to the prosperity of others? Do you find it easier to weep with those who weep rather than rejoice with those who rejoice? Perhaps you have "I" trouble too.

READ MATTHEW 20:13–16.

"But he answered one of them and said, 'Friend, I am doing you no wrong. Did you not agree with me for a denarius? Take what is yours and go your way. I wish to give to this last man the same as to you. Is it not lawful for me to do what I wish with my own things? Or is your eye evil because I am good?' So the last will be first, and the first last. For many are called, but few chosen." Matthew 20:13–16

1. How did the landowner address one of the complaining laborers?

2. In your own words, clarify why the landowner had done no wrong.

3. What advice did the landowner give the grumbling worker?

4. What reason did the landowner give for paying the last man equal wages?

5. a. The landowner reinforced his point by asking two probing questions. What was the underlying point of his first question?

b. Read Deuteronomy 15:7–9. Based on the information in these verses, why do you think the landowner asked, "Is your eye evil because I am good?"

6. Jesus ended this parable by returning to the same principle with which He began. Reread Matthew 19:30, and compare it to Matthew 20:16.

a. How did Jesus change the wording?

b. What phrase did Jesus add?

c. How do you think this applies to this week's parable?

LEARN ABOUT …

6 Lesson

The "called" are everyone invited to serve God. Like the first group of laborers, they prefer to serve on their own terms. The chosen are those who, rather than demanding a reward, trust the Master to be fair. "Masters, give your bondservants what is just and fair, knowing that you also have a Master in heaven" (Col. 4:1).

7. In order to fully understand the context of this parable, we need to read what happens *after* verse 16. Briefly skim Matthew 20:17–28.

a. What did the mother of Zebedee's sons (James and John, according to Mark 10:35) request?

b. How did Jesus' answer in verses 26–27 further illustrate the point of this week's parable?

c. What key lesson from these verses do you want to personally apply to your life?

LIVE OUT …

8. The landowner's response to the complaining laborers pointed to a deeper issue than the fairness of their wages—the envy in their hearts. What do the following verses say about the seriousness of envy?

LEARN ABOUT ...

9 Lay Aside

To lay aside means to cast off or put away like an old garment. Wearing envy does not befit a believer in Christ. Just as a person changes clothes, believers can change attitudes from sinful to saintly: "Put on tender mercies, kindness, humility, meekness, longsuffering" (Col. 3:12).

---

10 Lift up

The workers had families to feed, whether they had worked one hour or twelve hours. By caring for the workers, the landowner was caring for the workers' families. Scripture promises, "God shall supply all your need according to His riches in glory by Christ Jesus" (Phil. 4:19).

SCRIPTURE

Job 5:2

Proverbs 14:30

James 3:16

ENVY BRINGS ...

9. According to 1 Peter 2:1, what should we do with envy?

10. The landowner chose to treat those who had worked only one hour as if they'd worked all day. Journal about how God has been good to you when you deserved it the least.

11. a. How would you explain Jesus' purpose for telling this parable in Matthew 20:1–16?

    b. Now evaluate your own motives, and check the boxes to indicate your answer to the question, "Why do I serve God?"

    ❐ To impress others   ❐ Out of duty

    ❐ Out of guilt   ❐ Out of fear

    ❐ Out of gratitude and love ❐ Other _____

    c. Journal a prayer asking God to reveal any wrong motives you have for serving Him. Use Psalm 51:10, 12 as a guide: "Create in me a clean heart, O God. Renew a loyal spirit within me.... Restore to me the joy of your salvation, and make me willing to obey you" (NLT).

∘ ∘ ● ∘ ∘

One of our friends, Christy, tells this story: "I try to get my kids to let other people go first in line. They complained when they saw how other children were allowed to push ahead of them. Then I explained that God has a different standard—'The last will be first, and the first last.'"

Not long after that, Christy's family hosted a pool party. Her daughter Summer came in last in a race. She said, "That's okay! In God's eyes I came in first!"

The parable of the Laborers illustrates how God's divine economy vastly differs from the world's economy. Rather than rewarding the amount or length of service, God examines our hearts to see the motives and attitudes behind our service: "Men who have worked in Christ's service all their days may, by the spirit which they manifest at the last, make it too evident that … they never were chosen workmen at all."[13]

While we are all *called* to serve, may we never feel self-satisfied by the length of time we have worked in God's field. Instead, may we be found among those who are *chosen*—serving our Master not for selfish gain, but out of a sense of love and devotion. When we serve our heavenly Master from a pure heart, putting others' needs before our own, we move up to the front of the line in His eyes.

LISTEN TO …

Seek to live with such lucidity that the clarity of your motives becomes a lens which projects the image of Christ upon the screens of others' lives.

—*David Augsburger*

Actions Speak Louder Than Words

Matthew 21:28-46

The story is told of two men who were profoundly moved by a sermon. However, the first man refused to accept Jesus as Savior and enjoy the peace that comes with having one's sins forgiven. Later, he asked the second man, "Why did you respond right away?"

"My brother," the second man replied, "I can best explain it by this little story: At one time a rich prince wished to give us both a new coat. You shook your head and replied, 'I don't think so; mine looks good enough.' When he made the same offer to me, I looked at my coat and said, 'This coat is good for nothing,' and gratefully accepted the beautiful garment. You wouldn't give up your own righteousness. But knowing I had no goodness of my own, I immediately received the Lord Jesus Christ and His righteousness."[1]

The pious religious leaders of Jesus' day refused to give up their own righteousness to follow a lowly carpenter from Galilee. Jesus' declarations of deity and His revolutionary teachings had swayed the minds of the multitudes. But this only enraged the Pharisees and Sadducees. His sweeping temple reforms infuriated those who made a living from religious service. In short, Jesus was a threat to their power, and they hated Him for it. In their typically shrewd manner, the leaders confronted Him, saying, "By what authority are You doing these things? And who gave You this authority?" (Matt. 21:23).

This week we'll see Jesus, through the parable of the Two Sons and the parable of the Landowner, show these crafty men that their refusal to give up their self-righteous ways spoke volumes. Let's all learn the lesson that actions speak louder than words when it comes to accepting Christ as King.

Day 1: Matthew 21:28–32   **REFUSING THE FATHER**

Day 2: Matthew 21:33–36   **PERSECUTING THE PROPHETS**

Day 3: Matthew 21:37–39   **REJECTING THE SON**

Day 4: Matthew 21:40–43   **RECOVERING NEW FRUIT**

Day 5: Matthew 21:44–46   **STUMBLING ON THE STONE**

DAY 1

Refusing the Father

LIFT UP ...

Holy Spirit, so often I refuse the Father when I hear the Word; help me to obey Him. Give me a willing and grateful heart. Amen.

LOOK AT ...

During the period preceding this week's parables, Jesus and the twelve disciples traveled to Jerusalem to celebrate Passover. As they walked, Jesus taught His followers about His impending death and resurrection. He healed two blind men, made His triumphal entry into Jerusalem, cleansed the temple, and cursed a fig tree. While teaching in the temple, Jesus countered the religious leaders' questions regarding His authority with His own question: "Was John the Baptist sent from God, or not?" (Matt. 21:25 TLB). Unable to answer Him without exposing their hypocrisy, they answered, "We don't know!" So Jesus told the parable of the Two Sons, in essence forcing the men to testify against themselves.

There are several reasons why Jesus employed parables. Sometimes they graphically illustrated a truth. For believers, they made heavenly concepts easier to comprehend. However, His adversaries were often corrected and convicted by parables. In that case, a question served to expose wayward hearts. The prophet Nathan masterfully used a parable as a puzzle for King David to solve. In so doing, the king unwittingly condemned himself. Matthew Henry writes, "Reproving parables are appeals to the offenders themselves, and judge them out of their own mouths."[2] This is apparently Christ's intent as He begins today's parable with, "But what do you think?"

READ MATTHEW 21:28–32.

"But what do you think? A man had two sons, and he came to the first and said, 'Son, go, work today in my vineyard.' He answered and said, 'I will not,' but afterward he regretted it

LEARN ABOUT ...

3 Two Classes

Scholars agree that Jesus was depicting two classes of Jews: the outwardly sinful who repented and the religious leaders who rejected their Messiah. It can also speak to those in modern society who act like the ancient Jews. Jesus said, "I did not come to call the righteous, but sinners, to repentance" (Matt. 9:13).

6 Tax Collectors

The Jewish people despised tax collectors because they were allowed to collect more than the Roman government required and pocket the excess amount. The Jews viewed tax collectors as mercenaries employed by Israel's foreign oppressors. However, two notable followers of Jesus were tax collectors: Matthew and Zacchaeus.

and went. Then he came to the second and said likewise. And he answered and said, 'I go, sir,' but he did not go. Which of the two did the will of his father?" They said to Him, "The first." Jesus said to them, "Assuredly, I say to you that tax collectors and harlots enter the kingdom of God before you. For John came to you in the way of righteousness, and you did not believe him; but tax collectors and harlots believed him; and when you saw it, you did not afterward relent and believe him." Matthew 21:28–32

1. Read Matthew 21:23. Who confronted Jesus and why?

2. Knowing that Jesus was in dialogue with the above men, describe the main characters in this week's parable.

FIRST SON'S WORDS	HIS ACTIONS
SECOND SON'S WORDS	HIS ACTIONS

3. Who do you think each of these people might represent?

   First son

   Second son

4. In your own words, rephrase the question Jesus asked the religious leaders.

5. Note their response. Based on that response, what were they saying about themselves?

6. According to Jesus, who would enter the kingdom of God before the religious leaders? Why was that significant?

7. What do you think Jesus meant by saying John the Baptist "came to you in the way of righteousness"?

8. Why was it significant that the religious leaders rejected John the Baptist when notorious sinners believed him?

LIVE OUT ...

9. Scripture uses the vine or the vineyard to describe God's people. Summarize what the following verses teach you about the vineyard, the vine, the branches, and the vinedresser.

Jeremiah 2:3, 21

John 15:1, 4–5

10. Journal about how you are a worker in God's vineyard. Have you ever said, "I won't," only to obey later? If so, how were you blessed for your obedience?

11. John the Baptist's challenge to repentance was a painful jab at a society turning from God. John commanded his listeners to turn from their sin and obey God. Read the verses in the table below, and record the blessings of obedience.

SCRIPTURE	BLESSINGS OF OBEDIENCE
Isaiah 1:19–20	
Romans 5:19	
2 Corinthians 9:13	
Hebrews 5:9	

12. Though they saw the social outcasts come to salvation, the religious leaders still refused to relent and believe the truth. Think of

LEARN ABOUT ...

7 Tell He's Coming

John the Baptist was the forerunner of Jesus Christ who heralded the coming Messiah. God promised to send "My messenger before Your face, who will prepare Your way before You" (Mark 1:2). By rejecting the messenger, the leaders showed that they would also reject the Messiah.

9 Tender Care

In Scripture, the vineyard is a common symbol for the nation of Israel. "You brought us from Egypt as though we were a tender vine and ... planted us" (Ps. 80:8 TLB). Later, Gentiles were grafted into God's vineyard. "Branches were broken off that I might be grafted in" (Rom. 11:19).

11 True Commitment

Obedience relates to the sense of hearing, involving carrying out the word and will of another, especially God. Obedience is a positive, active response to verbal instruction: "Obey me, and I will be your God and you will be my people" (Jer. 7:23 NIV). Obedience reveals true commitment.

someone you know who has witnessed the power of salvation in your life but refuses to believe. Journal a prayer for the person you named based on the following Scripture:

"I will give them one heart, and put a new spirit within them. And I will take the heart of stone out of their flesh and give them a heart of flesh, that they may walk in My statutes and keep My ordinances and do them. Then they will be My people, and I shall be their God."
Ezekiel 11:19–20 NASB

○ ○ ● ○ ○

"I do love God," a little girl said to her father one Sunday after church when they were talking about what it means to love God.

"Perhaps you think so, Maria," he replied.

"I really, really do, Papa!" the girl adamantly insisted.

"Suppose, you should come to me, and say, 'Papa, I do love you,' and then go away and disobey me. Do you think I could believe you?"

"Well … no, Papa," the little girl hesitantly replied.

"Well, dear, how can I believe you love God when I see you doing things every day which He forbids? You know, the Bible says, 'If you love me, keep my commandments.'"[3]

The crowd of sinners had blatantly refused to obey God. Yet when they heard John's message of repentance, they saw their need for a Savior and obediently turned to do their Father's will. The religious leaders were too spiritually proud and blind to admit their sin. When confronted by John, they rejected the truth and refused to obey the Father. Though they daily recited Deuteronomy 6:5—"You shall love the LORD your God with all your heart, with all your soul, and with all your strength"—their actions spoke volumes. Their lip service failed to match their life service. The message of this parable is simple yet profound: Heed the Father's voice, obey His Word, and do His will. When we do these simple things, we reveal we really love Him.

LISTEN TO …

One act of obedience is better than one hundred sermons.

—*Dietrich Bonhoeffer*

DAY 2

Persecuting the Prophets

Years ago my (Lenya's) dad purchased a rundown home in Santa Ana, California, as an investment property. He and my stepmother worked hard to make it inhabitable and cozy for the new tenants. They replaced the toilets, put in new flooring, relandscaped the front yard, and updated the appliances. A woman responded to the ad in the paper and signed a rental agreement on behalf of her partner and herself.

When the rent checks didn't arrive, my folks drove to Santa Ana to visit the new tenants. They discovered that several couples had moved into the small abode. In the middle of the living room, on top of the brand-new carpet, the men had parked their motorcycles to change the oil. My dad clearly stated that this violated the lease agreement. He also demanded the past-due rent. That's when the men threatened my father with bodily harm. Dad left the premises to fight the battle another day, another way.

In the parable of the Landowner, Jesus tells the story of a man who invested in a rental property to build a fruitful vineyard. Then he leased it to a tenant farmer to cultivate the land for an agreed-upon amount. It was customary to set the rental fee as either (1) a specific cash advance; (2) a prescribed amount of the harvested crop regardless of the total yield; or (3) a specific percentage of each harvest, usually between 25 percent and 33 percent. However, just like in my father's case, the tenants did not live up to their agreement. And, being bullies, they persecuted the bill collectors, too.

LIFT UP ...

Jesus, when trouble comes my way—and I know it will—help me to have Your patience, faith, and love. Amen.

LOOK AT ...

Today, as we look at the parable of the Landowner, let's consider the landowner. He spent time preparing the land he intended to use for his vineyard. It was no small task but rather involved a substantial investment of thought, time, and resources. Owners were aware that

LEARN ABOUT ...

I A Hedge, a Press, and a Tower

A hedgelike wall was built around a vineyard to protect it from wild animals. Winepresses were square basins dug into a rock mountainside. At a slightly lower level on the slope, a second basin collected the grape juices. A watchtower served dual purposes: lodging for the vinedressers and a lookout for thieves during the harvest.

3 A Husbandman

God planted Israel and entrusted her to His appointed rulers and religious leaders. These people were responsible for cultivating and protecting the nation. "Now let me sing to my Well-beloved a song of my Beloved regarding His vineyard" (Isa. 5:1).

the vineyard would not produce fruit for several years, so he faithfully provided all that was needed to develop and maintain his investment. He built a wall to keep out people and animals, a tower where the vineyard keeper watched for thieves, and a winepress ready for future harvests. The wise landowner then leased his land to vinedressers to cultivate and encourage abundant growth. He asked nothing in return but his share of the vineyard's yield.

The landowner represents our generous and fair God, who patiently nurtures and provides for our needs, expecting us to flourish. When you produce fruit, do you give back what is required for His work, His people, and His glory? Are you being faithful to give a return on God's investment in you?

READ MATTHEW 21:33–36.

"Hear another parable: There was a certain landowner who planted a vineyard and set a hedge around it, dug a winepress in it and built a tower. And he leased it to vinedressers and went into a far country. Now when vintage-time drew near, he sent his servants to the vinedressers, that they might receive its fruit. And the vinedressers took his servants, beat one, killed one, and stoned another. Again he sent other servants, more than the first, and they did likewise to them." Matthew 21:33–36

1. Look at the four improvements the landowner made to his land. What impression of him do you get from his actions?

2. Recount what happened after the landowner improved the property.

3. a. Yesterday we learned that the vineyard represented Israel. In light of this knowledge, who do you think the vineyard landowner represents?

b. Who do you think the vinedressers represent?

4. a. Who did the landowner send to the vinedressers?

   b. Why did he send them?

   c. What happened to them?

5. a. What action did the landowner take when he heard of these servants' demise, and what was the result?

   b. If this happened in real life, what would you think about this as a response to murder? Why?

   c. Think about who the landowner represents. What do you think Jesus is saying about that person?

6. Read the following passages. In each case, explain who the passage is about and how their experience mirrors what happened to the servants in the parable.

   2 Chronicles 24:19–21

   Jeremiah 1:5; 37:15

   Jeremiah 26:20–23

LEARN ABOUT ...

4 A Harvest

A new vineyard took four to five years to produce fruit. As the fifth year—vintage-time—drew near, the vineyard owner sent his servants to collect the income. Contact between the owner and the vinedressers had probably been minimal during the first four years.[4]

7 A Hope

Patience in the New Testament is translated from a Greek word that expresses forbearance or endurance regarding people or circumstances. Biblically, patience grows best under trials—"The testing of your faith produces patience" (James 1:3).

LIVE OUT ...

7. The landowner could have easily become impatient with the vinedressers. Instead, he demonstrated patience when they persecuted his servants and stole his money. What causes you to feel impatient?

LEARN ABOUT ...

8 A Herald

Old Testament prophets spoke for God, communicating His message to the children of Israel. God repeatedly sent His messengers to convict the nation of sin and draw His children back to Him, but Israel repeatedly persecuted God's prophets: "They killed your prophets, who ... admonished them ... to turn them back to you" (Neh. 9:26 NIV).

❐ Irresponsible people

❐ Lack of control

❐ People who are stubborn

❐ Others' lack of honor and integrity

❐ Excessive duties/commitments

❐ Others' lack of effort

❐ Something else (name it):

8. Many of God's faithful prophets were persecuted for proclaiming His Word. Believers too are subject to persecution.

a. According to Matthew 5:11–12, how should we respond to persecution? Why?

b. According to Matthew 5:44, what should we do when mistreated?

c. Journal about a time you have felt persecuted because of your faith.

∘ ∘ ● ∘ ∘

Even in the United States, the land of supposed religious freedom and tolerance, Christians face subtle forms of persecution. A number of zoning cases have affected the right to worship in private homes. In Colorado Springs, minister Richard Blanche has been repeatedly cited for holding religious meetings in his home in violation of a city zoning ordinance. In Fairhaven, Massachusetts, local zoning officials ruled that Bible studies were home occupations and therefore prohibited under the town's property-use ordinances. In Los Angeles, officials ruled that home-occupancy regulations forbade Orthodox Jews from holding prayer meetings in their homes. Civil-liberties lawyers could not help but note in a Stratford, Connecticut, case that prayer in home Bible studies is penalized, while Tupperware parties enjoy the full protection of the Constitution.[5]

Most commentators agree that the ill-treated servants in today's parable represent the prophets who were sent to the nation of Israel. They were persecuted by society's rulers. When Jesus came to earth, He too was persecuted by society's elite. Therefore, it shouldn't surprise us when we are persecuted for our faith by the world we live in.

LISTEN TO ...

Wherever you see persecution, there is more than a probability that truth is on the persecuted side.

—*Hugh Latimer*

DAY 3

Rejecting the Son

Have you ever been bullied? Maybe someone on the playground left you out or made fun of you. We all know it's no fun. A bully is basically someone who hurts or intimidates another person. Bullying may include one of the following forms of intimidation: physical (hitting, shoving, or spitting), social (gossip, rumors, isolation, or humiliation), and oral (name-calling, mocking, or racial slurs). A bully utilizes these techniques to gain power, become popular, or obtain material possessions. Bullying is more prevalent than many realize:

"A recent study in the *Journal of the American Medical Association* demonstrated the seriousness of bullying in American schools. In a nationally representative sample of over 15,686 students in the United States (grades 6 through 10), 29.9% self-reported frequent involvement in bullying at school, with 13% participating as a bully, 10.9% as a victim, and 6% as both."[6]

One dangerous trend is evolving on school campuses: "the role that peers play in promoting bullying and victimization by either reinforcing the aggressor, failing to intervene to stop the victimization, or affiliating with students who bully."[7]

In this parable, we have seen the vinedressers acting like bullies. They have mocked, intimidated, and physically harmed the landowner's servants. It seems that everyone is going along with this harmful social behavior. Today we see the landowner send his son, the heir to the property, hoping to break up this destructive peer group. But the bullies prevail.

We discover that where bullies are concerned, there is no such thing as an innocent bystander. Paul told the Romans, "Although they know God's righteous decree that those who do such things deserve death, they not only continue to do these very things but also approve of those who practice them" (Rom. 1:32 NIV).

LIFT UP ...

Lord, because of Your rejection, crucifixion, and resurrection, I am a child of the King. Thank You for loving me more than I can comprehend. Amen.

Look at …

Yesterday we observed that the landowner sent several servants to the vinedressers to collect the fruit from his vineyard. Each servant who arrived was met with abuse. Nevertheless, the landowner continued to send messengers. Ultimately, the landowner sent his son and heir to convince the vinedressers of their obligation to pay what they owed. But the son was disrespected, rejected, and killed. The end of the story was as shocking as the death of Christ on the cross.

However, please do not overlook the mercy and grace exhibited by the landowner, who is a picture of God the Father. He didn't run the vinedressers off or cancel their agreement when they abused the servants, who are pictures of the prophets of old. Instead, through love and long-suffering, he continued his attempts to reach them, teach them, and forgive them. That persistence and patience continues today as God reaches out to us, offering us insight into His patient, long-reaching love.

READ MATTHEW 21:37–39.

"Then last of all he sent his son to them, saying, 'They will respect my son.' But when the vinedressers saw the son, they said among themselves, 'This is the heir. Come, let us kill him and seize his inheritance.' So they took him and cast him out of the vineyard and killed him." Matthew 21:37–39

1. As a last resort, the landowner sent his son to the vinedressers. What did he assume they would do?

2. What do you believe Jesus means us to think of a landowner who would do this? (For instance, is this landowner crazy? Explain your view.)

3. Describe how the vinedressers reacted to the son.

LEARN ABOUT …

2 Respect

Respect means to reverence. Reverence is a feeling of profound awe. Luke 20:13 best translates this verse: "Then said the lord of the vineyard, What shall I do? I will send my beloved son: it may be they will reverence him when they see him" (KJV). Perhaps he hoped these dangerous leopards would change their spots.

3 Revere

In this passage, "saw" means to gaze with wide-open eyes, as at something remarkable. An heir is someone who inherits the estate of another. "Now if we are children, then we are heirs—heirs of God and coheirs with Christ, if indeed we share in his sufferings in order that we may also share in his glory" (Rom. 8:17 NIV).

LEARN ABOUT ...

6 Repent

Jesus was crucified at Golgotha, a hill outside the walls of Jerusalem; "He was led like a lamb to the slaughter.... By oppression and judgment he was taken away...." (Isa. 53:7–8 NIV). God's hope for the people is the same as the landowner's: "Perhaps everyone will listen and turn from his evil way" (Jer. 26:3).

8 Recipient

An heir was the recipient of property as a gift or by legal right. To the Hebrew mind, the term *inheritance* had strong spiritual and national associations extending far beyond the family estate. The land of Canaan was regarded as an inheritance from the Lord, because God had promised it to Abraham's descendants.

10 Rejection

Jesus fearlessly confronted His foes who plotted to kill Him. Their rejection ultimately broke His heart: "When He approached Jerusalem, He saw the city and wept over it, saying, 'If you had known in this day, even you, the things which make for peace! But now they have been hidden from [you]'" (Luke 19:41–42 NASB).

4. What crime did they premeditate?

5. Describe the steps they took to commit this crime.

6. How do the following Scriptures confirm that Jesus was prophesying about His own death in the parable of the Landowner?

   Matthew 26:47, 50

   Matthew 27:31; Hebrews 13:12

LIVE OUT ...

7. The landowner believed the rebellious vinedressers would receive his son. According to John 1:11–12, what happened when God sent His Son?

8. Jesus was put to death on the cross, but three days later He came back to life. Those who believe in His death and resurrection become coheirs with Him and share in His inheritance. According to Hebrews 1:2, of what is Jesus the heir?

9. What parts of your heavenly Father's glorious inheritance do you most look forward to?

10. According to Ephesians 1:13–14, when did we become eligible for this inheritance and how is it guaranteed until Jesus returns?

⋅ ∘ ● ∘ ⋅

A true story is told of a man with disabilities cruelly nicknamed "Old Rattle Bones" by a group of boys on the street. Freddie, the main bully, became worried when the man headed straight toward his house. To impress his friends, the boy taunted, "Go on, Old Rattle Bones, see who cares if you visit my mother."

The man replied sadly, "You wouldn't call me names if you knew my condition."

He knocked on the door and was warmly welcomed by the boy's mother. She told her son to come inside too. Turning to Freddie, the man said, "When you were just a baby, your nurse took you on a carriage ride near the river. She accidentally let go of the handle, and the carriage careened downhill. Before she could stop it, the buggy plunged into the raging water. I jumped into the river and struggled to bring you safely to shore. The water that day was frigid, aggravating my rheumatic condition. Now, ten years later, I can scarcely hobble along."

Freddie hung his head and began to cry. "Thank you for saving me. And forgive me for calling you Old Rattle Bones. I didn't know who you were."[8]

Society is full of bullies. And most people play along. The world thinks nothing of using the Lord's name in vain. They don't realize that they are defaming the very One who died to rescue them from sin. Will you be the one to remind them who Jesus is and what He's done for them?

LISTEN TO ...

Our great honor lies in being just what Jesus was and is. To be accepted by those who accept him, rejected by all who reject him, loved by those who love him and hated by everyone who hates him. What greater glory could come to any man?

—*A. W. Tozer*

DAY 4
Recovering New Fruit

Since ancient times, landowners have used a technique called crop rotation to keep their land fertile and free of disease. Great ancient civilizations in Africa, Asia, and Rome record using this wise agricultural method of crop cultivation. Even today, modern agriculturalists rotate their fields.

The theory is simple: Two dissimilar types of fruit or vegetation are grown in sequence in the same location. Thus, the land is able to regenerate needed nutrients depleted by certain crops. Crop rotation also helps to rid the land of insects or disease that one plant group might attract.[9]

Jesus was, in a sense, practicing crop rotation. The old religious system had lost its vitality and grown diseased. The leaders did not even recognize the One who had planted them in the land, and they were spreading this disease of disbelief to the people. It was time for the old crop of those who rejected Messiah to be uprooted. A new crop would be planted in their place. The new harvest would be a hybrid mix of some Jews but primarily Gentiles who accepted Jesus as their Lord and Savior. They would become the church and bear spiritual fruit, building up the kingdom of God on earth.

However, it's important to remember that prophecy reveals that there will come a day when Jesus restores Israel as a viable crop in the end times. Though this parable does not speak of that time to come, believers are commanded to "pray for the peace of Jerusalem: 'May they prosper who love you'" (Ps. 122:6).

Now let's look at how the landowner recovers a new crop for the field of faith.

LIFT UP ...

Lord, I know Israel's rejection of You was part of Your plan to give me the gift of eternal life. Help me to bear fruit for Your kingdom. Amen.

LOOK AT ...

The parable of the Landowner is both a reminder of past behavior and a prophecy of coming events. It is a history of the relationship between the children of Israel and the prophets of God. At the same time it is a prophetic snapshot of Jesus' impending death at the hands of these religious leaders.

As this parable unfolds, we see that these hypocritical religious leaders, wittingly or unwittingly, pronounce sentence upon themselves. These men were wise in their own eyes and self-righteous in their attitudes. Matthew 23:28 says, "Even so you also outwardly appear righteous to men, but inside you are full of hypocrisy and lawlessness." God sees the real you. Don't settle for self-righteousness when God's righteousness is available to all who ask.

READ MATTHEW 21:40–43.

"Therefore, when the owner of the vineyard comes, what will he do to those vinedressers?" They said to Him, "He will destroy those wicked men miserably, and lease his vineyard to other vinedressers who will render to him the fruits in their seasons." Jesus said to them, "Have you never read in the Scriptures: 'The stone which the builders rejected has become the chief corner-stone. This was the LORD's doing, and it is marvelous in our eyes'? Therefore I say to you, the kingdom of God will be taken from you and given to a nation bearing the fruits of it." Matthew 21:40–43

1. Rephrase the question Jesus asked in conclusion to His parable.

2. What sentence did the religious leaders pass on the wicked vine-dressers and thus upon themselves?

3. Read Luke 19:43–44, and explain Jesus' prophecy about Jerusalem. Why would this calamity occur?

LEARN ABOUT ...

2 Sentenced

Wicked means worthless, depraved, or injurious to others. Because of their wickedness, the leaders would be destroyed. Literally, this means to cause to perish or punish by death. Thus, the rulers unknowingly pronounced a death sentence upon themselves for rejecting the Son.

3 Destroyed

In AD 70, the Romans destroyed Jerusalem and abolished Judaism. The situation escalated until "a Roman city was erected on the site and Jerusalem was regarded as forbidden ground for the Jews."[10] John MacArthur said, "Jerusalem's utter destruction was divine judgment for their failure to recognize and embrace their Messiah when He visited them."[11]

LEARN ABOUT ...

5 Positioned

The cornerstone is positioned at the bend of two walls, uniting and strengthening the structure. The stone is built into the corner of a building's foundation as its starting or end point. Jesus is "the Alpha and the Omega, the Beginning and the End" (Rev. 1:8) of the Christian and Jewish belief systems.

8 Rescued

God calls Israel "the apple of His eye" (Zech. 2:8); "His chosen ones" (Ps. 105:6); and "My people, the children of Israel" (Ex. 7:4). Because God loves her, He will not forsake her. When enemies come against Israel at Armageddon, Jesus will ride to her rescue on a white horse (see Rev. 19:11).

10 Reconciled

Unlike Israel, linked by geography and nationality, the new "nation" known as the church has no common race, creed, or color. We are bound by the Spirit and serve as ambassadors throughout the world: "We are ambassadors for Christ, as though God were pleading through us: we implore you on Christ's behalf, be reconciled to God" (2 Cor. 5:20).

4. Reread Matthew 21:41. Describe the religious leaders' solution for the operation of the vineyard.

5. Jesus then questioned them about Psalm 118:22–23.

   a. According to the psalm, what happened to the stone?

   b. Who orchestrated these events?

   c. Why are these events described as "marvelous"?

6. In your own words, describe the consequences for Israel's rejection of the Messiah.

7. Read Matthew 16:17–19. By what name would this new "nation" be called?

LIVE OUT ...

8. Though Israel rejected her Messiah, the Messiah has not forever rejected Israel. Journal a prayer praying "for the peace of Jerusalem" (Ps. 122:6).

9. A cornerstone is the starting point of a building and its foundational strength. In the columns provided, list some of the things Jesus has started and strengthened in you.

STARTED   **STRENGTHENED**

JESUS THE CHIEF CORNERSTONE

10. a. Jesus confirmed that the vineyard would be leased to new farmers who would bear fruit. According to Galatians 5:22–23, what fruit should we believers bear?

b. Ask a friend to describe evidence of specific spiritual fruit in your life. Write her answers.

∘ ∘ ● ∘ ∘

Grafting is a technique in which a section of a stem with leaf buds is inserted into the stock of a tree. The upper part of the graft (the scion) becomes the top of the plant. The lower portion (the understock) becomes the root system or part of the trunk.

Why graft? Because some seeds produce trees, though not of the original variety. The seed from a Haralson apple will produce an apple tree, but not produce a Haralson apple tree. In other words, some fruit trees cannot be reproduced "true" to the original from their seed. They can only reproduce by grafting. Grafting is also used to repair injured or unfruitful trees.[12]

Israel is represented in Scripture as an olive tree that had ceased to produce healthy fruit. Therefore, God grafted the Gentile church, known as a wild olive tree, into Israel to form a stronger tree from the two. Together, the Gentiles and the Jews would produce His kingdom and bear much fruit.

Although Paul was not a horticulturalist, he revealed the Master Gardener's plan to the Gentiles in Rome: "After all, if you were cut out of an olive tree that is wild by nature, and contrary to nature were grafted into a cultivated olive tree, how much more readily will these, the natural branches, be grafted into their own olive tree! I do not want you to be ignorant of this mystery, brothers, so that you may not be conceited: Israel has experienced a hardening in part until the full number of the Gentiles has come in" (Rom. 11:24–25 NIV). Even today, God is gathering a harvest of Gentiles and Jews.

LISTEN TO ...

My Spirit searches the deep things of the heart. I not only taste the fruit, I test the soundness of the tree. I do not look at the leaves, but examine the roots. I behold not the shape of the tree, but test the heart.

—*Frances J. Roberts*

DAY 5

Stumbling on the Stone

The Golden Gate Bridge is the portal to California. It is one of the most striking images of "The Golden State." It sits in tumultuous waters where powerful currents flow. Not only that, but it rests atop the infamous San Andreas fault—the famous tectonic plate that runs eight hundred miles up the California coast.

One thing that makes the Golden Gate Bridge so exceptional is its strong foundation. It has withstood wind, storms, and earthquakes. The Golden Gate Bridge was the first bridge ever constructed in the open ocean. Joseph Strauss, the chief engineer, sent teams of divers into bedrock as deep as 90 feet below the surface of the water. Finally, at 107 feet they inspected the bedrock and foundations and knew the bridge was safe.

As believers, we know that our foundation is Christ. With Christ as our bedrock, though earthquakes may come in the form of illness, economic loss, or personal tragedy, we will not be moved.

On the other hand, there are those whose preoccupation is not rock solid. They sway with every wind of false doctrine and philosophical fad. Jesus offers some firm warnings to these unbelieving people about their future fate—not to condemn them, but to offer hope: "God did not send His Son into the world to condemn the world, but that the world through Him might be saved" (John 3:17).

LIFT UP ...

Lord, You are my salvation, my glory, my refuge, and my rock of strength. I am so grateful I can trust You in all ways and at all times. Amen.

LOOK AT ...

It became apparent to the religious leaders that this parable was directed at them. They were the vinedressers who killed the Son; they were the builders who rejected the Cornerstone. They would pay the price as the kingdom of God would be taken from them. If this story had a happy ending, the chief priests and Pharisees would recognize the error of their ways,

turn from their prideful lives, and become believers in the Messiah, who labored in the vineyard. But they didn't react this way. Instead of eliminating their sinful behavior, they attempted to eliminate the Messenger.

As we meditate on this parable, let's examine our own hearts. Are there areas where we are too comfortable? Too prideful? Too stubborn? Don't make mistake of the Pharisees. Follow the guidance found in Lamentations 3:40: "Let us search out and examine our ways, and turn back to the LORD." When we return to the Lord, we reap a great harvest.

READ MATTHEW 21:28–46;
THEN FOCUS ON VERSES 44–46.

"And whoever falls on this stone will be broken; but on whomever it falls, it will grind him to powder." Now when the chief priests and Pharisees heard His parables, they perceived that He was speaking of them. But when they sought to lay hands on Him, they feared the multitudes, because they took Him for a prophet. Matthew 21:44–46

1. Describe what happens to anyone who falls on the stone.

2. What happens to anyone on whom the stone falls?

3. According to 1 Peter 2:8, why did Israel stumble over the Chief Cornerstone?

4. What did the chief priests and Pharisees perceive when Jesus finished speaking in parables?

5. How did the chief priests and Pharisees react to this parable?

6. Explain what prevented them from carrying out their plan.

LEARN ABOUT …

2 Broken

Broken means smashed into pieces or shattered. For instance, when glass falls on stone, it splinters into pieces. *To grind* refers to the process of milling grain to powder, separating the wheat from the chaff. Isaiah promises, "You shall winnow them, the wind shall carry them away, and the whirlwind shall scatter them" (Isa. 41:16).

4 Harden

To perceive means to understand or be aware of something. The chief priests and Pharisees recognized the messianic references in this parable. Rather than being convicted, they hardened their hearts. The author of Hebrews warns against this: "Today, if you will hear His voice, do not harden your hearts as in the rebellion" (Heb. 3:15).

6 Trepidation

An Old Testament prophet spoke God's Word and predicted the future. In this parable, Jesus referred to two passages: Isaiah 5, concerning the vineyard, and Psalm 118, concerning the cornerstone. He also foretold the religious leaders' future. The people saw Christ as a prophet, but they did not all perceive Him as their Savior.

LEARN ABOUT ...

7 Transformation

Sometimes God breaks us to make us. The angel of the Lord broke Jacob's hip to transform him into Israel. God used a thorn to break Paul's pride and bring utter reliance on God. Solomon said, "To everything there is a season ... a time to break down, and a time to build up" (Eccl. 3:1, 3).

8 Salvation

All people face one of two choices: willingly fall on and be broken by the stone of salvation or force the stone of judgment to fall on and condemn them. One day "every knee shall bow ... and every tongue shall confess that Jesus Christ is Lord, to the glory of God the Father" (Phil. 2:10–11 TLB).

LIVE OUT ...

7. a. Everyone who willingly falls on the stone, Jesus Christ, will be broken. But God promises restoration for those who cast themselves on Him. Read the following verses to discover God's promises of restoration.

SCRIPTURE	RESTORATION FOR THE BROKEN
Psalm 51:8–12	
Psalm 80:3	
Joel 2:25–26	

   b. Journal about some of the ways God has broken you spiritually, emotionally, or physically. How has brokenness made you stronger in your faith?

8. On judgment day, Jesus will grind and scatter to the wind all those who reject Him.

   a. Read John 5:24–25, and explain how people can avoid this fate.

   b. How will you help those in your sphere of influence avoid this horrible fate?

   ❏ Tell them what Christ has done in my life
   ❏ Invite them to church/Bible study
   ❏ Pray for them
   ❏ Other (name it)

   ° ° ● ° °

Over a hundred years ago in a Scottish seaside inn, some fishermen were relaxing after a long day at sea. As a serving maid walked past the fishermen's table with a pot of tea, one of the men made a sweeping gesture to describe the size of the fish he claimed to have caught. His hand hit the teapot, sending it crashing against the whitewashed wall, staining a large area. "That stain will never come out," the innkeeper said. "The whole wall will have to be repainted."

"Perhaps not." All eyes turned to the stranger who had spoken. "What do you mean?" asked the innkeeper. "Let me work with the stain," said the stranger. "If my work meets your approval, you won't need to repaint the wall." So he picked up a box and went to the wall. Opening the box, he withdrew pencils, brushes, and some glass jars of linseed oil and pigment. He began to sketch lines around the stain and fill it in here and there with dabs of color and swashes of shading. Soon a picture began to emerge. The random splashes of tea were transformed into the image of a magnificent stag. The man inscribed his signature on the painting, paid for his meal, and left.

"Do you know who that man was?" the innkeeper said in amazement. "E. H. Landseer!" Indeed, the famous wildlife painter, Sir Edwin Landseer, had visited the village.

God sent Jesus to take the stains and disappointments from our lives—not merely to erase them, but to turn them into a thing of beauty. Will we be like the religious leaders and reject Him as the cornerstone of our faith, or will we gladly accept Him as one who can transform our lives into a masterpiece?

LISTEN TO ...

Jesus is the foundation of my whole life. He is my strength.... He's the solid rock you can stand on every day. There's no problem you can't face if you have the love of Jesus to strengthen you.

—Johnny Cash

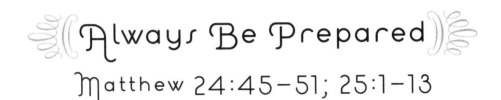

Always Be Prepared
Matthew 24:45–51; 25:1–13

When I (Penny) was in elementary school, my friend Kathy asked me to join her Girl Scout troop. I eagerly agreed. I really wanted to go with my friends to the meetings after school, wear the fun green outfit, and earn those merit badges. I went to my first troop meeting and received my *Girl Scout Handbook*. The troop mother instructed me to memorize the Girl Scout pledge and Girl Scout motto. I went home and began to study.

The next week, I went to our meeting and stood before the other girls dressed in my bright green Girl Scout uniform, knee socks, and cap. I solemnly raised the three fingers on my right hand and recited the pledge, "On my honor, I will try: to serve God and my country, to help people at all times, and to live by the Girl Scout Law." Then the troop mother asked, "And what is the Girl Scout motto?" I quickly replied, "Be prepared."

Jesus told the parable of the Servants and the parable of the Ten Virgins to teach His followers to always be prepared for His return. Scripture assures us that He *will* come again. One out of every thirty verses in the New Testament speaks of Christ's second coming as a literal and imminent event. For every prophecy in the Bible concerning Christ's birth, there are eight that look forward to His return.[1] This week's lesson will help you to answer the question "Are *you* prepared?"

Day 1: Matthew 24:45–47   **WAITING FAITHFULLY**

Day 2: Matthew 24:48–51   **LIVING RECKLESSLY**

Day 3: Matthew 25:1–4   **PREPARING WISELY**

Day 4: Matthew 25:5–9   **PACKING FOOLISHLY**

Day 5: Matthew 25:10–13   **ARRIVING TARDILY**

DAY 1
Waiting Faithfully

LIFT UP ...

Help me, Lord, to be faithful while I wait for You. I want to make an eternal impact while I walk in this world. Amen.

LOOK AT ...

After Jesus left the temple for the final time, He ended His public ministry. He then gave the Olivet Discourse to His followers, which included the parables we'll study this week. He also predicted the destruction of the temple, and that prediction confused the disciples. They thought the kingdom was coming immediately, so they asked, "What will be the sign of Your coming, and of the end of the age?" (Matt. 24:3). Knowing His crucifixion was only three days away, Jesus used this time to prepare the disciples for His death, resurrection, and ascension by detailing the end-time events that would precede His future kingdom. Jesus assured the disciples that the kingdom they hoped for would eventually come. He used the example of faithful servants to illustrate the believer's job until He comes: Wait faithfully for His return.

READ MATTHEW 24:45–47.

"Who then is a faithful and wise servant, whom his master made ruler over his household, to give them food in due season? Blessed is that servant whom his master, when he comes, will find so doing. Assuredly, I say to you that he will make him ruler over all his goods." Matthew 24:45–47

1. Read Matthew 24:42–44 for context. What two instructions did Jesus give the disciples?

2. Who did Jesus speak of in Matthew 24:45 to illustrate these instructions?

3. Describe the position the master gave this servant.

4. What specific duty did the ruler of the household have?

5. a. What word did Jesus use to describe the servant who was faithfully fulfilling his duties when the master returned?

   b. What do you think of when you hear this word?

6. What specific reward did Jesus say this servant would receive upon the master's return?

LIVE OUT ...

7. Like the faithful servant in today's story, believers are instructed, "As each one has received a gift, minister it to one another, as good stewards of the manifold grace of God" (1 Peter 4:10). With this in mind, complete the following exercise.

   a. Review the spiritual gifts listed below, and check the boxes to indicate which gifts you possess:
   - ❏ **Administration:** ability to lead and organize the gifts within a group
   - ❏ **Exhortation:** ability to bring out the best and encourage godliness in others
   - ❏ **Giving:** ability to discern and meet the material needs of others
   - ❏ **Healing:** being an instrument of God's grace to heal the body, mind, and emotions

LEARN ABOUT ...

2 Faithfulness

Faithful refers to one who is trustworthy and true. *Wise* speaks of someone cautious and thoughtful. Paul said, "Servants of Christ ... [are] entrusted with the secret things of God. Now it is required that those who have been given a trust must prove faithful" (1 Cor. 4:1–2 NIV). Are you trustworthy and thoughtful about the things of God?

4 Goodness

The household ruler oversaw the physical needs of the master's family and servants in his absence. He was to provide food and clothing for them "in due season," before it was too late or when the opportunity arose. As believers, "as we have opportunity, let us do good to all, especially to those who are of the household of faith" (Gal. 6:10).

6 Blessedness

The master of the household promoted this servant to rule over all of his goods because he proved faithful as ruler of the household. Jesus said, "Well done, good and faithful servant; you have been faithful over a few things, I will make you ruler over many things" (Matt. 25:23).

LEARN ABOUT ...

7 Giftedness

Spiritual gifts are supernatural abilities bestowed by the Holy Spirit on Christians to build up the church and glorify God. Spiritual gifts are gifts of grace and must be controlled by the greatest of all spiritual gifts—love. "Though I have the gift of prophecy, and understand all mysteries ... but have not love, I am nothing" (I Cor. 13:2).

9 Devotedness

Paul wrote, "It is required in stewards that one be found faithful" (I Cor. 4:2). It's impossible to serve God in a vacuum: Devotion to the Master will overflow to those around us. Serving God means serving others. Jesus said, "By this all will know that you are My disciples, if you have love for one another" (John 13:35).

❐ **Helps:** assisting others in practical ways so they are free to minister to others

❐ **Mercy:** sensing the emotional needs of others as if experiencing them firsthand

❐ **Service:** supplying materials and services to complete specific tasks

❐ **Shepherding:** leading, guiding, and nurturing others sensitively and sacrificially

❐ **Teaching:** ability to understand and clearly communicate the truth to others

b. Describe how you have been faithful to use your gifts to help others.

c. Now tell how others in the church have faithfully helped you through their spiritual gifts.

8. Journal a personal prayer asking God to make you a wise servant who is "a vessel for honor, sanctified and useful for the Master, prepared for every good work" (2 Tim. 2:21).

9. The master in this parable rewarded the servant's faithfulness with greater responsibility. According to the following Scriptures, what rewards will faithful servants of the Master receive?

SCRIPTURE	REWARDS FOR FAITHFUL SERVICE
John 12:26	
2 Timothy 2:12	
1 Peter 5:2–4	
Revelation 2:10	

○ ○ ● ○ ○

NBC's *Dateline* did a segment on a "revolutionary" idea for the business world: servant leadership. Stone Phillips wondered, "Can humility and faith be good for business? Was Jesus the ultimate CEO? It's an image nearly two thousand years old and a message that true leaders are servants first. It's an idea that's finding new disciples in corporate America."

Phillips interviewed Larry Spears, president and CEO of the Greenleaf Center, a worldwide nonprofit organization headquartered in Indianapolis, who challenged the pyramid model of business management with one based on sacrifice and service by those at the top:

> **Spears:** "What we're trying to encourage through servant leadership is showing your caring side in the workplace. Someone who is truly loving and caring at home with their family, with friends, neighbors, they have that capacity to bring that to the workplace. And servant-leadership sort of challenges people to be brave and courageous, and to bring ideas like friendship and perhaps even love to the workplace."
>
> **Phillips:** "The courage not just to be caring, but to be loving."
>
> **Spears:** "That's right. The word 'love' is something you rarely hear in the daily workings of most organizations, but in servant-led organizations you, in fact, do hear that."[2]

Corporate America is finally learning what Jesus taught over 2,000 years ago. God blesses those who lead by lovingly serving. May God find us faithful in our workplaces, our schools, and our churches. When He comes, may He find us faithfully serving and loving others.

LISTEN TO ...

The Possessor of heaven and earth ... placed you here not as a proprietor, but a steward.

—John Wesley

DAY 2

living Recklessly

"While the cat's away, the mice will play" is a cute way of saying that those who are not accountable to an overseer are vulnerable to making mischief—or when the person in charge is not there, the subordinates will take advantage of the absence. This phrase was used by Shakespeare in his play *Henry the Fifth*. If the statement was true during Shakespeare's time, it was true in biblical times, and it is still true today.

Just three months after the children of Israel were miraculously delivered from Egypt and Pharaoh's armies drowned in the Red Sea, Moses met with God on Mount Sinai. As he received the Ten Commandments, written on stone by the hand of God, the children of Israel got drunk and danced naked around their man-made calf of gold. While Moses was away, the children of Israel played the harlot with an idol.

Sadly, I (Lenya) learned that, just three months after graduating from a Christian high school, some of my son Nathan's friends abandoned the principles they once embraced in godly homes. One received a DUI violation. Another posted on her MySpace page that she was an atheist. Another friend admitted to Nathan that he was experimenting with marijuana. While away from their parents, these children are playing with fire.

In this parable we see how some unsupervised servants misbehaved. They mistakenly believed that what their master didn't see couldn't hurt them. But there's another saying that's equally true: "You may be sure that your sin will find you out" (Num. 32:23 NIV).

LIFT UP ...

Lord Jesus, help me to live what I know. Forgive me for being reckless with the opportunities You've given me. Amen.

LOOK AT ...

Yesterday in our parable we were introduced to a faithful servant. This servant loyally took care of business while his master was away. Today we will study a scenario involving a

servant with the opposite mind-set. He misrepresented his relationship to the master and abused his authority while the master was away.

In this parable Jesus called this worker an "evil servant." The Greek word translated "evil" is *kakos*. This word describes someone who is bad in character, intrinsically useless, and morally and ethically evil. The use of this word implies that this servant didn't simply have a brief lapse in judgment—he was truly evil in his heart. The evil servant only appeared to be faithful and trustworthy, but the Master was not fooled. First Samuel 16:7 warns, "For the Lord does not see as man sees; for man looks at the outward appearance, but the Lord looks at the heart." This is a strong warning for all of us. Though we may outwardly act one way, inwardly we can be completely different. Let's heed this warning and examine our hearts to "see if there is any wicked way in [us]" (Ps. 139:24). Then let's turn to the Lord to lead us "in the way everlasting" (Ps. 139:24).

READ MATTHEW 24:48–51.

"But if that evil servant says in his heart, 'My master is delaying his coming,' and begins to beat his fellow servants, and to eat and drink with the drunkards, the master of that servant will come on a day when he is not looking for him and at an hour that he is not aware of, and will cut him in two and appoint him his portion with the hypocrites. There shall be weeping and gnashing of teeth." Matthew 24:48–51

1. What did the evil servant secretly believe?

2. Supposing he would not have to give an account to his master, the evil servant engaged in what two behaviors?

3. How did Jesus describe the return of this servant's master?

4. Describe the evil servant's punishment.

LEARN ABOUT …

I Doubt

What we say in our hearts reflects what we think. "The fool has said in his heart, 'There is no God'" (Ps. 14:1). This servant doubted his master would return anytime soon. Peter warns that many will be like this servant: "Scoffers will come in the last days, walking according to their own lusts, and saying, 'Where is the promise of His coming?'" (2 Peter 3:3–4).

2 Wrong Behaviors

Beat means to strike repeatedly with the hand or other instrument. Stewards were not to lord authority over fellow servants. Eating and drinking with drunkards signified intimate fellowship and like-minded behavior. But Scripture warns us, "Do not follow evil men's advice …[or] hang around with sinners, scoffing at the things of God" (Ps. 1:1 TLB).

4 Dissected

Being cut in two was an ancient mode of punishment used in several countries. But Jesus probably spoke figuratively here about being "cut off" from God's people and receiving the punishment due a hypocrite—an actor or stage player. The Psalms promise, "Evildoers shall be cut off; but those who wait on the Lord … shall inherit the earth" (Ps. 37:9).

LEARN ABOUT ...

7 Distracted

It's easy to lose our eternal perspective in the hustle and bustle of daily life. Satan's most clever strategy is to convince us there's plenty of time to live for eternity—later. But John admonishes us to "abide in Him, that when He appears, we may have confidence and not be ashamed before Him at His coming" (I John 2:28).

5. *Hypocrite* is the Greek word for a stage actor. How did this evil servant behave like an actor?

6. Read the end of this parable as recorded in Luke 12:46–48.

   a. What word is used instead of hypocrites (v. 46)?

   b. What additional punishment did Luke record (vv. 47–48)?

   c. What do you think Jesus meant by saying, "Everyone to whom much is given, from him will much be required"?

LIVE OUT ...

7. The evil servant's belief about his master's return steered his behavior. Instead of living recklessly, the true believer lives as if Jesus could return at any moment.

   a. What kinds of things distract you, causing you to forget that Jesus could return at any moment?

   b. If He returned today, what would your response be?
      ❏ "Wait! I'm not finished with _____."
      ❏ "I never thought this would really happen."
      ❏ "This is my most embarrassing moment."
      ❏ "I have fought the good fight and finished the race."
      ❏ Other (name it)

8. Jesus described the evil servant as someone who drank with the drunkards. What do the following verses teach us to do *instead* of being drunk?

SCRIPTURE

Luke 21:34

Romans 13:13–14

Ephesians 5:18

1 Thessalonians 5:6–8

INSTEAD OF BEING DRUNK …

LEARN ABOUT …

9 Diabolical

Many commentators believe the evil servant represents unfaithful leaders who abuse their trust within the church. Severe punishment awaits these pretenders. Jesus condemned the religious leaders for "outwardly appear[ing] righteous to men" while they were "full of hypocrisy and lawlessness" on the inside (Matt. 23:28).

9. The evil servant abused his authority, neglected his responsibilities, and lived recklessly in the master's absence. He was a servant in name only—a hypocrite.

    a. How do you think others see you? Make a list of specific characteristics below.

    b. Now take an honest look in the mirror. Which of the above characteristics do you only "put on" when people are watching? Cross through them with your pen.

· · ● · ·

A young Christian businessman from Nashville was invited to speak at a local church. He chose for his text, "Thou shalt not steal," and he spoke unswervingly on the topic. The next morning he boarded a city bus for the ride to work. He handed a dollar bill to the driver and received some change, which he counted as he proceeded down the aisle of the bus. Before he reached his seat, he realized he had been given a dime too much. His first thought was that the transit company would never miss it. But deep inside he knew he should return it. So he went back to the driver and said, "You gave me too much change, sir." To the businessman's amazement, the driver replied, "I know … a dime too much. I gave it to you on purpose. Then I watched you in my mirror as you counted your change. You see, I heard you speak yesterday, and if you had kept the dime, I would have had no confidence in what you said."[3]

The walls may not have ears, but "the eyes of the LORD range throughout the earth to strengthen those whose hearts are fully committed to him" (2 Chron. 16:9 NIV). Whether or not people observe our actions, God sees everything. This concept should motivate us to behave well regardless of whether our supervisors, parents, or pastors can see us. God is watching, and He will reward *or* rebuke us for our actions, either good or bad.

LISTEN TO ...

Hypocrites in the church? Yes, and in the lodge, and at home. Don't hunt through the church for a hypocrite. Go home and look in the glass. Hypocrites? Yes. See that you make the number one less.

—Billy Sunday

DAY 3
Preparing Wisely

Being asked to be a bridesmaid is an honor that takes some preparation. Many of us have spent too much money on a dress in a color that didn't match our complexions or figure types and nodded knowingly as the bride said, "You can cut the dress off and wear it to parties!" We all know the sad truth. Those horrible dresses will sit in the back of the closet until we donate them to Goodwill. In modern America, it seems that the bridesmaid's job is to look frumpy so that the bride can look gorgeous. And we happily do this for our friends, knowing we'll get our turn later.

In Israel, the bridesmaids had a different job. All they had to do in order to prepare for the wedding was to have their lamps ready so they could light the way for the wedding party. They simply needed oil in their lamps.

If you've ever been in a wedding party, you know that some of the bridesmaids are always better prepared than others. In the dressing room there's always someone who says, "Oh, I lost my hairpins." Some flaky friends have even forgotten their dresses and delayed the wedding proceedings. Others are perfectly prepared. They have everything ready: bobby pins? Check. Hair spray? Check. Lipstick? Check. Those are the bridesmaids to have.

So it was in Israel. There were bridesmaids who were faithful and bridesmaids who were flaky. Today, we see the two kinds of bridesmaids: those who prepared wisely and those who did not.

LIFT UP ...

Lord, may I be found doing Your will when You come. And, Lord, please come quickly! Amen.

LOOK AT ...

In the parable of the Ten Virgins, we gain insight into the traditional Jewish wedding customs. After the marriage proposal was accepted, the bridegroom would leave to prepare for the wedding. It could take as long as one year, but the groom would return

LEARN ABOUT ...

I End Times

"Then" in Matthew 25:1
indicates when the kingdom
of heaven will become like
these virgins. Rather than
His usual "the kingdom of
heaven is like" where Jesus
spoke of the present phase
of the kingdom, Jesus spoke
in the future tense— "shall
be likened to"—turning our
attention to the next phase
in God's kingdom: the end
of the age.[4]

for his bride after the work was complete to bring the bride to his home. Though there was no exact date, as the time drew near the bride and her attendants would prepare for the bridegroom. The bride would keep her veil and a lamp by her bed in anticipation of the groom's visit. The attendants would collect their lamps and oil so they could accompany the couple.

The bridegroom would come to retrieve his bride usually around midnight. As he approached, the wedding party would begin to shout, "Behold, the bridegroom cometh!" to warn the bride that she should be ready. The duty of the bridesmaids was to honor the bridegroom by lighting the way for the wedding party as they returned to the wedding chamber. This is probably where modern couples got the idea for candle-light weddings. For the virgins *not* to be prepared spoke to their lack of belief in the ultimate return of the bridegroom for his bride. As you read this parable, ask yourself which member of the wedding party you most relate to. Are you ready for the bridegroom to return?

READ MATTHEW 25:1–14.

"Then the kingdom of heaven shall be likened to ten virgins who took their lamps and went out to meet the bridegroom. Now five of them were wise, and five were foolish. Those who were foolish took their lamps and took no oil with them, but the wise took oil in their vessels with their lamps."
Matthew 25:1–4

1. What key word serves as a transition between the previous parable and this one? Read the sidebar about the end times, and talk about how you feel when you read about the end of the age.

2. Jesus said the kingdom of heaven would be like ten virgins who did what two things?

3. Into what two categories did Jesus separate these ten virgins, and what differentiated them from one another?

4. Who do you think each set of virgins represents?

5. Proverbs is known as the book of wisdom. Draw a line connecting the verses from Proverbs with the characteristics they describe; then classify each as wise or foolish.

SCRIPTURE *	CHARACTERISTIC	WISE OR FOOLISH?
Proverbs 12:15	Prays before speaking	
Proverbs 15:5	Enjoys arguments	
Proverbs 20:3	Does whatever feels right	
Proverbs 29:11	Seeks biblical advice	
	Rebels against authority	
Each verse may have more than one answer.	Accepts correction	
	Is a peacemaker	
	Speaks his or her mind	

LEARN ABOUT ...

3 Wise Living

To be *wise* means to have spiritual and practical understanding. *Foolish*—from the Greek word *moros*—means dull or stupid, literally a blockhead. How much better to live wisely than to live worthlessly, especially when it comes to spiritual matters.

4 Responsible People

The oil in one of these outdoor torches was depleted within fifteen minutes, especially if the torch's wick burned without oil. A responsible bridesmaid wouldn't forget her oil, since lighting the way for the procession was one of her chief responsibilities. A bridesmaid forgetting her oil was unthinkable: "Can a virgin forget her ornaments, or a bride her attire?" (Jer. 2:32).

LIVE OUT ...

6. Jesus characterized the virgins who didn't prepare ahead as foolish. Look at your answers to the previous question. Place a – beside any of the foolish characteristics that you tend to have and a + beside your wise attributes. Based on this assessment, do you tend to be more wise or foolish?

7. Now journal a prayer confessing some ways you've been foolish.

Ask God for "the wisdom that comes from heaven [which] is first of all pure; then peace-loving, considerate, submissive, full of mercy and good fruit, impartial and sincere" (James 3:17 NIV).

8. The bridesmaids were responsible for carrying torches to light the way. Jesus said, "You are the light of the world.... Let your light so shine before men, that they may see your good works and glorify your Father in heaven" (Matt. 5:14, 16).

    a. Who is the source of "your light" according to John 8:12?

    b. How do you know if you have the light of life inside you?

    c. How would you describe your torch?

    ❏ Shining bright   ❏ Flickering   ❏ Out cold

9. a. The wise virgins kept oil in their lamps so they could continue to shine brightly. List some ways God's light shines through your life. Who, specifically, does it shine on?

    b. What blocks God's light in your life, causing it to be hidden under a basket?

    ❏ Unforgiveness   ❏ Pride   ❏ Lack of self-control
    ❏ Filthy language   ❏ Materialism   ❏ Selfish ambition
    ❏ Jealousy   ❏ Anger   ❏ Other (name it)

    c. How will you seek to affect others in a way that enriches and preserves, like salt?

○ ○ ● ○ ○

Little Bonnie came home from Sunday school after learning the verse, "Let your light so shine before men, that they may see your good works and glorify your Father in heaven" (Matt. 5:16). She asked her mom what it meant. Her mother replied, "It means that when you are good and kind and obedient, you are letting Christ's light shine upon all who see you."

The next week in Sunday school, Bonnie got in a tussle with Sara, and the girls began calling each other names. The teacher ran to find the mothers to take the disruptive classmates home. Bonnie's mother was so concerned about her behavior that she asked on the way home, "Sweetie, don't you remember about letting your light shine for Jesus before others?" The girl blurted out, "Mom, I got so mad I blew myself out." It only took little Bonnie one week to lose sight of her purpose.[5]

So too, the foolish bridesmaids lost sight of their purpose in serving at the wedding by letting their lamps burn out. When the winds of life blow against our lamps, it's tempting to give up and let them fade. But if we'll hold our empty vessels out to God, He is willing to replenish our hearts with the oil of His Spirit: "'He who believes in Me, as the Scripture has said, out of his heart will flow rivers of living water.' But this He spoke concerning the Spirit" (John 7:38–39).

LISTEN TO ...

God will never fail to give light when we have no other plan than to please him and to act in love for him.

—Brother Lawrence

DAY 4
Packing Foolishly

With the onset of Braxton-Hicks contractions and a sudden burst of energy, it was obvious that the arrival of our (Lenya's) baby was imminent. The doctor said, "It could be any day. Don't forget to pack your hospital suitcase." The big question was, *When?!* What day and hour would our firstborn arrive? Surprisingly, he came early—two weeks before his due date. As Skip backed down the driveway, I shouted, "Don't forget the suitcase!" We were prepared for Nathan's appearance.

Most birthing coaches recommend you pack some of these items in your suitcase to prepare for your hospital visit during birth:

- Your insurance paperwork
- Phone numbers of friends and family
- Camera equipment
- Your eyeglasses. Even if you wear contacts, you'll probably want to take them out at some point
- A headband and barrettes to keep your hair out of your face
- Lip balm
- Your robe, nightgown, and slippers
- Your own pillow
- Something to use as a focal point
- Your favorite music to listen to during labor

The bridesmaids were instructed to have their belongings ready for a great arrival—the appearance of the bridegroom. They knew what they needed and should have been watching and waiting for his arrival. Some had prepared wisely while others packed foolishly. The foolish needed to turn back to get vital supplies. Sadly, by packing foolishly, they'd miss the anticipated event.

LIFT UP ...

Dear Lord, please help me to keep my focus on the clouds as I go about my daily business. Remind me that You could come for me today. Amen.

Look at ...

Today in our parable we see that the bridesmaids fell asleep while waiting for the bridegroom. The implication is that they left their lamps burning but failed to have any oil to refill them once he actually arrived. Perhaps they only burned the wicks and did not use any oil at all.

In this parable, Jesus tells us that the bridegroom was delayed. The word translated *delayed* literally means to while away time by lingering or tarrying. This does not mean that the bridegroom wasted precious time. We know that our heavenly Bridegroom's return is perfectly timed. *Delayed* does imply, however, that the bridegroom did not follow the bridesmaids' expected timetable. Nor will Jesus Christ's return come according to a human timetable. Jesus said, "Watch therefore, for you do not know what hour your Lord is coming.… Therefore you also be ready, for the Son of Man is coming at an hour you do not expect" (Matt. 24:42, 44). The question is, do you have oil in your lamp? Ask yourself: are you ready for His return?

Learn about ...

3 Procession

Eastern tradition required the bridegroom to fetch the bride at her house. The time of his arrival was unknown to the bride. Since the bride isn't mentioned specifically, it's also possible she was already with the bridegroom as the wedding procession began en route to the marriage feast.[6]

Read Matthew 25:5–9.

"But while the bridegroom was delayed, they all slumbered and slept. And at midnight a cry was heard: 'Behold, the bridegroom is coming; go out to meet him!' Then all those virgins arose and trimmed their lamps. And the foolish said to the wise, 'Give us some of your oil, for our lamps are going out.' But the wise answered, saying, 'No, lest there should not be enough for us and you; but go rather to those who sell, and buy for yourselves.'" Matthew 25:5–9

1. How many of the bridesmaids nodded off to sleep while waiting for the bridegroom?

2. When and how were the bridesmaids awakened?

3. Explain the instructions they received.

LEARN ABOUT ...

4 Proper Order

To trim literally means to arrange or adorn; to put in proper order. Upon awakening, the bridesmaids put themselves and their lamps in order. But the foolish had nothing to put in order; their lamps were in disarray. Christ tells us, "Be dressed in readiness, and keep your lamps lit" (Luke 12:35 NASB).

6 Purchase Oil

If the wise bridesmaids had agreed to share their oil, none of the lamps would have lasted throughout the procession. Instead, they suggested what the foolish bridesmaids should have done in the first place— purchase extra oil.

7 Postponed

Jesus, our Bridegroom, has delayed His coming for now. One day, He will return in the clouds for His bride: all who have believed in Him. This event, known as the rapture and described in I Thessalonians 4:15–17, will usher in the tribulation. Seven years later, Jesus will return with His bride to establish an earthly kingdom (Rev. 19:14).[7]

4. Describe how the bridesmaids prepared for the bridegroom's arrival.

5. What did the foolish bridesmaids realize, and how did they seek to remedy the situation?

6. Recount how the wise bridesmaids responded.

LIVE OUT ...

7. Read John 3:28–29. How do these verses confirm who the bridegroom in this parable represents?

8. The bridesmaids in this parable seemed alike outwardly. But when the time came to meet the bridegroom, their differences became obvious—their supply or lack of oil. Oil often represents the Holy Spirit in Scripture.

   a. What does Romans 8:9 say about those who do not have the Spirit of Christ?

   b. Are you prepared to meet the Bridegroom based on this Scripture?

   c. Journal a prayer to God revealing your anticipation or anxiety—whichever applies—about Christ's return. Ask Him to show you how to be ready for His return.

9. The wise bridesmaids were prepared when the bridegroom arrived because they packed extra oil. What items are packed in every believer's suitcase in preparation for eternity?

SCRIPTURE

Isaiah 61:10

Ephesians 6:14–17

1 Peter 5:5

PACKING LIST

Our absent Lord has given special commendation to those who not only *wait* for His return, but also earnestly *watch* for Him. The distinction between these terms can be better understood through the story of a fishing vessel returning home after many days at sea. As the boat neared the shore, the sailors gazed eagerly toward the dock where a group of their loved ones had gathered. The skipper looked through his binoculars and identified some of them: "I see Bill's Mary, and there is Tom's Margaret and David's Anne." One man became concerned because his wife was not there. Later, he left the boat with a heavy heart and hurried up the hill to his cottage. As he opened the door, she ran to meet him, saying, "I have been waiting for you!" He replied with a gentle rebuke: "Yes, but the other men's wives were watching for them!"[8]

Planning for our heavenly Bridegroom's arrival is infinitely more important than any journey. Jesus said, "I am going ... to prepare a place for you.... I will come back and take you to be with me" (John 14:2–3 NIV). Jesus *is* coming to take us home. We, His bride, should be waiting and watching for His return. Don't just wait for Him—*watch* for His arrival. Be sure you are filled with faith in Christ and the Holy Spirit in your heart so you'll be ready for His coming.

LISTEN TO ...

They who work hardest watch best for the Lord's return.

—Unknown

DAY 5

Arriving Tardily

There is an awe-inspiring inscription in the dome of the Capitol in Washington that few people know about. It reads: "One far-off divine event toward which the whole creation moves." A visitor saw this inscription and asked the guide what it meant. He said: "I think it refers to the second coming of Christ." Amazingly, when the dome of our Capitol was erected, some God-fearing official ordered that inscription to be etched in the dome of the seat of government of the United States of America, believing that its truth was vital to the nation.[9]

It's been well said that history is *His* story. And one day soon, that story will culminate in Christ first coming for His church and later coming in power to conquer His enemies. When Christ comes, He will take us to an amazing feast called the marriage supper of the Lamb. On the island of Patmos, the apostle John was given a vision of this marvelous event. The angel who revealed it to him told him to "write: 'Blessed are those who are called to the marriage supper of the Lamb!'" (Rev. 19:9).

Our parable serves as a grave warning that only those who are prepared will go with the Bridegroom to this supper. But those who arrive tardily will be left out of the festivities. Make sure *you* are ready for the "one far-off divine event toward which the whole creation moves." You don't want the Bridegroom to close the door and leave you out.

LIFT UP ...

Heavenly Father, thank You for loving me enough to send Jesus to die for and rejoice over me. I look forward to Your return. Amen.

LOOK AT ...

As we complete this week's study, we find that this wedding celebration doesn't end well for everyone. The five foolish virgins missed the one vital element required to claim their seat at the marriage supper—the undeserved grace or oil of salvation through the presence of the indwelling Holy Spirit in their hearts.

The ten bridesmaids (virgins) outwardly appeared to be similar to each other. They all had their lamps; they all had their wedding clothes—in other words, they were all outwardly religious. But only five recognized their need for salvation and the gift of the Holy Spirit.

Please don't be like the foolish virgins. Don't wait until it is too late. Make sure that you are thoroughly prepared for our heavenly Bridegroom's coming. Make sure that you have confessed your need for a Savior and that your heart is filled with the Holy Spirit. Make no mistake—He *is* coming again. Don't you want to be wise and waiting?

READ MATTHEW 25:10–13.

"And while they went to buy, the bridegroom came, and those who were ready went in with him to the wedding; and the door was shut. Afterward the other virgins came also, saying, 'Lord, Lord, open to us!' But he answered and said, 'Assuredly, I say to you, I do not know you.' Watch therefore, for you know neither the day nor the hour in which the Son of Man is coming." Matthew 25:10–13

1. What three things happened while the foolish bridesmaids went to purchase oil?

2. What did the foolish bridesmaids say when they returned to find the door shut?

3. How did the bridegroom respond?

4. Explain how Jesus' words in Matthew 7:21–23 mirror this parable.

5. What did Jesus say to do in light of the parable of the Ten Virgins?

LEARN ABOUT …

1 Recognition

A wedding banquet at the bridegroom's home traditionally followed the procession through the village. When Jesus returns from heaven with His bride, many Jews will recognize Him as Messiah and be invited to the wedding celebration: "'Blessed are those who are called to the marriage supper of the Lamb!'" (Rev. 19:9).[10]

---

2 Separation

The shut door symbolizes the separation destined to take place at the end of the age, a truth Jesus taught in many of the parables: "He is coming to judge the earth. He shall judge the world with righteousness, and the peoples with His truth" (Ps. 96:13).

---

3 Relation

The word *know* implies a relationship. The bridegroom assured the bridesmaids that they weren't related to him and therefore did not belong at the wedding banquet.[11] "If anyone loves God, this one is known by Him" (1 Cor. 8:3).

---

5 Consideration

Watch means to be spiritually alert. It involves being vigilant and considerate in prayer regarding the day of His return: "Therefore, beloved, looking forward to these things, be diligent to be found by Him in peace, without spot and blameless" (2 Peter 3:14).

LEARN ABOUT ...

6 Preparation

Watchfulness and preparedness go hand in hand. If we believe His Word and we're longing for His return, we cannot help but live as if our "our citizenship is in heaven ... and we eagerly await a Savior from there, the Lord Jesus Christ" (Phil. 3:20 NIV).

---

7 Recognition

Although the foolish bridesmaids appeared to belong at the wedding, the bridegroom recognized them as imposters: "God's truth stands firm ... with this inscription: 'The LORD knows those who are his,' and 'All who belong to the LORD must turn away from evil'" (2 Tim. 2:19 NLT).

6. Why did Jesus stress the importance of watchfulness?

LIVE OUT ...

7. The bridegroom refused to let the foolish bridesmaids in because they weren't related to him. Read John 10:27–28.

   a. How does Jesus know who belongs to Him?

   b. What assurance do we have if we are truly His sheep?

8. While the foolish bridesmaids searched for merchants to sell them oil, they missed the wedding feast. Some commentators believe the oil could also symbolize God's Word. Many today refuse to carry the truth of Scripture with them, seeking answers elsewhere instead.

   a. Identify the places—other than God's Word—where you sometimes seek comfort, truth, peace, and strength.

   b. Journal a prayer asking God's forgiveness for trusting in these things instead of Him.

○ ○ ● ○ ○

Believers can view Christ's return in at least two ways. A. B. Simpson says,

> There is a looking FOR it and a looking AT it. We
> may regard it with a keen intellectual interest and yet
> have it mean nothing to us personally. On the other

hand, we may know little about the theology involved in the subject and still enjoy a deep longing for the Lord's appearing. Let me illustrate. When a wedding occurs, the public looks AT it, but the bride has been looking FOR it.

May the theme of the return of Christ not only be our study but also our personal hope, for "unto them that look for Him shall He appear the second time without sin unto salvation." An unknown poet has written:

> What would He find, should He come just now:
> A faded leaf, or a fruitless bough;
> A servant sleeping, an idle plow?
> What would He find, should He come just now?
> What would He find should He come tonight?
> Your garment soiled, or a spotless white;
> Your lamps all burning, or with no light?
> What would He find, should He come tonight?[12]

When the door is shut on this age, it will be too late to respond to the Bridegroom's invitation. The table will be set. Engraved place cards will mark each seat. Only those belonging to God's family will be allowed. Until the end comes, He's ready and waiting to adopt all who want to be part of the celebration. Won't you come in and let the Bridegroom rejoice over you?

LISTEN TO ...

The Bible opens and closes with a wedding.

—Selwyn Hughes

Use It or Lose It
Matthew 25:14–30

Aesop told the fable of the Miser who sold all that he had to buy a lump of gold. He buried the gold in a hole in the ground beside an old wall. Every day he went to look at his treasure. One of his workmen observed his frequent visits to the spot and decided to watch where his employer went. He soon discovered the secret of the hidden treasure. Digging down, he came to the lump of gold and stole it. On his next visit, the Miser found the hole empty and began to tear his hair and to cry loud lamentations. A neighbor, seeing him overcome with grief and learning the cause, said, "Pray do not grieve so; but go and take a stone, and place it in the hole, and fancy that the gold is still lying there. It will do you quite the same service; for when the gold was there, you had it not, as you did not make the slightest use of it." As in all of Aesop's fables, there is a moral to be learned. The moral of the Miser is simple: The true value of money is not in its possession but in its use.[1]

Jesus told the parable of the Talents to make a similar point. God has given His people talents that are more precious than gold. But Christ strongly makes the point that we must not hoard them like the Miser, or they are worth no more than a chunk of stone. Instead, we must use our talents for other people's good and for God's glory. The moral to the parable of the Talents is short and sweet: Use it or lose it.

Day 1: Matthew 25:14–15	SERVANTS ENTRUSTED
Day 2: Matthew 25:16–18	PROFITS GAINED
Day 3: Matthew 25:19–23	FAITHFULNESS REWARDED
Day 4: Matthew 25:24–27	TRUTH DISTORTED
Day 5: Matthew 25:28–30	JUSTICE DISTRIBUTED

DAY 1

Servants Entrusted

LIFT UP ...

Lord, I cannot begin to thank You for the wonderful gifts You have given us. Teach me to be good steward of all that You have bestowed upon me. Amen.

LOOK AT ...

Last week in the parable of the Ten Virgins we learned to *watch* for our Bridegroom's return. As Jesus continues the parables in the Olivet Discourse, we learn in the parable of the Talents to *work* diligently for the kingdom of heaven until He comes again.

This parable is one of the longest spoken by Jesus in the gospel of Matthew. Clearly, Jesus was preparing His disciples for His death and the period of time after His death. He wanted to make sure that all believers would be busy about kingdom business as they waited for Christ's return. When Jesus spoke of talents in this parable, He was referring not to a person's natural abilities or gifts, like an artistic talent or the gift of song. He was referring to a unit of currency common during the Roman occupation. However, Jesus expects us to be good stewards of both our natural talents and our financial resources until He comes again.

READ MATTHEW 25:14–30;
THEN FOCUS ON VERSES 14–15.

"For the kingdom of heaven is like a man traveling to a far country, who called his own servants and delivered his goods to them. And to one he gave five talents, to another two, and to another one, to each according to his own ability; and immediately he went on a journey." Matthew 25:14–15

1. Read Matthew 24:3 to gain context for the parable of the Talents.

a. To whom was Jesus speaking?

b. Where were they?

c. What questions did they have for Jesus?

2. To whom did Jesus compare the kingdom of heaven in this parable?

3. Describe what this man did.

4. a. Who do you think this man and his servants represent?

   b. What time period in history do you think this parable is talking about?

5. Recount what each servant received and how the man determined what to give.

6. Explain where the man went and when.

LIVE OUT ...

7. The servants were amply supplied so they could have "purchasing power" to wisely invest their master's money. With this in mind, complete the following exercise.

   a. Multiply $40,000 times 20 to get an idea of what one talent would be worth today. This is what the third servant received: $40,000 x 20 =_____

   b. Multiply the answer in letter "a" by 2 to get the equivalent of the two talents that the second servant received.

LEARN ABOUT ...

3 Delivered

In this context, *to deliver* means to surrender or entrust. In Jesus' day, when a wealthy man left home for a period of time, he would often enter into an agreement with his servants to manage his affairs.[2] "Let a man so consider us, as servants of Christ and stewards of the mysteries of God" (I Cor. 4:I).

5 Dynamite

Ability comes from *dunamis*, where we get the word *dynamite*. It speaks of miraculous power or strength. God supernaturally bestows different gifts and abilities on His servants through the power of the Holy Spirit: "The same Spirit works all these things, distributing to each one individually as He wills" (I Cor. 12:II).

4 Delayed

The time between Christ's first coming and second coming is known as the church age or the age of grace. Before He traveled to heaven, Christ instructed His followers to fulfill the Great Commission: "Go therefore and make disciples of all the nations ... teaching them to observe all things that I have commanded" (Matt. 28:19–20).

LEARN ABOUT ...

7 Dollar Amount

A talent was an amount of silver—about seventy-five pounds, worth about twenty years' wages. It was a heavy weight to carry—think of trying to haul around a purse that size! According to the US Census Bureau, 2000 Census, the median income of a full-time, year-round male worker was almost $40,000.[3] The master in this parable entrusted his servants with a fortune to administrate.

---

8 Director

Steward originally referred to the director or manager of a household or estate. Metaphorically, it came to indicate those who preach the gospel or teach God's Word. Steward also signifies anyone who serves Christ. Peter tells us, "As each one has received a gift, minister it to one another, as good stewards of the manifold grace of God (1 Peter 4:10).

c. Again multiply the answer in letter "a" by 5 to get the equivalent of the five talents the first servant received.

d. What does this reveal about the master's character?

8. a. What has God generously entrusted you with?

❏ Financial Resources   ❏ Spiritual Gifts   ❏ Mental Abilities
❏ Physical Abilities   ❏ Special Talents   ❏ Other (name it)

b. Journal a prayer asking God to make you a good steward of that which He has entrusted to you.

9. a. We have all been entrusted with various gifts, talents, and resources. What spiritual principle for these resources does Jesus give in Luke 12:48?

b. How have you have seen this spiritual principle at work?

∘ ∘ ● ∘ ∘

Most of us think of Florence Nightingale as a compassionate nurse—and she was. But in addition to being a nurse, she was a statistician. Florence had a flair for collecting, arranging, and presenting facts and figures. This was the secret ability that made her a legend in the field of nursing. She used the data she collected to improve the sanitary conditions in hospitals worldwide. In 1837, she said that God told her she had a mission. Though she didn't realize it at the time, Florence Nightingale used her God-given abilities to reform her chosen profession and, more importantly, to lower mortality rates in hospitals.[4]

In her book *My Heart Sings* Florence wrote, "If I could give you information of my life it would be to show how a woman of very ordinary ability has been led by God in strange and unaccustomed paths to do in His service what He has done in her. And if I could tell you all, you would see how God has done all, and I nothing. I have worked hard, very hard, that is all; and I have never refused God anything."[5]

You may have abilities that don't *seem* spiritual. You may be good at math, mending, or memorization. But every skill and spiritual gift you have can be used to minister to others and spread the good news of the gospel. If you surrender your will to God and work with all your might, God will use your talents for His kingdom.

LISTEN TO ...

There is something that is much more scarce, something rarer than ability. It is the ability to recognize ability.

—Robert Half

DAY 2

Profits Gained

The *Christian Science Monitor* carried this headline praising workers in the airline industry: "American uses workers' expertise." The story told how one company used its employees' knowledge to ensure it gained a profit:

> Two American Airlines mechanics didn't like having to toss out $200 drill bits once they got dull. So they rigged up some old machine parts—a vacuum-cleaner belt and a motor from a science project—and built "Thumping Ralph." It's essentially a drill-bit sharpener that allows them to get more use out of each bit. The savings, according to the company: as much as $300,000 a year.
>
> And it was a group of pilots who realized that they could taxi just as safely with one engine as with two. That was instituted as policy and has helped cut American's fuel consumption even as prices have continued to rise to record levels. From the maintenance floor to the cockpit, American Airlines is daily scouring operations to increase efficiency and find even the smallest cost savings. It's paid off: Last week, the company announced its first profit in almost five years."[6]

As we continue studying the parable of the Talents, we discover that Jesus clearly understood what corporate America is now finally learning: Entrusting one's servants with resources can be very profitable for the wise employer. However, we will also discover that some employees are not very wise in the way they utilize their master's resources.

LIFT UP ...

Lord, sometimes serving You means engaging in hard work. Thank You for the promise that we will reap a harvest if we don't lose heart. Amen.

LOOK AT ...

Yesterday we learned that God has entrusted us with a wealth of gifts. Through His divine will He has distributed gifts according to our ability. Today we discover what profits are gained when we put our gifts to work.

In Jesus' day, slaves or workers were often allowed to enter into business with their masters and make a profit. They would be entrusted with a sum of money and allowed to engage in free enterprise in the hopes of making a high earning. In this case, the master trusted the servants so much that he went to a "far country." We know that the "far country" where Jesus went was heaven. The "talents" He bestowed upon His servants were spiritual and natural gifts meant to advance the kingdom. He continues to entrust each generation with these gifts to spread the gospel message. As you continue to study this parable, ask yourself how many talents you have received and how much return you are making for your Master. One day He will require an accounting.

LEARN ABOUT ...

I Trading

Trade literally means to toil or labor continuously and untiringly. Paul used the same root word when he urged believers to "increase more and more; that you also aspire to lead a quiet life, to mind your own business, and to work with your own hands, as we commanded you" (I Thess. 4:10–11).

READ MATTHEW 25:16–18.

"Then he who had received the five talents went and traded with them, and made another five talents. And likewise he who had received two gained two more also. But he who had received one went and dug in the ground, and hid his lord's money." Matthew 25:16–18

1. Describe what business the first servant entered into.

2. What kind of profit did he receive for his work? Do you think this would be pleasing to the master?

   ❏ 10%   ❏ 50%

   ❏ 25%   ❏ 100%   ❏ No Profit

LEARN ABOUT ...

3 Gaining

To gain means to win or get through diligence or work. Unlike investing in the stock market, when we invest in the Lord's kingdom, a profit is guaranteed: "Therefore, my beloved brethren, be steadfast, immovable, always abounding in the work of the Lord, knowing that your labor is not in vain in the Lord" (I Cor. 15:58).

5 Hiding

To hide means to conceal or keep secret. Like the master in the parable, Christ gives gifts to benefit His kingdom. Hiding our gifts accomplishes nothing. "No one, when he has lit a lamp, puts it in a secret place or under a basket, but on a lampstand, that those who come in may see the light" (Luke 11:33).

7 Loving

We can use our five fingers, toes, and senses as talents from God. But there's another five you may not have thought about. In *The Five Love Languages*, Dr. Gary Chapman identifies five ways people express and receive love: (1) Quality Time; (2) Words of Affirmation; (3) Gifts; (4) Acts of Service; (5) Physical Touch. Ask God to help you use these five special gifts to speak and understand the love languages of those around you.

3. Describe what the man who received two talents did.

4. What kind of profit did this man receive for his work? How do you think the master felt about this?

☐ 10%   ☐ 50%
☐ 25%   ☐ 100%   ☐ No Profit

5. Describe what the man who received one talent did.

6. What kind of profit did this man receive from hiding the talent?

☐ 10%   ☐ 50%
☐ 25%   ☐ 100%   ☐ No Profit

LIVE OUT ...

7. The master gave one servant five talents and he gained five more. List some ways to use the human "fives" to profit God's kingdom.
   Five fingers:
   Five toes:
   Five senses:

8. One servant was given two talents and gained two more. List some ways to use the human "twos" to profit God's kingdom.
   Two eyes:
   Two ears:
   Two hands:
   Two feet:

9. One servant was given one talent and hid it in the ground. Journal about how we, as believers, can hide our "ones" (one heart, one voice, one body, one gospel, etc.) so that no one profits spiritually. Be creative.

As a lad, James M. Gray had a friend whose father was very wealthy. Having already made a fortune, the man sought to add to it by purchasing a large tract of real estate in upper Manhattan Island. At that time, it was known as Harlem Flats. One day Gray's young companion said, "Let's go up and see the land Dad bought." Recounting the incident years later, Dr. Gray said, "I remember how I laughed when we got there. He couldn't show me a single spot of dry ground. The property was completely covered over with tidewater. I didn't see much of an investment in that for anybody. But, of course, his father did not acquire it for what it was worth then, but for its value in decades to come." Today that land has all been filled in and is heavily populated. It represents millions and millions of dollars to its present owners.[7]

It's hard to imagine that when Christ looks at our lives—the fives, twos, and ones that He has bestowed upon each of us—He sees something amazing. After all, we're sinful human beings. But God looks beyond our present state to what we can become through His powerful presence dwelling within us. With the Holy Spirit's help, Jesus invests in us to turn the swampland of a sinful life into a valuable asset for the kingdom of heaven.

LISTEN TO ...

Those who give much without sacrifice are reckoned as having given little.

—Erwin Lutzer

LEARN ABOUT ...

8 Multiplying

Jesus can multiply our "fives" and "twos." When the multitudes followed Jesus to a deserted place, a boy brought five loaves and two fish to Christ: "He took the five loaves and the two fish, and looking up to heaven, He blessed and broke and gave the loaves to the disciples.... They all ate and were filled" (Matt. 14:19–20).

DAY 3
Faithfulness Rewarded

A newspaper article described the kind of "delayed rewards" we should be living for. The story told of a car dealer who went out of his way to give a foreign student an honest deal on a new automobile. Fifteen years later, the young man had become the sole purchasing agent for the contractors' association in his country. He showed his gratitude for the kindness he had received by placing a multimillion-dollar order with the honest dealer for 750 heavy dump trucks and 350 pickups. "It's unbelievable!" exclaimed the businessman. The good he had done was rewarded years later beyond his wildest imagination.[8]

The time span between verses 15 and 19 represents the period between Jesus' first and second comings. At His first coming, Jesus shared this parable with the disciples—His innermost circle of trusted friends. Just three short days after speaking these words, He entered Jerusalem for His final days on earth. He knew He would make a far journey after His death. Before departing, He imparted spiritual wealth to His disciples, instructing them to make the most of it before His return. At the Lord's second coming, He will establish the new city of Jerusalem. At that time, the apostles' faithfulness will be rewarded: "Now the wall of the city had twelve foundations, and on them were the names of the twelve apostles of the Lamb" (Rev. 21:14). They will enter into the joyous celebration of their Master and Lord—and all who believe will be there to celebrate with them.

LIFT UP ...

Lord, thank You for the privilege of being called Your servant! I sing for joy! Amen.

LOOK AT ...

Yesterday we learned that Jesus enters into a partnership with His followers and works with them to further His kingdom until He returns. We've seen that the servants were given talents in different proportions. The servant given five talents gained five more. The servant who received two talents earned two more. Sadly, the servant with only one talent hoarded his. Now we see that the lord of the servants returned to settle accounts and rewarded his servants for their work.

We might wonder how the master decided what amount to give each servant. But it is not ours to wonder how much each received. The master knew his servants, and two of the three doubled his investment. In the same way, only God determines which gifts and abilities we receive. Paul wrote, "There are diversities of gifts, but the same Spirit. There are differences of ministries, but the same Lord" (1 Cor. 12:4–5). The question is what are you doing with the gifts and abilities God has given to you? When He returns, will He sing your praises?

LEARN ABOUT ...

2 Settle

Settling accounts refers to the judgment seat of Christ. There, many will be commended, but others will be condemned: "For we must all appear before the judgment seat of Christ, that each one may receive the things done in the body, according to what he has done, whether good or bad" (2 Cor. 5:10).

READ MATTHEW 25:14–30;

THEN FOCUS ON VERSES 19–23.

"After a long time the lord of those servants came and settled accounts with them. So he who had received five talents came and brought five other talents, saying, 'Lord, you delivered to me five talents; look, I have gained five more talents besides them.' His lord said to him, 'Well done, good and faithful servant; you were faithful over a few things, I will make you ruler over many things. Enter into the joy of your lord.' He also who had received two talents came and said, 'Lord, you delivered to me two talents; look, I have gained two more talents besides them.' His lord said to him, 'Well done, good and faithful servant; you have been faithful over a few things, I will make you ruler over many things. Enter into the joy of your lord.'" Matthew 25:19–23

1. What period of time had passed between verses 18 and 19?

2. Explain what the lord came to do.

3. First we see the lord's reckoning with the one who received five talents. Describe what he reported.

4. What two words of praise did the lord give, and what two words did he use to describe his servant?

    Words of praise:

    Descriptive words:

5. What was the servant promised because of his faithfulness?

6. Summarize the results of the conversation between the lord and the second servant.

    Servant's report:

    Words of praise:

    Descriptive words:

    What was promised:

LIVE OUT ...

7. If today were the day that you were to settle accounts with your Master, what would you have to show? Fill in the following chart to discover some things you give an account for.

SCRIPTURE	TO YOUR ACCOUNT
Matthew 12:36–37	
Romans 4:20–22	
Romans 14:11–13	
Philippians 4:15–18	

8. We learned that *faithful* means one who is dependable or loyal. It can also mean full of faith. With what do you fill your life? List the things you will remove or add to your life so that you can be full of faith.

    EMPTY OUT   FAITHFUL   **FILL UP**

9. a. The faithful servants who multiplied the Lord's investment were invited to enter into the joy of the Lord. Check the box that best describes the way you have entered the Lord's presence today.

☐ "Enter into His gates with thanksgiving" (Ps. 100:4).

☐ "Enter … into His courts with praise" (Ps. 100:4).

☐ "Enter in at these gates to worship the Lord!" (Jer. 7:2).

☐ "Enter into His glory" (Luke 24:26).

☐ "Through many tribulations enter the kingdom of God" (Acts 14:22).

☐ "Let us therefore be diligent to enter that rest" (Heb. 4:11).

☐ "Enter the Holiest by the blood of Jesus" (Heb. 10:19).

b. Journal a prayer to God, using a Scripture from above, to express your entrance into His presence. Ask Him to take account of your life.

○ ○ ● ○ ○

LEARN ABOUT …

8 Unequal

One servant received five talents and the other only two. Although the two servants began with unequal sums, they multiplied and overflowed to the same proportion—double the amount they received originally. The psalmist said that God provided him with an overflowing life: "My cup overflows" (Ps. 23:5 NIV).

9 Boldness

The way the servants joyfully came forward foreshadows believers' boldness on the day of judgment. Because they had something to show for their labor, their master made them rulers over more. If we are good stewards of God's gifts, He will make "us kings and priests to our God; and we shall reign on the earth" (Rev. 5:10).

The truth of the parable is that each servant did not receive an equal amount of talents. The same is true today. We have each been given different gifts, abilities, assets, and opportunities. Perhaps, like Susannah Wesley, your greatest asset is the child God has entrusted to you.

Susannah Wesley spent the time she was given praying one hour daily for her seventeen children. In addition, she took each child aside for a full hour every week to discuss spiritual matters. No wonder two of her sons, Charles and John, were used of God to bring blessing to all of England and much of America. Here are a few rules she followed in training her children: "(1) Subdue self-will in a child and thus work together with God to save his soul. (2) Teach him to pray as soon as he can speak. (3) Give him nothing he cries for and only what is good for him if he asks for it politely. (4) To prevent lying, punish no fault that is freely confessed, but never allow a rebellious, sinful act to go unnoticed. (5) Commend and reward good behavior. (6) Strictly observe all promises you have made to your child."[9]

When Susannah gives an account for her stewardship as a mother, she will certainly hear, "Well done." What about you? Are you wisely investing into the lives God has entrusted to you?

LISTEN TO ...

He that does good for God's sake seeks neither praise nor reward; he is sure of both in the end.

—*William Penn*

DAY 4
Truth Distorted

The folly of human nature is summed up by the case of the middle-aged schoolteacher who invested her life savings in a business enterprise that had been invitingly explained to her by a swindler.

When her investment disappeared and the wonderful dream was shattered, she went to the office of the Better Business Bureau. "Why on earth," they asked, "didn't you come to us first? Didn't you know about the Better Business Bureau?"

"Oh yes," said the woman sadly, "I've always known about you. But I didn't come because I was afraid you'd tell me not to do it."[10]

The third servant in our parable was also foolish with his failed investment and made excuses for his folly. Like in the schoolteacher's case, fear motivated the poor choice he made. Cowardice caused them to hide the truth and the talent. Fear blinds us from trusting others. Fear is the opposite of faith.

There's another obvious trait displayed in these failed investments: Both made excuses for their blunders. The servant's reason for squandering his talent was to blame the master for possessing a flawed and ferocious reputation. There is a correlation between what we believe and how we behave. Many today distort the truth of God's character. Some use predestination as an excuse not to evangelize, failing to keep the Great Commission. Some focus on God's judgment and wrath over His love and mercy, accusing God of inequity. Have you distorted the truth about God? Are you foolishly hiding your talent behind a shoddy excuse?

LIFT UP ...

Lord, please fill me with understanding that I may conduct my works with wisdom. Help me to use the gifts You have given to me for Your glory. Amen.

LOOK AT ...

Yesterday we learned that God's faithful servants will be rewarded and filled with joy. Today we turn our attention to the unfaithful servant, who hid his talent and did not gain any return

LEARN ABOUT ...

3 Accusation

The word *hard* can be translated "harsh." The servant's own accusation convicted him—he knew the lord wanted the best from the servant. He acted like a petulant child blaming others for his misconduct. Good thoughts of our heavenly Master will produce love and a willingness to serve Him. Harsh thoughts of Him produce fearfulness, laziness, and unfaithfulness.

4 Afraid

"Afraid" comes from the Greek word *phobeo*, which gives us our word *phobia*. It means alarmed or exceedingly fearful. *The Message* translates it this way, "I was afraid I might disappoint you" (Matt. 25:24–25).

for his lord. The scene is much different from that of the two faithful servants. There, the scene was filled with joy and praise. In this case, the scene is filled with distortion and discord. The servant immediately began to heap recriminations upon his master, blaming the master for his failure to prosper. We see in this servant a picture of those who have a false view of God. There are many who see God as capricious and harsh, when in fact God is loving and tenderhearted. How tragic that it is possible to have such a distorted vision of God. Remember that "every good gift and every perfect gift is from above, and comes down from the Father of lights, with whom there is no variation or shadow of turning" (James 1:17).

READ MATTHEW 25:24–27.

"Then he who had received the one talent came and said, 'Lord, I knew you to be a hard man, reaping where you have not sown, and gathering where you have not scattered seed. And I was afraid, and went and hid your talent in the ground. Look, there you have what is yours.' But his lord answered and said to him, 'You wicked and lazy servant, you knew that I reap where I have not sown, and gather where I have not scattered seed. So you ought to have deposited my money with the bankers, and at my coming I would have received back my own with interest.'" Matthew 25:24–27

1. How do you think this third servant might have been feeling when he was called to appear before his master?

2. In your own words, describe how he viewed his master.

3. What was the basis for the servant's view of his master?

4. How did the servant's belief affect his behavior?

5. According to the servant, what justified his actions?

6. Restate the lord's description of this third servant.

7. Explain what the servant could have done instead and what the results would have been.

LIVE OUT ...

8. Today we saw how the servant's erroneous thoughts regarding his lord paralyzed his service. Sometimes what we perceive as truth may be distorted.

   a. Have your thoughts about God ever been distorted? Explain your answer.

   b. How do you think we can dispel erroneous thoughts about God?

   c. Fill in the blanks using the Scriptures below to learn the truth about our Lord.

   God is _____. (2 Chron. 30:9)

   God is _____. (Job 9:4)

   God is _____. (Ps. 46:1)

   God is _____. (Ps. 62:7)

   God is _____. (1 John 1:5)

9. a. The servant's thoughts caused him to fear his master. Read 1 John 4:18. What cannot be found in love?

   b. What does perfect love do?

   c. What does fear involve?

d. What does this verse say about those who have fear?

10. The servant didn't truly know his lord, and that ignorance led to fear. Ultimately, the servant was ineffective in his lord's service. His unwillingness to take a risk proved he was unworthy of his lord's trust.

a. How has fear of failure kept you from taking a risk for God?

b. Where is God asking you to take a risk on His behalf?

❏ Sharing the gospel with others   ❏ Tithing
❏ Leading or stepping out in a ministry   ❏ Other (name it)

c. Ask someone in your small group to keep you accountable and pray with you regarding this step of growth.

○ ○ ● ○ ○

If the wealth of spiritual riches is available to all saints, why do so few enjoy them? Spurgeon told this story:

> A young woman from a poor family married a wealthy merchant. After their wedding the timid bride pleaded with her husband for money to buy a modest dress. To her great surprise, he flatly refused!
>
> "But why?" she asked.
>
> "All I have is yours. I won't have my wife begging for rags when she could dress like a countess! The money is in the bank. All you need to do is write the checks!"[12]

The Lord Jesus Christ "has given to us all things that pertain to life and godliness" (2 Peter 1:3). We are "joint heirs" to His wealth. This does not excuse a lazy, inactive Christian lifestyle. Because Jesus placed the endowment for spiritual victory in our spiritual bank account, we have the responsibility (and privilege) to appropriate these resources by cashing in on our inheritance through faith and obedience. If we're so rich in Christ, why do we act as if we were spiritual paupers?[13]

The lazy servant distorted the truth and lost financial profit. He claimed to do nothing because he was afraid. But if that were truly the case, shouldn't he have been all the more diligent to make his work pleasing to the master? Unfortunately, we see this in the body of Christ. We make excuses for our laziness. Rather than doing the least we can, we choose to do nothing at all. The lord described the servant as lazy and wicked—let's not be accused of the same.

LISTEN TO ...

You can best reward a liar by believing nothing of what he says.

—Aristippus

DAY 5

Justice Distributed

Growing up, I (Lenya) admit that my dad spoiled his kids. All four of us were given cars on or before graduation. My brothers, Scott and Michael, each received a Nissan pickup truck. My sister, Suzanne, and I both drove a Chevrolet Monza off the new-car lot.

However, the boys were hard on their cars. Amazingly, Dad graciously provided them with a second automobile, better than the first! Mike rode a BMW and Scott sported a MGB convertible. Sadly, they treated their second autos as poorly as their first. Once, when Scott received a traffic violation, Dad took away his MGB and gave it to me to drive. That incident reminds me of this parable—taking that which one possesses and giving it to the one who already has plenty. It was a lesson neither of us forgot.

This parable teaches us to use it wisely or lose it. The central message is faithfulness. What do you do with what you have? The unprofitable servant was not judged for failing to gain as much as the other two servants. He was judged for failing to use what he had. The gifts and resources given by God that are unexercised or unappreciated will fall away. Also, that very gift that one loses, another will receive. Are you using or losing the precious resources God has provided you?

LIFT UP ...

Thank You, Lord, that You promise to come quickly. Thank You for Your magnificent reward. Make me faithful in the work You have given me. Amen.

LOOK AT ...

The unprofitable servant distorted the truth to hide his laziness and believed it was too difficult to serve his master. Now we see how the master, who is a picture of God, handles both types of servants by distributing rewards and taking away rewards. Throughout Scripture, God is portrayed as both merciful and just. His mercy is the aspect of God's love that causes Him to help the miserable, just as grace is the aspect of His love that moves Him to forgive the guilty. God's justice is seen throughout Scripture. *Nelson's Illustrated Bible Dictionary* says, "As Lord and Judge, God brings justice to nations and sets things right: in behalf of the poor, the oppressed, and the victims of injustice (Ps. 103:6; 146:6–9). For the wicked, the unjust, and the oppressor, God as supreme Judge of the earth is a dreaded force."[14]

As we close this parable, we see that God, the master, blends mercy with justice in His dealings with humanity. Rest assured that you can trust God to be merciful. But if you are not a true follower, one day you will stand in His presence and face His divine judgment. Isn't it time to run to His mercy seat?

READ MATTHEW 25:28–30.

"So take the talent from him, and give it to him who has ten talents. For to everyone who has, more will be given, and he will have abundance; but from him who does not have, even what he has will be taken away. And cast the unprofitable servant into the outer darkness. There will be weeping and gnashing of teeth." Matthew 25:28–30

1. What happened to the unprofitable servant's talent?

2. Do you think this was just? Why or why not?

3. In your own words, explain how to achieve spiritual abundance.

4. In your own words, explain how to become spiritually bankrupt.

5. How does the verse describe the servant?

6. What was his fate?

LEARN ABOUT ...

4 Revoked

Take means to take for oneself or to choose. "A man can receive nothing unless it has been given to him from heaven" (John 3:27); therefore, anything that doesn't profit the kingdom, God reserves the right to take away. As Scripture tells us, "Every branch in Me that does not bear fruit He takes away" (John 15:2).

3 Accomplished

God gives us abundance so that we will use it to accomplish more good works: "And God is able to make all grace abound toward you, that you, always having all sufficiency in all things, may have an abundance for every good work" (2 Cor. 9:8).

5 Trampled

Unprofitable means without usefulness. Many of us keep useless things buried in closets or drawers, but God doesn't: "You are the salt of the earth; but if the salt loses its flavor, how shall it be seasoned? It is then good for nothing but to be thrown out and trampled underfoot by men" (Matt. 5:13).

LEARN ABOUT ...

7 Anointed

Joseph's faithfulness caused him to be "set over all the land of Egypt" (Gen. 41:43). Moses led God's people out of bondage after forty years of small things in the wilderness. King David didn't become king overnight—at least fifteen years passed between his anointing and assuming the throne.

---

8 Enabled

Liberality means bountifulness or generosity. God's generosity enables us to be generous toward others. When we give in liberality, God gets the glory: "For the administration of this service not only supplies the needs of the saints, but also is abounding through many thanksgivings to God" (2 Cor. 9:12).

LIVE OUT ...

7. The servant lost his opportunity to serve God because he wasn't faithful in the small things. We must prove ourselves in the small things before God can entrust us with more. Let's explore some godly men who were faithful in the small things.

    a. Joseph is an example of a person who was faithful in the little things. How was he brought to Egypt, according to Genesis 37:27–28 and Genesis 39:1–3?

    b. What does Exodus 3:1 tell you Moses was doing when the Lord revealed to him His calling for his life?

    c. In what occupation was David first found faithful according to 1 Samuel 16:11?

8. We have learned that God abundantly blesses those who prove themselves faithful in the small things. Read 2 Corinthians 9:10–11, and explain why we are given abundance or "enriched in everything" (v. 11).

9. If we prove ourselves unfaithful in few things, even what we have will be taken away. Based on your stewardship, evaluate whether you use or will lose the items in the following list. Place them in the appropriate column: time, money, resources, talents, home, automobile, education, opportunity, relationships, citizenship, and church.

USE IT	LOSE IT

10. Look back at what you've learned from the parable of the Talents. What is one thing you've been given that you believe God wants you to use better than you are using it now? How can you do that?

○ ○ ● ○ ○

Faithfulness isn't momentary; it should last a lifetime. The master in this parable traveled far away and was gone a long time. The five- and two-talent servants remained faithful during his extended absence. The one-talent servant was shortsighted and stingy. Although delayed, the day of reckoning was coming. Likewise, the reward for our faithfulness may not come today, tomorrow, or next week. But when our Lord returns, He'll richly compensate us for our faithfulness if we don't give up.

The admonition to be faithful in the long haul in this parable is similar to the story of a chaplain who ministered to a seriously wounded soldier. The dying man requested him to write a letter to his former Sunday school teacher. "Tell her I died a Christian because of what she taught me in class," he said. "Her earnest pleas and love caused me to accept Jesus as my Lord. Tell her I'll meet her in heaven." The message was sent, and some time later the chaplain received this reply: "May God forgive me. Just last month I resigned my position and abandoned my Sunday school class because I felt my work had been fruitless. Now I regret my lack of faith! I shall ask my pastor to let me go back to teaching. I have learned that when one sows for God, the reaping is both sure and blessed!"[15]

Paul encouraged long-term faithfulness to the worn-out Galatians: "Let us not grow weary while doing good, for in due season we shall reap if we do not lose heart. Therefore, as we have opportunity, let us do good to all" (Gal. 6:9–10). Don't lose heart. Someday soon your Master will proclaim, "Well done, good and faithful servant."

Listen to ...

Well done is better than well said.

—Benjamin Franklin

LESSON EIGHT

The Best Things in Life Aren't Things

Luke 12:13–34

A tightfisted old man sat in the front pew of the church every time he went to church. Because he was nearly deaf, he'd cup his hand around his ear so he could catch the preacher's sermon. One morning the pastor chose the topic of "Cheerful Giving." The old man muttered to himself, "I'll give $10." But as the sermon continued, he became more deeply convicted and mumbled, "No, I'd better make it $50!" When the ushers started passing the collection plates, his conscience began to rage. He began an inner dialogue as the congregation watched. He had no idea his whispers were loud enough for people to hear him.

When the collection plate finally reached the miserly man, those sitting nearby could see the agony of his struggle with the green monster. Suddenly, he gained the victory. Putting his well-filled billfold into the offering plate, he muttered, "Now squirm, old nature!" Joy immediately flooded his soul. He had given 'til it felt good. That experience became a turning point in his Christian life. The once stingy saint had finally conquered covetousness.[1]

While money is important in our lives, as believers we must continually evaluate our attitude toward it. Our affluent and materialistic age tempts us to trust in earthly riches. Instead, as we learn in the parable of the Rich Fool, we must learn to trust in our heavenly Father's perfect provision. Like the miserly man in the story, won't you pray to gain victory over your old nature and experience the joy of conquering covetousness?

Day 1: Luke 12:13–15   **GREEDY GRUMBLER**
Day 2: Luke 12:16–21   **SELFISH STOCKPILES**
Day 3: Luke 12:22–26   **WORTHLESS WORRIES**
Day 4: Luke 12:27–31   **FATHER'S FORTUNE**
Day 5: Luke 12:32–34   **GODLY GUARANTEES**

DAY 1

Greedy Grumbler

LIFT UP ...

Lord, I want to be free from the love of money and the craving for earthly possessions. Help me to be content with what You have provided and to trust in Your unfailing ways. Amen.

LOOK AT ...

On His journey to Jerusalem and the cross, Jesus traversed Israel's countryside, ministering to His followers and the townspeople along the way. One day a massive crowd gathered, the sheer number paralleling those at modern rock concerts. People pushed and shoved their way to the front while others were trampled underfoot. Out of the multitude, someone with an inappropriate demand rudely interrupted Jesus. "Make my brother divide my deceased father's inheritance evenly," he said. The crowd—previously mesmerized by a discussion about hypocritical religious people versus sincere seekers—must have been annoyed.

Crowds are made up of members with mixed motives. Some who followed Jesus were sincerely seeking truth, some selfishly elbowed their way into the in-crowd, and others held not-so-hidden agendas. The next time you're at church, take a look around and ask yourself, *Why are these people here and what are their motives?* But more importantly, search your heart. Why do you attend church? To be a social conservative? To receive a tax deduction? To network so that you increase your net worth? Or are you there to worship the Lord?

READ LUKE 12:13–34;

THEN FOCUS ON VERSES 13–15.

Then one from the crowd said to Him, "Teacher, tell my brother to divide the inheritance with me." But He said to him, "Man, who made Me a judge or an arbitrator over you?" And He said to them, "Take heed and beware of covetousness, for one's life does not consist in the abundance of the things he possesses." Luke 12:13–15

LEARN ABOUT ...

2 Divide

A double portion of a deceased father's inheritance went to the eldest son, who was responsible for maintaining the family's property. Apparently, the man calling out to Jesus was the younger son asking for his portion of the inheritance. "Every tribe of the children of Israel shall keep its own inheritance" (Num. 36:9).

---

4 Dispute

Jesus came to earth the first time to save mankind from sin and death, not to judge petty disputes. That was a job for civil authorities. However, at His second coming, He will come as judge of all the earth, as John tells us: "And the Father leaves all judgment of sin to his Son" (John 5:22 TLB).

---

6 Danger

Jesus warned against the dangers of covetousness: (1) Take heed—discern clearly or recognize it—and (2) beware—guard against or avoid it. Jesus admonished the disciples and others (including us!) to clearly recognize and guard against greed's temptation—to avoid it completely. Scripture tells us, "If riches increase, do not set your heart on them" (Ps. 62:10).

1. How did the man from the crowd address Jesus?

2. Explain what he wanted Jesus to do.

3. Prior to the man's outburst, Jesus was teaching the people about confessing or denying the Savior before others. What do you think the man's abrupt change of topic revealed about him?

4. In your own words, recount Jesus' response.

5. Review Luke 12:1, and describe to whom Jesus redirected His attention here.

6. What warning did Jesus give, and what was His reasoning?

LIVE OUT ...

7. God included covetousness in His Top Ten list of things He hates, right beside murder and adultery. What additional information does Ephesians 5:3–7 give you about covetousness and those who practice it?

8. Read 1 Timothy 6:6–10, and answer the following questions to discover the difference between greed and contentment.

   a. What is the greatest form of wealth or gain and why (vv. 6–8)?

   b. What do you learn about those who desire abundant earthly riches (v. 9)?

   c. Is money in itself evil? Explain why or why not (v. 10).

d. Describe the two things that can happen when greed takes root (v. 10).

9. Though Job was a very wealthy man, God allowed Satan to strip him of everything—people and possessions alike—to prove Job's devotion to God. Despite utter devastation, Job remained faithful and was fully restored.

    a. List the people and earthly possessions you most treasure.

    b. Put yourself in Job's shoes. If you were stripped of all these people and possessions, could you, would you still praise God? Explain your answer.

    c. Journal a prayer based on Philippians 4:11–13, thanking God for your spiritual and material blessings. Ask Him to help you learn to be content regardless of your circumstances:

I have learned how to be content with whatever I have. I know how to live on almost nothing or with everything…. For I can do everything through Christ, who gives me strength." Philippians 4:11–13 NLT

∘ ∘ ● ∘ ∘

LEARN ABOUT …

7 Desire

Covetousness is an inordinate desire to have more, a desire for what one does not have, in the negative sense. It is sometimes translated "greed." It springs from a discontentment with what one has. It can be manifested in several ways: overeagerness to obtain money, unwillingness to part with money, or meanness in dealing with money.

8 Depends

Contentment means freedom from anxiety or worry. It comes from a Greek word meaning independence or self-sufficiency. Those who depend on God are free from worldly concerns and find their sufficiency in Him: "Not that we are sufficient of ourselves … but our sufficiency is from God" (2 Cor. 3:5).

A person more interested in finances than faith, who rudely interrupted Jesus, prompted this parable. Jesus was teaching on matters of life and death, heaven and hell, when this man blurted out his question about his earthly inheritance. By doing so, he revealed that his obsession with worldly wealth was more important to him than spiritual insight.

Jesus refused to judge civil problems—Scripture tells us He has set up governments for those matters. Instead, during His first incarnation He maintained His focus on moral issues. Preferring to work from the inside out, He dealt with the heart. Jesus knew that if the heart was changed, appropriate actions would follow. Jesus sternly rebuked the man, not for interrupting Him but for caring more about gold than God. It's a good gut check for all of us. We should all ask the question, *What defines me? Possessing stuff or professing the Savior as my personal Lord?*

A cemetery in England holds a tombstone inscribed, *She died for want of things.* Alongside this stone stands another, which reads, *He died trying to give them to her.*[2] These epitaphs remind us of the folly of living and working for worldly goods alone. To think of life solely in terms of material possessions is not only foolish but also fatal. Abundant life consists of more than accumulating wealth; it rests on gaining spiritual and eternal riches. Listen to the Master's words, and avoid becoming a greedy grumbler.

LISTEN TO ...

All you are unable to give possesses you.

—*André Gide*

DAY 2

Selfish Stockpiles

Jesus talked a great deal about money. Sixteen of the thirty-eight parables were concerned with how to handle money and possessions. In the Gospels, an amazing one out of ten verses (two hundred eighty-eight in all) deals directly with the subject of money. The Bible offers five hundred verses on prayer, fewer than five hundred verses on faith, but more than two thousand verses on money and possessions![3]

Sadly, rather than using their resources wisely, many people misuse them. I (Lenya) have a dear friend who grew up the third child in a family of four. During his childhood, his family lived on a tight budget. His dad resorted to hunting in order to supplement the grocery budget. After hard work and wise investments, the family enjoyed prosperity. But the youngest brother never forgot the lean times. Despite a full refrigerator, he was constantly caught hoarding food underneath his bed. One day it was cookies, another day his favorite box of cereal. One morning my friend was pushed out of bed by his furious brother, who shouted, "Where did you put my Popsicles?" Of course, this perishable treat had melted away. His hidden stash disappeared into thin air.

Today we see a rich man who also schemed about ways to selfishly stockpile his goodies. Would he build bigger barns for his bumper crop? Would he party hardy instead of caring and sharing with those in need? In the parable of the Rich Fool, God awakens him from his folly by reminding him that you can't take it with you.

LIFT UP ...

Lord, I confess that I am oftentimes a selfish person. Forgive me when I hoard my time, talents, and treasures. Please give me a continual and heartfelt spirit of generosity toward others. Amen.

LOOK AT ...

Yesterday we realized that not everyone following Jesus was there for spiritual reasons. One young man wanted Jesus to change time-honored laws about inheritance regarding the

LEARN ABOUT ...

1 Plenty

To *yield plentifully* means to be fertile and bring forth abundantly. God desires to bless people abundantly, but there are those unfortunates who are ignorant of the divine source of their prosperity. But we know from Scripture that "[God] did good, gave us rain from heaven and fruitful seasons, filling our hearts with food and gladness" (Acts 14:17).

firstborn. But the Lord wasted no time filling pocketbooks when it was the human soul that was poverty-stricken.

Sadly, humans do not evaluate sin the same way God does. We tend to rank sins as slightly wrong, really wrong, and dead wrong. Historically, terms like *venial* (slight) and *mortal* (serious) were applied to transgressions. While people think some sins like robbery and murder are universally sinful, they glance over or, worse yet, glorify other sins. These slight sins include partying, spreading rumors, or accumulating wealth and status. There are whole industries built around these transgressions: nightclubs for the drunks, tabloids for the gossips, and Wall Street for the covetous. Society actually rallies around the mascots of missteps, from Paris Hilton to Donald Trump. But Jesus tackled what we might call mini and mortal sins with equal disdain. Today He colorfully illustrated the sinfulness of covetousness in the parable of the Rich Fool.

READ LUKE 12:16–21.

Then He spoke a parable to them, saying: "The ground of a certain rich man yielded plentifully. And he thought within himself, saying, 'What shall I do, since I have no room to store my crops?' So he said, 'I will do this: I will pull down my barns and build greater, and there I will store all my crops and my goods. And I will say to my soul, "Soul, you have many goods laid up for many years; take your ease; eat, drink, and be merry."' But God said to him, 'Fool! This night your soul will be required of you; then whose will those things be which you have provided?' So is he who lays up treasure for himself, and is not rich toward God." Luke 12:16–21

1. Who is the central character of this parable, and what blessing did he receive?

2. What dilemma did he ponder in his heart?

3. a. What solution did he propose to his problem?

b. What personal pronoun did he continue to use in his problem solving? What do you think this reveals?

4. Having solved his problem, who would he address, and of what would he boast?

5. In this parable, unlike some others, God is not depicted as a character but as a divine being.

   a. Why did God call the rich man a fool?

   b. What question did God ask the man to consider? How might you rephrase it?

6. Explain the key lesson Jesus wanted the people to learn.

7. Who do you think the rich fool represents in this parable?

LIVE OUT ...

8. a. We can either stockpile our riches or spread them around and be rich toward God. In what ways have you been or would you like to be rich toward God?

   ❑ Supporting a missionary
   ❑ Supporting others with prayer
   ❑ Sharing time with others
   ❑ Supporting my church financially
   ❑ Sharing my gifts/talents
   ❑ Other (name it)

   b. Journal a prayer of thanksgiving for all the riches God has blessed you with. Ask Him to give you a heart of generosity: "So

LEARN ABOUT ...

5 Pitiful

A *fool* is one who is mindless, ignorant, or unbelieving. It signifies a person lacking the common sense and awareness of natural and spiritual realities. Foolish people order their lives recklessly, especially in regard to salvation. Jesus said, "You Pharisees are so careful to clean the outside of the cup and the dish, but inside you are filthy—full of greed and wickedness! Fools!" (Luke 11:39–40 NLT).

4 Personality

Soul refers to a person's inner or thought life. The soul is the seat of personality and is best explained as "self." However, our souls are not our own, for God has said, "Behold, all souls are Mine" (Ezek. 18:4). And sadly, there are many culprits attempting to steal yours.

8 Possessions

Generosity speaks of liberality in spirit, especially regarding the needy. All believers should generously share their possessions with the poor. "Happy ... is [she] who is kind and merciful to the poor" (Prov. 14:21 AB). You are never more like God than when you're giving: "For God so loved the world that He gave" (John 3:16).

9 Piled Up

To *lay up* means to heap or
hoard. Hoarders usually
regard their wealth as the
product of their own work
and not as a God-given
blessing. Accordingly, they
do not seek His guidance in
the use and distribution of
their wealth. But the Bible
teaches, "It is more blessed
to give than to receive"
(Acts 20:35).

let each one give as he purposes in his heart, not grudgingly or of
necessity; for God loves a cheerful giver" (2 Cor. 9:7).

9. People who hoard money or possessions usually do so because
    those things represent something powerfully attractive to them.
    What does money represent to you? For instance:

    ❏ Security. Money is what guarantees food on my table, a roof
      over my head, and health care if I get sick. I'm afraid of not
      having enough.
    ❏ Status. Money buys the things that make other people think
      I'm successful and okay.
    ❏ Pleasure. Money buys the things and experiences that help me
      enjoy life.
    ❏ Love. Getting things makes me feel loved.
    ❏ Other (name it)

10. Giving to the Lord and His work requires sacrifices on our part.
    Read the following verses, and record what you learn about our
    spiritual sacrifices.

Scripture	Our Spiritual Sacrifices
Psalm 107:22	
Psalm 141:2	
Romans 12:1	
Hebrews 13:15	
Hebrews 13:16	

∘ ∘ ● ∘ ∘

We often put our affection on things that come with a price tag. The
story is told of a miserable rich man who visited a happy rabbi who lived
modestly. The rabbi tried to illustrate what caused the difference in their

dispositions. Leading the man to his window, he said, "Look out the window and tell me what you see." The man said, "I see some men, women, and a few children." The rabbi then led him to a mirror and said, "Look there and tell me what you see." Frowning, the man replied, "Obviously I see myself." "Interesting," the rabbi commented. "The window and the mirror are both made of glass. But the glass of the mirror is backed by a little bit of silver. No sooner is the silver added than you cease to see others, and only yourself." Maybe our troubles start when just a little bit of silver is added, and we stop looking through and start looking at.[4]

The personal pronouns *I* and *my* are used eleven times in today's parable. Instead of worshipping the Holy Trinity of God the Father, God the Son, and God the Holy Spirit, the rich fool worshipped the unholy trinity of *me, myself,* and *I.* He lived a fool's life without God in his heart and then died a fool's death, forever separated from the One who could give him eternal life.

LISTEN TO ...

I have held many things in my hands, and I have lost them all; but whatever I have placed in God's hands, that I still possess.

—*Martin Luther*

DAY 3

Worthless Worries

In *The Skylark's Bargain*, G. H. Charnley tells the story of a young skylark that discovered a man who would give him worms in exchange for a feather. He made a deal—one feather for two worms. The next day the lark was flying high in the sky with his father. The older bird said, "You know, son, we skylarks should be the happiest of all birds. See our brave wings! They lift us high in the air, nearer and nearer to God." But the young bird did not hear, for all he saw was an old man with worms. Down he flew, plucked two feathers from his wings and had a feast. Day after day this went on. Autumn came and it was time to fly south. But the young skylark couldn't do it. He had exchanged the power of his young wings for worms.[5]

We humans are guilty of the skylark's sin. We exchange our worship of God for worthless worries. God has given us everything in the world we need to make us happy. Scripture teaches, "His divine power has given to us all things that pertain to life and godliness, through the knowledge of Him who called us by glory and virtue" (2 Peter 1:3). Yet somehow, we manage to pluck our happiness away like feathers, one or two worries at a time, keeping us digging in the dirt. Isn't it better to trust God to provide for all of our needs and then offer Him the praise He is due? Today, let's learn a lesson from the birds, which don't have worthless worries. Why should we settle for the worms of worry when we can soar in the sky with songs of praise?

LIFT UP ...

Lord, forgive me for the sin of worry. I know nothing good comes from it. Please help me to spend my time in worship rather than worry. Amen.

LOOK AT ...

Through the parable of the Rich Fool, Jesus warned the crowds about the folly of hoarding wealth and being stingy toward God. The greatest mistake the wealthy farmer made was eliminating God from the equation. There was nothing wrong with his decision to build bigger barns. A good farmer has the foresight to plan ahead. Sadly, in all his meticulous plans he did not consult God. James warned, "Come now, you who say, 'Today or tomorrow we will go to such and such a city, spend a year there, buy and sell, and make a profit'; whereas you do not know what will happen tomorrow. For what is your life? It is even a vapor that appears for a little time and then vanishes away. Instead you ought to say, 'If the Lord wills, we shall live and do this or that.' But now you boast in your arrogance. All such boasting is evil" (James 4:13–16).

Now we discover two polar opposites concerning money—either amassing too much or anxiety about possessing too little. Money is not the issue; instead it is the human heart. Money, like a knife, is neutral. A blade can slay or perform surgery. Paul warned, "For the *love* of money is a root of all kinds of evil, for which some have strayed from the faith in their greediness, and pierced themselves through with many sorrows" (1 Tim. 6:10). Those who lack money can be as guilty of greed as those who have millions. Today Jesus gives instructions concerning anxiousness, something we *all* need to learn from the Master's lips.

LEARN ABOUT …

2 Worried

Worry means to strain, tear, or rip asunder. Believers are commanded not to mentally or emotionally strain over material necessities or rip themselves apart over their physical needs. The Bible promises, "God will meet all your needs according to his glorious riches in Christ Jesus" (Phil. 4:19 NIV).

READ LUKE 12:22–26.

Then He said to His disciples, "Therefore I say to you, do not worry about your life, what you will eat; nor about the body, what you will put on. Life is more than food, and the body is more than clothing. Consider the ravens, for they neither sow nor reap, which have neither storehouse nor barn; and God feeds them. Of how much more value are you than the birds? And which of you by worrying can add one cubit to his stature? If you then are not able to do the least, why are you anxious for the rest?" Luke 12:22–26

1. To whom did Jesus direct His next instructions?

2. a. What did He command about their lives?

   b. What did He command about their bodies?

LEARN ABOUT ...

4 Winged

Judaism considers ravens unclean. Ravens are scavengers that will eat almost anything, even dead animals. Their symbolism as bad omens may have begun when Noah sent one from the ark never to return, or it may be due to their deep caw. Yet, God "provides food for the raven, when its young ones cry" (Job 38:41).

---

6 Worthless

A cubit is the distance from the elbow to the fingertip—about eighteen inches long. In biblical times, the cubit was the standard unit of length and was the common designation of a person's height, or stature. Jesus was simply reminding us not to let the things we have no control over control us.

---

8 Weighty

To be anxious is to have a distracting care about things. Rather than lightening our lives, anxiety weighs us down. It distracts us from focusing on God and diminishes our capacity for abundant living. The author of Hebrews exhorts us to "fix our eyes on Jesus, the author and perfecter of our faith" (Heb. 12:2 NIV).

c. How were these commands connected to His teaching about hoarding?

3. What does it mean to say that "life is more than food"?

4. What creature did Jesus ask the disciples to consider and why?

5. How did Jesus compare us to the raven?

6. Considering the definition of cubit, rephrase Jesus' questions to explain why worry is useless.

LIVE OUT ...

7. We are commanded not to worry about our lives. Check the box or boxes that describe the things that make you anxious and cause you to be torn from God in your heart and mind.

   ❏ Finances
   ❏ Health
   ❏ Children
   ❏ Marriage
   ❏ Safety
   ❏ Death
   ❏ War
   ❏ Friendships
   ❏ Other_____

8. Journal about the box or boxes you checked. How much of your time is consumed by these worries? Why?

9. a. Jesus commanded us not to worry about what we will eat or

what we will put on. When was the last time you did not have something to eat?

b. When was the last time you did not have anything to wear—literally?

c. Talk about how you have experienced God taking care of your needs and even some of your greeds.

10. Wild creatures don't plant, harvest, or store their food. They live, trusting God to provide. Fill in the chart to discover some of the ways you can trust God.

Scripture	Believers Can Trust God ...
1 Chronicles 5:20	
Psalm 18:2	
Psalm 34:22	
Psalm 56:4	

Learn About ...

9 What Ifs

We worry about what-ifs. *What if there's not enough to eat? What if I don't have something to wear?* But that really means: *What if I'm not dressed in the latest style?* Perspective check: UNICEF reports that 30,000 children "die quietly [every day] in some of the poorest villages on earth, far removed from the scrutiny and the conscience of the world."[6]

∘ ∘ ● ∘ ∘

A wealthy employer overheard one of his workers exclaim, "If I only had a hundred dollars, I would be perfectly content." Knowing that his own money had not given him peace, he told her, "Since I would like to see someone who is perfectly contented, I'm going to grant your desire." He gave her the money and left, but before he was out of earshot, he heard her remark almost bitterly, "Why didn't I say two hundred dollars?"[7]

One root cause of worry is discontentment with what God has provided. Add in a little bit of distrust that God might not provide in the future, and you end up with disbelief in God's goodness. That really is something to worry about!

King David wrote, "I have been young, and now am old; yet I have not seen the righteous forsaken, nor his descendants begging bread." (Ps. 37:25). As God's children, we can be content with our lot and trust in our heavenly Father to take care of our physical, spiritual, and emotional needs. Worrying is not only a waste of time; it is an insult to our loving Father. Heed Solomon's counsel: "Trust in the LORD with all your heart, and lean not on your own understanding; in all your ways acknowledge Him, and He shall direct your paths" (Prov. 3:5–6). Don't let worthless worries strangle the life out of you.

LISTEN TO ...

Every increased possession loads us with a new weariness.

—John Ruskin

DAY 4
Father's Fortune

"Consider the lilies," Jesus admonished the disciples, lest they worry about what to wear. These flowers were probably anemones or windflowers. They grew profusely in the fields of Galilee, coloring them brilliantly with reds and purples, the royal colors.[8] Solomon's most expensive regal robes paled in comparison to how God had adorned these delicate flowers.

Some wildflowers may be a dime a dozen. But these days a pocketful of posies can be hard on the pocketbook. The hydrangea averages about $7 per stem. The lily of the valley is roughly $50 per bunch. And exotic orchids can be over $25 per stem. These flowers are for adorning bouquets and nosegays. But if you're looking for an expensive flower that is edible, then the saffron ranks as the most expensive spice in the world. Derived from the dried purple blossom saffron crocus, it takes between 70,000 and 250,000 flowers to make one pound of saffron. Moreover, the flowers have to be individually handpicked in the autumn when fully open. The New York market price for saffron in March 2003 was $365 per pound. Among fragrant flowers for perfume, the Damascene Rose is one of the most expensive, selling for $2,990 per kilogram. The amazing thing about these designer flowers is that, although they are costly, they are temporary and inanimate.

In today's lesson, Jesus reminds us of His Father's fortune. If God clothes these fading flowers so gloriously, you can be sure that He will also adorn you, His special creation, with beautiful apparel.

LIFT UP ...

Jesus, thank You for giving me access to the Father's fortune now and forever. Help me to live by faith and to trust You for everything I need. Amen.

LOOK AT ...

Jesus instructed the disciples not to worry about their lives or what they would eat. As an illustration, He used God's perfect provision even for scavenging birds. Through another example of creation, flowers, Jesus continued to teach the importance of depending on God. Jesus draws

one huge contrast between flocks, flowers, and folks like you and me. The former have a Creator, the latter have a Father. A creator might denote detachment, but a father portrays a close relationship. If birds don't worry, then certainly God's children have no excuse to stress about the future. Because we have someone to watch over us, we don't need to waste energy seeking worldly advantage. Instead, we can seek first God's kingdom for His glory. We have a choice. We can focus on here or the hereafter.

READ LUKE 12:27–31.

"Consider the lilies, how they grow: they neither toil nor spin; and yet I say to you, even Solomon in all his glory was not arrayed like one of these. If then God so clothes the grass, which today is in the field and tomorrow is thrown into the oven, how much more will He clothe you, O you of little faith? And do not seek what you should eat or what you should drink, nor have an anxious mind. For all these things the nations of the world seek after, and your Father knows that you need these things. But seek the kingdom of God, and all these things shall be added to you." Luke 12:27–31

1. Describe what Jesus asked the disciples to consider.

2. With whom did He compare the flowers, and what phrase did He use to describe him?

3. Explain what happened to the grasses from one day to the next.

4. a. What rhetorical question did Jesus ask?

   b. What did this question reveal?

5. What three commands did Jesus give?

   a. Do not seek _____.

b. Do not seek _____.

c. Do not have _____.

6. a. Who seeks these things?

   b. Why shouldn't believers seek them?

7. Explain what we are to seek and the benefits of this pursuit.

LIVE OUT ...

8. a. When we seek things or people above God, we make them into idols. What earthly goods, pursuits, or people have you craved?

   ❑ Automobiles
   ❑ Clothing/Jewelry
   ❑ Vacations
   ❑ Children/Spouse
   ❑ Other Relationships
   ❑ Hobbies/Interests
   ❑ Prestige/Reputation
   ❑ Home Furnishings
   ❑ Other _____

   b. Journal about how seeking these things affects you spiritually. (For example, "I spend so much energy on my kids, I don't take time for God.")

9. If you have fallen into the trap of idolatry, write a prayer of confession and repentance. Ask God to forgive you and give you clean hands and a pure heart, for "[she] who has clean hands and a

LEARN ABOUT ...

7 Telling

Our number one priority in life should be to worship God and spread the gospel. God will take care of everything else. Peter encourages us, "Like newborn babies, crave pure spiritual milk, so that by it you may grow up in your salvation, now that you have tasted that the Lord is good" (1 Peter 2:2–3 NIV).

8 Tempting

Seek is a verb that can also be translated as *worship, desire* ... or *crave*. Craving material possessions is a form of idol worship or idolatry and displays a heart of unbelief. Scripture warns, "You shall worship no other god, for the LORD ... is a jealous God" (Ex. 34:14). Are you making God jealous by the things you're pursuing?

9 Trading

An idol is anything or anyone who trades places with God in the mind of a believer. Idolatry is a dangerous and deceitful sin. It is imperative that all believers be constantly on guard against anything that comes between them and God: "Put to death ... covetousness, which is idolatry" (Col. 3:5).

pure heart, who does not lift up [her] soul to an idol … will receive blessing from the LORD" (Ps. 24:4–5 NIV).

10. Throughout the parables, we've learned in detail about the kingdom of God. Use the word SEEK as an acrostic to describe some things you'll pursue for God's kingdom.

S

E

E

K

○ ○ ● ○ ○

A pastor won $5 million in the Reader's Digest sweepstakes. Lonnie Harris, forty-seven, leads the thirty-five-member independent Bethel House of Prayer in Clovis, South Carolina. He, his wife, and four children flew—all for the first time—to Digest headquarters in suburban New York to pick up a check for $287,000, the first installment of a projected twenty-nine-year payout, Religious News Service reported. Harris was replacing the door hinge of his 1975 Ford van when the letter arrived. He said he planned to buy a new van large enough to carry the amplifiers used by his traveling gospel music group and "maybe some new clothes." Harris also wants to help the needy in his community.[9] Even though this pastor won millions of dollars, he kept his priorities righteous: He sought first the kingdom of God.

Having wealth and wanting material possessions are not sins. However, focusing on wealth and acquiring possessions can keep us from worshipping God, which *is* a sin. Do you have a God-sized faith that trusts in the Father's unfathomable fortune, or do you trust only in yourself? Since God feeds the birds and clothes the lilies, you can be sure that He will "supply all your need according to His riches in glory by Christ Jesus" (Phil. 4:19). And if He provides "exceedingly abundantly above all that we ask or think"

(Eph. 3:20), be sure to share the wealth with others. Your hands can become the Father's in the life of somebody else.

LISTEN TO ...

Theirs is an endless road, a hopeless maze, who seek for goods before they seek for God.

—*Bernard of Clairvaux*

DAY 5

Godly Guarantees

In the late nineteenth century, John Wanamaker opened a department store in Philadelphia called the Grand Depot to house a series of 129 specialty shops under one roof. It was "the largest space in the world devoted to retail selling on a single floor." The store soon became one of the most successful businesses in the country. Wanamaker came to be known as "the Merchant Prince" because of his innovative sales and advertising techniques. A deeply religious man, Wanamaker refused to advertise on Sundays. He was the first person to use the price tag. Before then, most buying was done by haggling. A devout Christian, Wanamaker believed that if everyone was equal before God, then everyone should be equal before price. He became postmaster general of the United States, president of the YMCA, and superintendent for the largest Sunday school in the world at Bethany Presbyterian Church.[10]

When asked how he could hold all those positions, he explained, "Early in life I read, 'Seek ye first the kingdom of God, and His righteousness, and all these things shall be added unto you.' The Sunday school is my business; all the rest are the things."

Wanamaker had a specially constructed soundproof room in his store. Every day he spent thirty minutes praying and meditating on God's Word in that room. He left a multimillion-dollar empire, but more importantly, a deep spiritual legacy, giving enormous sums to charities, such as the Children's Wing of Philadelphia's Presbyterian hospital, and he devoted Sundays to religious work. "If you once have the joy and sweet pleasure of bringing one soul to Christ, you will be hungry to get another."[11]

Wanamaker could have put his business first and worried about every little detail of his life. But he had his priorities right. He put the fear of the Lord first, and God honored that. Not all of us will be as successful in business as Wanamaker, but when we fear the Lord, we can all be as spiritually successful as this spiritual seeker.

LIFT UP …

Lord, thank You so much for teaching me the truth about earthly and heavenly riches. Help me not to fear the troubles in the world, but to set my sights on heaven's treasures and joys. Amen.

LOOK AT ...

This week Jesus taught us that as believers we are commanded not to covet, worry, or be anxious about the things of this world. When Christians engage in these corrosive behaviors, we give God a bad name. To call Him Father and then complain about His provision diminishes His reputation to a watching world. Why would they desire a Father we portray as neglectful? God may not provide your greeds, but He will always provide your needs. Perhaps instead of pouting about what you don't have, you should praise Him for all that you do have. Then you can proclaim with Paul, "I know what it is to be in need, and I know what it is to have plenty. I have learned the secret of being content in any and every situation, whether well fed or hungry, whether living in plenty or in want. I can do everything through him who gives me strength" (Phil. 4:12–13 NIV).

Today He will reveal more about how to give up our fears so that we can have the faith to rely on His godly guarantees and enjoy life here and in the hereafter, for our good and for the good of others.

READ LUKE 12:32–34.

"Do not fear, little flock, for it is your Father's good pleasure to give you the kingdom. Sell what you have and give alms; provide yourselves money bags which do not grow old, a treasure in the heavens that does not fail, where no thief approaches nor moth destroys. For where your treasure is, there your heart will be also." Luke 12:32–34

1. a. What command did Jesus give?

   b. To whom did He give it?

2. In your own words, explain why we are not to fear.

3. What did Jesus instruct His followers to do for others?

LEARN ABOUT ...

2 Pleased

The words *good pleasure* come from a compound Greek word that means to be well pleased or delighted. Why be afraid of anything when our loving, gracious Father is well pleased to give us everything we need? James tells us, "Every good gift and every perfect gift is from above, and comes down from the Father of lights" (James 1:17).

---

3 Poor

Alms are charitable offerings given to the poor: "He who has pity on the poor lends to the LORD, and He will pay back what he has given" (Prov. 19:17). It is sinful not to share. However, there is nothing sinful about saving: "The children ought not to lay up for the parents, but the parents for the children" (2 Cor. 12:14).

LEARN ABOUT …

4 Permanent

Acquiring and maintaining earthly wealth consumes time and energy. Believers are to invest their hearts, minds, and souls in heavenly wealth that will last forever: "So we fix our eyes not on what is seen, but on what is unseen. For what is seen is temporary, but what is unseen is eternal" (2 Cor. 4:18 NIV).

---

7 Pastures

By nature, sheep are helpless creatures in need of shepherds to lead them to water and to pasture and to defend them from wild beasts. Even more helpless are the little lambs in the flock. Isaiah prophesied that Jesus would "feed His flock like a shepherd; He will gather the lambs with His arm, and carry them in His bosom" (Isa. 40:11).

---

8 Possessions

Just as the early church provided charity, we too should be charitable. The term *charity* means brotherly kindness or love for all humanity. Our outward support of others is but a manifestation of our inward love for God. Paul notes, "If I give all my possessions to feed the poor, and if I surrender my body to be burned, but do not have love, it profits me nothing" (1 Cor. 13:3 NASB).

4. Describe what believers are to provide for themselves and why.

5. What do the things we treasure reveal?

6. How have you discovered this to be true in your life?

LIVE OUT …

7. Jesus used "little flock" as a term of endearment to comfort His disciples. They were constantly worried about what to eat, what to wear, or where to go, like baby lambs following a shepherd. Read Psalm 23 aloud.

   a. Now list all of the benefits our Great Shepherd provides for His sheep.

   b. What have you been afraid of lately?

   c. How does Psalm 23 help you to "fear not"?

8. a. The early church did charitable deeds and sold its possessions to support the poor. Name some of the underprivileged and poor in your community.

   b. Journal about how you will endeavor to give alms to these people.

9. We learned that while some treasures on earth are destroyed or robbed from us, treasures in heaven do not fail. In the columns below, list some of both kinds of treasure that you have stored up.

   TARNISHED TREASURES   **TRUE TREASURES**

○ ○ ● ○ ○

A rich man learned that he would die in a few days. He called his three friends—a doctor, preacher, and lawyer—to his bedside. He said, "The preacher has told me that you can't take it with you, but I believe I have worked out a way so that I can. Doc tells me that I won't live long, so I have prepared three sealed envelopes, each containing $10,000. When I die, I want each of you to walk by the casket and drop in your envelope with the $10,000." A short time later, they attended his funeral and then met together. The preacher said, "I've got a confession to make. We've been needing to repair the organ in the church for a long time, and I took $2,000 out of Bill's envelope and used it on the organ." The doctor said, "This makes it easier for me, because I took $5,000 out and used it for my new clinic and only dropped in $5,000." The lawyer said, "Well, my conscience is clear. I did just what Bill said. I kept my envelope, picked up both of yours, and dropped in a check for the whole amount of $30,000." The lesson is simple: Many people have tried to take it with them, but none have accomplished that task.[12]

God desires for us, His children, to keep our hearts fixed on His kingdom and the work He has called us to do. If we seek to please God first, then our thoughts will not be carried away with excessive cares, worries, and anxieties over the things of this world. When we seek God's kingdom first, we can rest assured that "all these things shall be added to you" (Luke 12:31).

LISTEN TO ...

As the purse is emptied, the heart is filled.

—Victor Hugo

There's No Place Like Home

Luke 15:1–32

A father and his son worked for months to build a toy sailboat. When it was finished, they traveled to a nearby lake for the boat's trial run. Before launching it, the father tied a string to its stern to keep the boat from sailing too far. It performed beautifully, but before long a motorboat crossing the lake cut the string, and the sailboat drifted out of sight. Attempts to find it were fruitless. Both father and son wept over its loss.

As the boy walked home from school one day, he passed his favorite toy store and noticed a toy sailboat in the window—*his* sailboat! He ran inside to claim the boat, telling the owner of his experience on the lake. The owner explained that he had found the boat during a fishing trip. "You may be its maker," he said, "but as its finder, I am its legal owner. You can buy it back for fifty dollars." The boy was stunned at how much it would cost him to regain his boat, but since it was so precious to him, he was determined to earn the money to buy it back. Months later, the boy walked into the toy store and handed the owner fifty dollars. The day he brought his sailboat home was the happiest day of his life.[1]

Although God made man and woman, they sailed away to sin in the garden of Eden. But God willingly paid the ultimate cost—His Son's life—to buy back each lost soul who has followed the example of Adam and Eve—wandering from God's grace. This week in the parables of Lost Things, we will see God continually pursue all who are lost and witness His boundless joy when each one returns home.

Day 1: Luke 15:1–7   **SHEEP WANDERED**

Day 2: Luke 15:8–10   **TREASURE RECOVERED**

Day 3: Luke 15:11–16   **INHERITANCE SQUANDERED**

Day 4: Luke 15:17–24   **REALITY PONDERED**

Day 5: Luke 15:25–32   **BEGRUDGINGLY HONORED**

DAY I

Sheep Wandered

LIFT UP ...

Lord, I was a lost and wandering sheep when You found me. Thank You for carrying my sin on Your shoulders to the cross. Keep me ever mindful of the price You paid for me. Amen.

LOOK AT ...

Both Matthew and Luke include the parable of the Lost Sheep in their gospels. Their outlines are identical but differ in some of the details. Since the days of the patriarchs, shepherding had been an integral part of Israel's commerce and society. It is likely Jesus knew that this touching tale would tug on the hearts of the listeners, especially children who could visualize being carried on someone's shoulders. Even today many nursery rhymes and hymns—from "Baa Baa Black Sheep" and "Mary Had a Little Lamb" to "Savior, Like a Shepherd Lead Us"—call this parable to remembrance. Isn't it wonderful to observe this tender side of the Savior?

This week we'll discover the meaning behind three vanishing acts: the lost lamb, the missing money, and the backslidden boy. Herbert Lockyer said, "The key to most of Christ's parables hangs on the front door."[2] In other words, the circumstances and setting surrounding the parables hold the key to understanding their meaning. The Pharisees' view of "sinners" as trash deserving to be thrown away prompted Jesus to tell these parables, illustrating that God does not see lost souls as garbage worth tossing but as priceless treasure worth finding. We begin today with the parable of the Lost Sheep.

READ LUKE 15:1–7.

Then all the tax collectors and the sinners drew near to Him to hear Him. And the Pharisees and scribes complained, saying, "This Man receives sinners and eats with them." So He spoke this parable to them, saying: "What man of you, having a hundred sheep, if he loses

Learn about ...

2 Outcast

The outcasts came close to Christ while the religious leaders stood afar. Tax collectors were shunned by Jews and Greeks. The Pharisees referred to people of ill repute as "sinners." But Romans 3:23 says, "All have sinned and fall short of the glory of God." All people should draw near to Jesus, whether religious or of ill repute.

3 Outcome

To the religious leaders, anyone who disagreed with them was a sinner. Because they believed physical contact with sinners defiled them, the intimate activity of eating together was unthinkable. The outcasts who were shunned by the religious leaders were attracted to Jesus because He "received," or welcomed, them as friends.

4 Outlook

When a sheep wanders from the flock, it becomes disoriented and immobilized with fear. An attentive shepherd regularly counts his sheep. If one is missing, he immediately looks for it. God, our attentive Shepherd, counts things too: "The very hairs of your head are all numbered" (Matt. 10:30).

one of them, does not leave the ninety-nine in the wilderness, and go after the one which is lost until he finds it? And when he has found it, he lays it on his shoulders, rejoicing. And when he comes home, he calls together his friends and neighbors, saying to them, 'Rejoice with me, for I have found my sheep which was lost!' I say to you that likewise there will be more joy in heaven over one sinner who repents than over ninety-nine just persons who need no repentance." Luke 15:1–7

1. In Luke 14, Jesus instructed people about what it meant to be His disciples. Read Luke 14:25, 35 to discover the context of today's text.

   a. To whom was Jesus speaking (v. 25)?

   b. What did He admonish them to do (v. 35)?

2. According to Luke 15:1, who else drew near to hear Him speak on discipleship?

3. What two complaints did the Pharisees and scribes make against Jesus?

4. Jesus began this parable with a question. Rephrase the question in your own words.

5. Describe what happened when the shepherd found the lost sheep.

6. What spiritual application did Jesus make to this parable?

7. According to Jesus' interpretation in Luke 15:7, match each letter with the correct answer to show who you think the following represent in this parable.

a. The one lost sheep   ___ Heavenly hosts

b. Those who rejoiced over   ___ Repentant sinners

   finding the sheep

c. The ninety-nine sheep   ___ Self-righteous people who

   left in the field   don't see their need for a Savior

LIVE OUT ...

8. Sinners and outcasts were drawn to Jesus because He had compassion for them. Romans 2:4 says, "The goodness of God leads [us] to repentance." Describe a time when God's goodness drew you toward Him and away from sin.

9. a. Believers are often compared to sheep in Scripture. Psalm 119:176 says, "I have strayed like a lost sheep. Seek your servant, for I have not forgotten your commands" (NIV). In which of the following ways have you strayed from His commands?

   ❒ Thoughts   ❒ Behaviors   ❒ Priorities

   ❒ Attitudes   ❒ Words   ❒ Other (name it)

b. Journal a prayer thanking God that He is attentive and faithful to seek you when you stray. "O LORD, you have searched me and you know me. You know when I sit and when I rise; you perceive my thoughts from afar. You discern my going out and my lying down; you are familiar with all my ways" (Ps. 139:1–3 NIV).

10. The shepherd carried the lost sheep home on his shoulders. Psalm

LEARN ABOUT ...

7 Outsider

The Pharisees had a common saying that demonstrated their contempt for sinners: "There is joy in heaven when one sinner is obliterated." In contrast, "when [Jesus] saw the multitudes, He was moved with compassion for them, because they were weary and scattered, like sheep having no shepherd" (Matt. 9:36).[3]

8 Outpour

God is good and pours out His love on His people. In common use, goodness is the opposite of badness. It's the character quality that makes its possessor lovable. In Scripture, goodness carries the idea of kindness and unfailing love. The Psalmist declared, "Oh, how great is Your goodness" (Ps. 31:19).

9 Outbound

As the shepherd in this parable left the ninety-nine to search for the one lost sheep, Jesus—the "Good Shepherd [who laid] down his life for the sheep" (John 10:11 TLB)—left heaven and came to earth "to seek and to save that which was lost" (Luke 19:10).

100:3 says, "We are His people and the sheep of His pasture." Fill in the chart to describe specifically how and when the Shepherd carries His people.

Scripture	How?	When?
Psalm 18:48		
Psalm 94:18–19		
Isaiah 46:3–4		

○ ○ ● ○ ○

'Twas a sheep, not a lamb, that strayed away,

In the parable Jesus told;

A grown-up sheep that had gone astray

From the ninety and nine in the fold.

Out on the hillside, out in the cold,

'Twas a sheep the Good Shepherd sought;

And back to the flock, safe into the fold,

'Twas a sheep the Good Shepherd brought.

And why for the sheep should we earnestly long,

And as fervently hope and pray?

Because there is danger, if they go wrong,

They will lead the lambs astray.

And so with the sheep we tenderly plead,

For the sake of the lambs today;

If the sheep are lost, what terrible cost

Some lambs will have to pay![4]

There is safety in numbers. A stray sheep becomes a prime target for hungry predators. The shepherd must find the lost sheep, pick it up, and carry it home to the flock. Likewise, Jesus, the Good Shepherd, longs to carry us tenderly back to safety. Sadly, we often choose to stay isolated from the flock and vulnerable to devouring enemies. Today, find a quiet place to contemplate the small ways you have strayed from the Shepherd. Close your eyes and picture Jesus carrying you on His strong shoulders. Rest in His arms: "Be still, and know that [He is] God" (Ps. 46:10).

LISTEN TO ...

God's salvation takes into account the lost, the last, and the least.

—Unknown

DAY 2

Treasure Recovered

A rock hound named Rob Cutshaw owns a little roadside shop outside Andrews, North Carolina. Like many in the trade, he hunts for rocks, then sells them to collectors or jewelry makers. He knows enough about rocks to decide which to pick up and sell, but he's no expert. He leaves the appraising of his rocks to other people. As much as he enjoys the work, it doesn't always pay the bills. He occasionally moonlights cutting wood to help put bread on the table.

On a dig twenty years ago, Rob found a rock he described as "purdy and big." He tried unsuccessfully to sell the specimen and, according to Cutshaw, kept the rock under his bed or in his closet. He guessed the blue chunk could bring as much as $500, but he would have taken less if something urgent came up, like paying his power bill. That's how close Rob came to hawking for a few hundred dollars what turned out to be the largest, most valuable sapphire ever found. The blue rock that Rob had abandoned to the darkness of a closet two decades ago—now known as "The Star of David" sapphire—weighs nearly a pound and could easily sell for $2.75 million.[5]

Just as Rob Cutshaw was a rock hound, God hounds humans. In the parable of the Lost Coin we'll see God, the Holy Spirit, diligently searching for lost souls like some people search for lost treasure.

LIFT UP …

Lord, Your love for me is unfathomable. It's amazing to think You'd number the hairs on my head. Thank You for caring about every detail of my life. Help me to value others like You value me. Amen.

LOOK AT …

Yesterday we saw the importance of the one over the many. In the cold calculations of percentages, losing one lamb out of one hundred is a measly 1 percent. Statistically it's marginal. Factor in that as the flock continued to mate and breed it's likely that many newborns would take the place of the missing sheep—eventually increasing the bottom line. But God is a stickler for details, especially when the numbers represent a human soul. Jesus emphasized that His "Father in heaven is not willing that any of these little ones should be lost" (Matt. 18:14 NIV). Not one stray is ignored. Jesus would have died on the cross even if you were the only one to be saved. That's the power of one!

Jesus used three parables to illustrate a key truth: God searches for lost people as we would search for valuable treasure. All of heaven rejoices when they're found. Today's parable sheds a different light on the same truth as we see a treasure recovered by God working through the church empowered by the Holy Spirit.

READ LUKE 15:8–10.

"Or what woman, having ten silver coins, if she loses one coin, does not light a lamp, sweep the house, and search carefully until she finds it? And when she has found it, she calls her friends and neighbors together, saying, 'Rejoice with me, for I have found the piece which I lost!' Likewise, I say to you, there is joy in the presence of the angels of God over one sinner who repents." Luke 15:8–10

1. To whom did Jesus next turn His attention?

2. Explain what the woman had and what she lost.

3. What three actions did the woman take when she lost this coin?

4. Describe the woman's reaction upon finding the coin and how it was similar to the shepherd's response to finding the lost sheep.

5. What spiritual truth did Jesus want the people to take home?

LEARN ABOUT …

2 Precious

The lost coin was probably a Greek drachma. It was equal in value to a Roman denarius, about fifteen cents, or a day's wage. The coin probably came from the woman's headpiece—a symbol of marriage or betrothal. Losing this coin would be as traumatic as a woman losing a stone from her wedding ring.

3 Persistent

The men in the audience would have related to the shepherd's plight in the previous parable. But Jesus used an example a woman working in her home could truly appreciate. Homes in the ancient East were small and windowless, with dirt floors. Searching for one coin in this dark atmosphere required considerable effort.

5 Praiseworthy

The shepherd's joy over finding his sheep and the woman's joy over finding her coin both symbolize God's joy when a soul returns to His kingdom. "He will rejoice over you with gladness.… He will rejoice over you with singing" (Zeph. 3:17). His joy reverberates throughout heaven, and the angels rejoice when a sinner repents.

LEARN ABOUT ...

7 Portrays

Herbert Lockyer said, "The woman sweeping the house for her lost coin is an illustration of the Holy Spirit working through His Church (the saved) to save others. The Spirit's work naturally follows the Shepherd's task."[6] Symbolically, God's Word is the light, and the Holy Spirit is God's cleansing breath working through the living body of the church.

---

9 Prayer

To *intercede* means to light upon, to converse with, to petition, or to pray. When you light upon God through the power of the Holy Spirit, He can shine the light of His love on someone who has wandered into the darkness: "The Spirit also helps in our weaknesses. For we do not know what we should pray for as we ought" (Rom. 8:26).

6. Who do you think the woman and the coin represent in this parable?

LIVE OUT ...

7. The woman in this parable lit, swept, and searched the house diligently until she found the lost coin. Similarly, God takes these same steps to recover us. Match each of the following verses with the step to which it corresponds in this parable:

    a. Luke 19:10   ____ Provides light in the darkness

    b. John 12:46   ____ Sweeps the dirt away

    c. 1 John 1:7–9   ____ Searches diligently

8. When we hear about missing children or lost hikers, we hope and pray for their safe recovery. God is in the search-and-rescue business—He pursues lost people every day.

    a. How often do you think about and pray for those who are lost spiritually?

    ❏ Daily   ❏ Weekly   ❏ Monthly   ❏ Rarely   ❏ Never

    b. Read 2 Corinthians 4:3–4. How does our Enemy, "the god of this age," seek to keep the lost from being found?

    c. How can you play an active role on God's search-and-rescue team according to 2 Timothy 4:2?

9. Hebrews 7:25 says Jesus "is able to save completely those who come to God through him, because he always lives to intercede for them" (NIV). Journal a prayer interceding for someone you know

whose eyes have turned from the light of the gospel and who is sitting in a corner gathering dust.

∘ ∘ ● ∘ ∘

If the sheep was lost because of its own foolishness, the coin seems to have been lost because of the owner's carelessness. Thus, the coin might symbolize a person who has fallen away from the faith. In the book of Revelation, Jesus spoke to the church at Ephesus and said: "Nevertheless I have this against you, that you have left your first love" (Rev. 2:4).

This is similar to when you first fall in love. You can't wait to talk to the object of your affections. You long to be in the presence of the one you love. You do everything to look your best and be on your best behavior. But after a while, maybe the luster wears off. Maybe a little dust starts to gather in the corner of your relationship. Maybe, like the woman, even a coin falls off the headpiece. It's up to you to make a conscious effort to spend time and energy on your relationship with your spouse—to keep it alive and fresh.

The same is true in our relationship with God. As believers, we must be careful not to be like the church at Ephesus. Jesus told them, "You have left your first love.… Repent and do the first works" (Rev. 2:4–5). Are you spiritually gathering dust, or is your love story with God fresh and new? If your coin of worship is hanging by a thread, go back and do the first works—repent of your sins, read the Word, and worship the Lord. Remember that God is diligently searching for you.

LISTEN TO ...

Just as a strong wind will blow through an open window and stir things up in a house, the Holy Spirit will blow new life into your church (or your life) if you give Him access.

—*Anonymous*

DAY 3

Inheritance Squandered

I (Penny) am not proud of the fact that I was a prodigal. I grew up in a family of faith. My great-grandfather was a Baptist evangelist. My mother played the piano in the church. You might say I was a church rat. I was saved at an early age and knew that God called me into His family.

Sadly, in high school, I answered the world's allure and walked away from my family's faith. Despite my parents' and grandparents' protests, I left my church and began to walk in the ways of the world. I squandered my spiritual inheritance "to enjoy the passing pleasures of sin" (Heb. 11:25).

Thankfully, neither my earthly family nor my heavenly Father gave up on me. My folks continued to love me unconditionally while upholding the godly standards of Scripture—they wouldn't allow me to bring my sinful lifestyle home. And my heavenly Father waited patiently for me to return to His family fold. It took a great deal of pain and sorrow for me to recognize my need for the powerful living God rather than relying on my own meager resources. But He welcomed me back with open arms.

My biggest regret is the years I spent wandering from God. I think of how much time I wasted learning about the world's philosophies when I could have been seeking heavenly truth. I wonder how much wiser I might be if I hadn't thought I was smarter than my parents. For a time I squandered my inheritance. Thankfully, God has restored the spiritual riches He intended for me. He has been gracious to "restore … the years that the swarming locust has eaten" (Joel 2:25). He did it for me. He can do it for you.

Lift up …

Heavenly Father, thank You for the inheritance You've prepared for me. Help me to remember how quickly earthly rewards fade away. Keep my eyes on serving and pleasing You alone. Amen.

LOOK AT ...

In the parable of the Lost Sheep we saw Jesus contrast the religious leaders' contempt toward sinners with heaven's joy over one who repents. In the parable of the Lost Coin we saw the church join with the Holy Spirit in bringing the errant sinner to repentance. In Jesus' final parable in this trilogy, the parable of the Prodigal Son, Jesus movingly demonstrates how much God the Father longs for each of us to return home, regardless of what we've done.

Notice that with each parable, the lost item increases in value. It seems that Jesus wanted to emphasize His point and reach a crescendo. These stories build in intensity with ever more complicated plotlines. It's not unusual for a sheep to go astray or for a coin to slip through the cracks. But witnessing a son willfully jumping into the abyss must have startled the audience. The father didn't lose his son at a crowded market. The boy, unlike Hansel and Gretel, did not become disoriented while hiking through a thick forest. No, this prodigal determinedly marched off into oblivion. The father could have tried to reason with his son. He could have denied the boy's demand. He could have sent servants to spy on the lad. But instead, the father allowed his son to learn a lesson the hard way, through trial and error. There are times in our children's lives when we too must let go and let God work in their hearts. Sometimes saying no only delays the inevitable. However, when we say "go," we allow our offspring to grow.

READ LUKE 15: 11–16.

Then He said: "A certain man had two sons. And the younger of them said to his father, 'Father, give me the portion of goods that falls to me.' So he divided to them his livelihood. And not many days after, the younger son gathered all together, journeyed to a far country, and there wasted his possessions with prodigal living. But when he had spent all, there arose a severe famine in that land, and he began to be in want. Then he went and joined himself to a citizen of that country, and he sent him into his fields to feed swine. And he would gladly have filled his stomach with the pods that the swine ate, and no one gave him anything." Luke 15:11–16

1. Describe the characters in this parable.

Learn about ...

2 Premature

The father likely gave the younger son two-ninths of the estate's value. Upon the father's death, the younger brother would have received one-third. Because he received his inheritance early, he could no longer lay claim to the larger amount. He lost his name and his status in the community. He was cut off and considered dead.[7]

3 Prodigal

The younger son "gathered all together" as if he didn't plan to return. Journeying to a far country indicated a desire to leave behind the life he had with his father. Augustine describes the far country as "forgetfulness of God."[8] Prodigal living is riotous behavior, extravagant spending, and fulfillment of one's lusts.

6 Pigsty

Jews were forbidden to raise swine since they were considered unclean. This once-prosperous Jewish boy had sunk as low as possible: He was reduced to feeding pigs and even longed to fill his stomach with their food—fruit from the locust or carob tree.

2. Explain what the younger son requested and how the father responded to this outrageous request.

3. What period of time passed and what three things did the younger son do when he left?

   time period:

   first:

   second:

   third:

4. What two things happened when he ran out of money?

5. From whom did the prodigal son seek help, and how did this person respond?

6. Describe the son's condition despite his employment.

7. Who do you think the younger son and the father represent in this parable and why?

Live out ...

8. Instead of waiting patiently for his full inheritance, the younger brother demanded to receive a lesser amount immediately. Do you demand short-term gratification over long-term goals? Using the words NOW and THEN, list some instances where you either demanded something meager now or waited for something better later.

N   T
O   H
W   E
             N

LEARN ABOUT …

8 Pleasure

Those who live for momentary pleasure often miss out on lasting benefits. Spending rather than saving is shortsighted. Indulging instead of dieting leads to an unhealthy lifestyle. Solomon warned, "An inheritance gained hastily at the beginning will not be blessed at the end" (Prov. 20:21).

9 Provision

The Prodigal Son suffered because he left his family and his God for a foreign land. In contrast, "there is no want to those who fear Him. The young lions lack and suffer hunger; but those who seek the LORD shall not lack any good thing" (Ps. 34:9–10).

10 Promises

You are never too far away to draw near to God. If you take one step toward God, He will come from heaven to forgive your sins. In fact, Jesus left His heavenly dwelling place and took a long journey to "seek and to save that which was lost" (Luke 19:10). The Bible promises, "Draw near to God and He will draw near to you" (James 4:8).

9. The father didn't refuse the son's request or keep him from leaving. God allows us to exercise free will—He won't stop those intent on prodigal living. According to Romans 1:28–32, how does God respond to those who reject Him, and what is the result?

10. The Prodigal Son relocated to a far-off country, leaving his family and his religion behind. Read Ephesians 2:12–13 (NIV), and fill in the phrases from the verse under the proper headings: *separate from Christ; excluded from citizenship; foreigners to the covenants of the promise; without hope; without God in the world; in Christ Jesus; once were far away; brought near; through the blood of Christ.*

FAR   **NEAR**

○ ○ ● ○ ○

Robert Robinson had been saved out of a tempestuous life of sin through George Whitefield's ministry in England. Shortly after that, at the age of twenty-three, Robinson wrote the hymn "Come, Thou Fount." The words are timeless and moving:

> Come, Thou Fount of ev'ry blessing
> Tune my heart to sing Thy praise
> Streams of mercy, never ceasing
> Call for songs of loudest praise.

Sadly, Robinson wandered far from the streams of mercy and, like the Prodigal Son, journeyed to the distant country of apostasy … even questioning whether God was a Trinity (Father, Son, and Spirit). Then one day he was traveling by stagecoach and sat beside a young woman engrossed in her book. She ran across a verse of a song she thought was beautiful and asked him what he thought of it:

> Prone to wander, Lord, I feel it
> Prone to leave the God I love
> Here's my heart, Lord, take and seal it
> Seal it for Thy courts above.

Bursting into tears, Robinson said, "Madam, I am the poor, unhappy man who wrote that hymn many years ago, and I would give a thousand worlds, if I had them, to enjoy the feelings I had then."[9] In an article concerning Robinson, Doug Kutilek said, "The pride of life and the allurement and siren song of 'intellectual' speculations loosed him from his theological moorings until he drifted far from shore, and became shipwrecked in heresy."[10]

Let's learn the lesson from this sad prodigal. We are never too far off to return home to the heavenly Father we love. There is always a longing in our hearts for not only our heavenly Father but also our heavenly home. If you have wandered into the far country, won't you turn your heart toward home?

LISTEN TO …

The moment may be temporary, but the memory is forever.

—Anonymous

DAY 4

Reality Pondered

God wants all prodigals to know that there is no place like His home. C. S. Lewis describes his experience:

> You must picture me alone in that room in Magdalen, night after night, feeling, whenever my mind lifted even for a second from my work, the steady, unrelenting approach of Him whom I so earnestly desired not to meet. That which I greatly feared had at last come upon me. In the Trinity Term of 1929 I gave in, and admitted that God was God, and knelt and prayed: perhaps, that night, the most dejected and reluctant convert in all England. I did not then see what is now the most shining and obvious thing; the Divine humility which will accept a convert even on such terms. The Prodigal Son at least walked home on his own feet. But who can duly adore the Love which will open the high gates to a prodigal who is brought in kicking, struggling, resentful, and darting his eyes in every direction for a chance of escape? … The hardness of God is kinder than the softness of men, and His compulsion is sour liberation.[11]

When C. S. Lewis pondered the reality of God being God, he surrendered his life to the heavenly Father. The Prodigal Son also had a reality check. When "he came to himself," he returned to his earthly father. Hearts follow intellect. Belief leads to behavior. Have you pondered your reality? God loves prodigals and with open arms waits for them to come home.

LIFT UP ...

Lord Jesus, thank You for lighting the way home to my heavenly Father. Help me to walk in the light and truth of Your Word rather than in the filth of this world. Amen.

LEARN ABOUT ...

5 Compassion

Compassion is a deep, visceral distress over another's pain. The father recognized his son's distress, laid aside his dignity, ran toward him with open arms, and covered him with kisses. Our heavenly Father will treat His wandering children the same way: "Love will cover a multitude of sins" (I Peter 4:8).

LOOK AT ...

In the parable of the Prodigal Son, we've seen the extent to which this son was lost. He descended to the "guttermost," landing in the mud and eating food fit for pigs. Some folks just take a long time to hit rock bottom. As with any prodigal, a number of elements factored into the boy's fall. In the first place, he was young. Some commentators speculate that he was merely a teenager. Second, he came from the country. There is speculation that the savvy city folks took advantage of his naïveté. It's likely that he knew how to manage cows but not how to manage cash, so he was careless rather than careful. Third, nature worked against him. While his stash of cash dwindled, a famine developed. He had no place else to turn. Sometimes God will allow us to fall so low that there is no place else for us to look except up. And when we do, we find that God was there all the time, watching and waiting for us to take His hand. Today we'll discover how the prodigal found his way back home to his faithful father.

READ LUKE 15:17–24.

"But when he came to himself, he said, 'How many of my father's hired servants have bread enough and to spare, and I perish with hunger! I will arise and go to my father, and will say to him, "Father, I have sinned against heaven and before you, and I am no longer worthy to be called your son. Make me like one of your hired servants."' And he arose and came to his father. But when he was still a great way off, his father saw him and had compassion, and ran and fell on his neck and kissed him. And the son said to him, 'Father, I have sinned against heaven and in your sight, and am no longer worthy to be called your son.' But the father said to his servants, 'Bring out the best robe and put it on him, and put a ring on his hand and sandals on his feet. And bring the fatted calf here and kill it, and let us eat and be merry; for this my son was dead and is alive again; he was lost and is found.' And they began to be merry." Luke 15:17–24

1. Describe the mental state the son reached and how he arrived there.

2. With whom did he compare himself and in what ways?

3. Describe:

   what action the son decided to take

   what he would confess

   what he would request

4. a. Next, the Prodigal Son headed home. Where was he when his father saw him?

   b. What does this tell you about the father?

5. Describe in detail the father's response to his son's return.

6. The father and son had an amazing exchange.

   a. In your own words, what did the son confess?

   b. How did the father cover the son's sins?

   c. How did the father provide for his son's needs?

   d. Make a spiritual application: How does this resemble your relationship with your heavenly Father?

7. How did the father describe his son?

LEARN ABOUT ...

6 Community

The father wanted to publicly reconcile his son to his community, so he gave him the best robe reserved for honored guests. The ring signified authority, and the sandals were a symbol of status—only the poor and slaves went barefoot. A fatted calf was reserved for important celebrations.[12] Truly, the prodigal was welcomed home.

7 Conversion

The son had figuratively returned from the dead because he had been given up as lost to his family. Now he was alive, revived, or returned to life. Spiritually, those who repent of sin are truly born again. Scripture teaches us to "offer yourselves to God, as those who have been brought from death to life" (Rom. 6:13 NIV).

8 Common Sense

Many have described the idea of the Prodigal Son leaving his father and rebelling against God as a kind of madness. The phrase "he came to himself" indicates not only that he repented but also that his mental faculties were restored. When you come to your senses, you will quickly return to your God.

---

9 Constant

The father was waiting and watching for his son "while he was still a great way off." Similarly, "the eyes of the Lord search back and forth across the whole earth, looking for people whose hearts are perfect toward him, so that he can show his great power in helping them" (2 Chron. 16:9 TLB).

LIVE OUT ...

8. When the Prodigal Son "came to himself," he had a change of mind—from warped to worshipful thinking. Using the "call outs" provided, (a) write one of your warped thoughts in the left box, and (b) write how you changed your thoughts to worshipful ideas in the right box.

9. When the Prodigal Son decided to leave the pigsty and return home, his father compassionately ran toward him.

    a. Describe a time when God ran toward you even though you deserved to be cut off.

    b. Read Psalm 103:13–14, and explain how His compassion comforts you.

10. The father rejoiced over the return of his son, who'd been given up as dead. As God's children, we've been revived from the dead. Read Ephesians 2:1–5 and Colossians 2:13–14; then explain how this is possible.

○ ○ ● ○ ○

In his book, *God, in My Disbelief,* J. W. Stevenson tells how Dr. Christopher, an old minister, had gone south to London to seek for his son who had left home and dishonored his father and mother. There was no address to guide him. After many days the old, white-haired minister discovered the name of the street. He stood at one end and realized he could never go from door to door because of its great length. Just then a street musician came by. Dr. Christopher asked him to play one of his son's favorite tunes from childhood. So they went slowly, the street musician and the old minister. The compassionate father held his hat in his hand so that his face could be seen. This was the last slender chance to find the son who had no use for him, seeking him who had no understanding of the love in his father's heart.[13]

We've all been prodigals at one time or another. But the moment we realize "there's no place like home," our heavenly Father comes running to meet us. He longs to smother us with kisses, clothe us with honor, and celebrate our status as His child: "My heart yearns for him; I will surely have mercy on him, says the LORD" (Jer. 31:20). If you're still wandering around a foreign land, what are you waiting for? Run home to Daddy—He's watching and waiting for you.

LISTEN TO ...

Like the father of the Prodigal Son, God can see repentance coming a great way off and is there to meet it; the repentance is the reconciliation.

—Dorothy L. Sayers

DAY 5

Begrudgingly Honored

After the Sunday school teacher told the story of the Prodigal Son to the class, she asked, "Was anyone sorry when the Prodigal Son returned?" One boy answered, "The fatted calf."[14] However, there was someone else who had a hard time with the prodigal's homecoming—the older sibling.

The parable of the Prodigal Son could have ended with a celebration. But it did not, because this father had two prodigals—one who had strayed from home and the other who had strayed from his father's heart. By refusing to enter the home, the elder son broke with cultural customs. As the firstborn, he was expected to assume the role of host upon arriving home. His absence was a personal affront to the father. This jealous man saw himself as a servant rather than a son, saying, "These many years I have been serving you; I never transgressed your commandment."

The kind father had gone out to meet the son from a far country, and now he went out to meet the son who was so close and yet so far away. He treated them both equally. The younger had come home, and now the father pleaded for the older son to come inside the house to join the celebration.

Perhaps you have never strayed far away from God's house. But have you ever wandered from His heart? Do you dishonor Him with railing accusations? If so, He will run out to meet you and invite you to enter into the joy of the Lord: "In Your presence is fullness of joy; at Your right hand are pleasures forevermore" (Ps. 16:11).

LIFT UP ...

Lord, please remind me how much mercy I've received from Your good hand. Help me to show that same mercy to others as I walk through this world. Amen.

LOOK AT ...

Yesterday's lesson illustrates another difference between the first two parables and the last: The father did not seek his son to save him. The shepherd combed the countryside, searching for his lost sheep. The woman swept her home clean, looking for a lost coin. Yet this father stayed home. However, out of sight was not out of mind for this man. He watched and waited for his son to repent and return. One day his prayers were answered as his son appeared on the horizon. And more than his heart leaped as the man bolted from his lookout. He laid aside all dignity to run barefoot to embrace the boy. In ancient Near Eastern cultures, a wealthy landowner who ran demonstrated a lack of self-respect. The father literally ran the gauntlet of ridicule and reason to greet his prodigal. Recognizing that this earthly father represents our heavenly Father is a humbling realization. Jesus implied that God runs toward sinners with open arms and a tender heart. If you have strayed from the Savior, isn't it time to return to Him with reckless abandon? He'll run to meet you.

Although we witnessed a joyous celebration upon the prodigal's return, not everyone rejoiced. Today we'll see how Jesus used the older son to reveal the hardness of the religious leaders' hearts.

READ LUKE 15:25–32.

"Now his older son was in the field. And as he came and drew near to the house, he heard music and dancing. So he called one of the servants and asked what these things meant. And he said to him, 'Your brother has come, and because he has received him safe and sound, your father has killed the fatted calf.' But he was angry and would not go in. Therefore his father came out and pleaded with him. So he answered and said to his father, 'Lo, these many years I have been serving you; I never transgressed your commandment at any time; and yet you never gave me a young goat, that I might make merry with my friends. But as soon as this son of yours came, who has devoured your livelihood with harlots, you killed the fatted calf for him.' And he said to him, 'Son, you are always with me, and all that I have is yours. It was right that we should make merry and be glad, for your brother was dead and is alive again, and was lost and is found.'"
Luke 15:25–32

1. Explain where the older son was, what he heard when he got home, and what he did in response.

2. Summarize the servant's explanation.

3. Describe the older son's response.

4. What two things did his father do?

5. How did the older son commend himself and complain against his father?

6. What disrespectful title did he give his brother, and what accusation did he make?

7. How did the father both reassure and rebuke his older son?

LIVE OUT ...

8. Blind to his own sin, the older son lacked forgiveness and mercy for his brother. Think of someone to whom you have difficulty showing mercy. Use your Bible concordance to find a verse about forgiveness or mercy. How will you change your attitude or behavior based on this verse?

9. a. The older son stayed close to home, but he had a prodigal heart. He assumed the worst about his brother and focused on his history rather than on his repentant heart. Which of the following usually shape your opinions of others?

❒ Clothes/ House/Car   ❒ Education/ Profession   ❒ Cultural background

❒ Personality   ❒ Church affiliation   ❒ Other (name it)

b. Journal a prayer asking God to help you believe the best about your brothers and sisters in Christ. Commit to obey

Philippians 4:8: "Fix your thoughts on what is true and good and right. Think about things that are pure and lovely, and dwell on the fine, good things in others. Think about all you can praise God for and be glad about" (TLB).

10. How does Jesus' example encourage you to treat those who are wandering or lost?

LEARN ABOUT ...

8 Parallel

The older son's behavior parallels the behavior of the religious leaders of Christ's day: Both were angered when sinners received unmerited favor. In each case, the destiny of the sinner's soul—which matters most to God—was the least of their concern. Jesus rebuked people like this: "You have a reputation of being alive, but you are dead" (Rev. 3:1 NIV).

○ ○ ● ○ ○

Dwight L. Moody once told the fable of an eagle who was envious of another that could fly better than he could. One day the bird saw a sportsman with a bow and arrow and said to him, "I wish you would bring down that eagle up there." The man said he would if he had some feathers for his arrow. So the jealous eagle pulled one out of his wing. The arrow was shot, but it didn't quite reach the rival bird because he was flying too high. The first eagle pulled out another feather, then another—until finally he had lost so many feathers that he himself couldn't fly. The archer took advantage of the situation, turned around, and killed the helpless bird. Moody made this application: If you are envious of others, the one you will hurt the most by your actions will be yourself.[15]

The older son had complete access to his father's wealth, but he was envious because he had never received a goat or a party like his younger brother. The Pharisees and scribes were given the riches of God, but when their promised Messiah came, they complained about Him. And so when Jesus was turned over to the Romans, His beard was plucked out and His heart pierced through. They succeeded in shooting down the Son of Righteousness. But when Christ rose from the dead, the actions of the religious leaders would come back to bite them.

Envy chokes out compassion and mercy. All of God's riches belong to those of us who've been found. Let's joyfully share the wealth!

LISTEN TO ...

In jealousy there is more self-love than love.

—*François, Duc de La Rochefoucauld*

Good Things Come to Those Who Wait

Mark 13:1–37

All of us have probably taken a bite of fruit that hasn't had a chance to ripen. What's the result? You probably spit the sour morsel out. Let's face it, underripened fruit is disappointing. But good things come to those who wait. The taste of ripe fruit is sweet and juicy.

How can you tell when fruit is ripe? As fruit ripens, it goes from hard, sour, and inedible to brilliant colored, sweet, juicy, and aromatic. Here are some indicators of ripeness:

Color: Some fruits reveal ripeness through color. As the acidity changes, the green chlorophyll breaks down. Bananas, apples, and tomatoes have bright colors underneath the chlorophyll layer. Berries become a deeper, more intense red as they ripen.

Aroma: Scent hints strongly at flavor. Most melons change chemically when ripening, causing a sensuous, luscious scent.

Feel: As fruits ripen, the substances that hold the cells together break down, making them softer. Squeeze a plum, avocado, or pear. If it's rock hard, it isn't ripe.

Weight: It generally means that the fruit is fully mature, which leads to ripeness. A heavy tomato or grapefruit, for example, is usually a good one.[1]

In this parable we see Jesus examining His fig tree—Israel. He knows exactly the right time to pluck His people, the church, from this planet. Like fruit, the world has indicators to reveal ripeness: False christs, rumors of war, famine, and frequent earthquakes are a few key signs. The good One will come to those who are waiting for His return!

Day 1: Mark 13:1–4   QUESTIONS ASKED
Day 2: Mark 13:5–13   SIGNS AND WARNINGS
Day 3: Mark 13:14–23   COMING CRISIS
Day 4: Mark 13:24–27   SECOND COMING
Day 5: Mark 13:28–37   WATCH AND WORK

DAY 1
Questions Asked

LIFT UP ...

Father, I have so many questions. Thank You for Your patience in listening to me and answering with compassion and understanding. Amen.

LOOK AT ...

Our text this week comes from the book of Mark. It is taken from the famous Olivet Discourse that Jesus gave from the Mount of Olives before His crucifixion. Here Jesus responded to His disciples' questions concerning the fate of the temple. The disciples believed that the temple would be destroyed and that Messiah would immediately appear. They did not understand that there would be a period of time between Christ's two appearances. This event, recorded in Matthew, Mark, and Luke, answered two questions: (1) "When will these things be?" and (2) "What will be the sign of Christ's return?" Jesus answered that His followers must "take heed."

The temple was indeed destroyed in AD 70. But this did not bring Christ's second coming. There are other signs of His return, as we will see in this week's lesson. The parable of the Fig Tree was primarily intended for the people of Israel, to warn them of the dangers of rejecting their Messiah. But it also has relevance for us today. We too must take heed. We are living in the signs of the times. Are you ready for Christ's return?

READ MARK 13:1–4.

Then as He went out of the temple, one of His disciples said to Him, "Teacher, see what manner of stones and what buildings are here!" And Jesus answered and said to him, "Do you see these great buildings? Not one stone shall be left upon another, that shall not be thrown down." Now as He sat on the Mount of Olives opposite the temple, Peter, James, John, and Andrew

LEARN ABOUT ...

1 Gladness

While He was teaching and answering questions, Jesus exposed the hypocrisy and incompetence of the religious leaders entrusted with the temple. Christ's coming had been the hope of Judaism since its inception. While the common people "heard Him gladly," these leaders didn't recognize that their Messiah had already come.

3 Gold

About forty years later, in AD 70, the Romans terrorized Jerusalem, killed a million Jews, and demolished the temple. The heat from the flames melted the golden rim of the temple. The Roman soldiers overturned the stones to get to the gold that had run between the cracks, thus fulfilling the words Jesus had spoken.

4 Gloominess

Jesus and His disciples crossed the Kidron Valley (*Kidron* means gloomy) to the Mount of Olives. The mount stands directly opposite the temple and offers a panoramic view of Jerusalem. From here, Jesus foretold future events. This speech is known as the Olivet Discourse.

asked Him privately, "Tell us, when will these things be? And what will be the sign when all these things will be fulfilled?" Mark 13:1–4

1. Skim Mark 12:35–40. Where was Jesus, and what was He doing?

2. As He left the temple, how did one of the disciples address Jesus, and what did he point out to Jesus?

3. Jesus often answered a question with a question. Recount His question and answer.

4. Where did Jesus go next, and who accompanied Him?

5. It seems the disciples assumed that Jesus would imminently usher in the kingdom. What two questions did they ask in reference to this?

6. Matthew remembered different details about this incident. Compare and contrast the conversations in Matthew 24:3 and Mark 13:4.

LIVE OUT ...

7. The disciples revered the temple because it was considered the dwelling place of God. When we surrender our lives to Jesus, *we* become the temple of the Holy Spirit, the very place where God lives. Mark the boxes below that indicate how you care for the place God calls home—your spirit.

   ❏ Food: I'm fed daily by His Word.
   ❏ Water: I drink from the Living Water—Jesus.
   ❏ Rest: I rest in the Lord.
   ❏ Exercise: I exercise my spiritual gifts.

8. Perform an honest appraisal of God's temple based on your answers to question 7.

   a. Which of the above, if any, are lacking in your life?

   b. How and why do you neglect those areas?

   c. Journal a commitment to diligently maintain God's temple.

9. Paul says, "If anyone defiles the temple of God, God will destroy him. For the temple of God is holy, which temple you are" (1 Cor. 3:17). *Defile* means to spoil, corrupt, or decay.

   a. Are you allowing anything to defile your temple? If so, what?

   b. Journal a prayer asking for God's forgiveness. Ask Him to empty you of rubbish and fill you to overflowing with His Holy Spirit.

∘ ∘ ● ∘ ∘

One thing that impressed me (Lenya) about Skip Heitzig when I met him was his casual attitude toward material possessions. One day we left a restaurant to discover that someone had dented his pickup truck. Instead of an outburst of anger, words of perspective and praise poured out: "It's all going to burn anyway. Thank God, He's provided transportation."

We've been married for nearly twenty-five years, and Skip still has a light touch on the things of this world. Just before we left New Mexico for California, we had built our dream house in the foothills of the Sandia Mountains. It was a secluded sanctuary on five wooded acres with three porches overlooking the wilderness. Skip's office was a pastor's dream: perched on the third floor with inspiring views, bottom-to-top

LEARN ABOUT …

6 Grace Period

The disciples were familiar with Zechariah 14, which predicted the day of the Lord, when Messiah would defeat Israel's enemies and establish an earthly kingdom. Because their perspective was limited, they weren't aware that there would be a period of time between the destruction of the temple and the end of the age.

7 Gold Plated

The temple was a magnificent structure. The stones weighed four hundred tons, measured forty-five feet in length, and were cut by hand. Made of white marble, the eastern wall was gold plated and visible from miles away. But that temple does not compare to the human body, which is "fearfully and wonderfully made" (Ps. 139:14).

8 God Filled

The builders spared no expense in building the temple in Jerusalem. Similarly, God spared no expense when He built His temple inside you: "Your body is a temple of the Holy Spirit, who is in you.… You are not your own; you were bought at a price. Therefore honor God with your body" (1 Cor. 6:19–20 NIV).

built-in bookcases and a library ladder, a fireplace, and vaulted ceilings. But when God said, "Go," Skip willingly let go.

The disciples were amazed at the brilliance of the temple, but Jesus predicted that it would be torn down. Just as He said, it was burned to the ground, and no stone was left on top of another.

Like the disciples, we get distracted by the temporary objects in our lives. We forget that our earthly possessions will eventually burn: "But the day of the Lord will come as a thief in the night, in which the heavens will pass away with a great noise, and the elements will melt with fervent heat; both the earth and the works that are in it will be burned up" (2 Peter 3:10). Let's not get too attached to the temporal—even our physical bodies. Jesus teaches us to have an eternal perspective. Only what we do in our physical bodies for His glory will last forever.

LISTEN TO ...

Wherever souls are being tried and ripened, in whatever commonplace and homely way, there God is hewing out the pillars for his temple.

—*Phillips Brooks*

DAY 2
Signs and Warnings

When I (Penny) was a little girl, I heard about the signs of Christ's second coming. I remember hearing sermons about the things that would indicate when the time would be near. For instance, I knew that Joel prophesied, "The sun shall be turned into darkness, and the moon into blood" (Joel 2:31). I can remember watching in fascination in autumn as the full moon changed colors over the cottonfields of Texas. I'd wonder aloud, "Is now the time? Will Jesus come tonight?" But my grandmother, who was a very wise woman, would say, "No, dear, that's just the orange light of the harvest moon. It happens every year at this time." Then we'd sing, "Shine On, Harvest Moon." She didn't try to explain the church age or the rapture. She knew one day I'd understand.

As I grew up, I became more and more fascinated with prophecy. I still long for Christ's return. I know that believers in every generation have seen signs that could indicate His return. And that's a good thing—we should all long to see Christ return for His church.

As we'll learn today, when He does return, the signs and warnings will come closer and closer like the birth pangs of a laboring woman. The things predicted throughout Scripture will be crystal clear to those who have studied God's Word. The Bible is a road map of the things to come, telling us what will come in the physical world, the political world, and the spiritual world. When, like my grandmother, you know the signs of the times, you can discern whether you are living in the times of the signs.

LIFT UP ...

Father, please help me to be spiritually aware and not deceived. Though there may be signs and warnings, I put my trust in You. Amen.

LOOK AT ...

We left the disciples asking Jesus, "When will these things be?" Jesus answered by revealing the signs preceding the coming tribulation. He was not referring to the everyday trials and tribulations we have as believers in Christ. Rather, He was speaking of a time in the

LEARN ABOUT ...

2 False Prophets

False messiahs and false prophets have always been around. In the past century, more than 1,100 people of national notoriety have publicly proclaimed to be the messiah.[2] One sign of the end times is people claiming to be the messiah: "Many antichrists have come, by which we know that it is the last hour" (1 John 2:18).

future when there will be intense suffering and persecution. He began by warning Christ's followers of spiritual deceivers. It's very important to check God's Word to make sure that what people say aligns with God's Word. But Christ warned that in the end times, deception will increase just as the birth pains of a woman in labor increase. In a parenthetical comment, Jesus warned the disciples that they would be brought before authorities for their faith in Christ. This prophecy proved true, as we read in the accounts of the persecution of Christ's disciples in the book of Acts.

We can take comfort in knowing that Christ's words are true. His comfort will sustain us through any tribulation. His disciples never wavered in their faith. When hard times come, He'll make sure that you don't either.

READ MARK 13:5–13.

And Jesus, answering them, began to say: "Take heed that no one deceives you. For many will come in My name, saying, 'I am He,' and will deceive many. But when you hear of wars and rumors of wars, do not be troubled; for such things must happen, but the end is not yet. For nation will rise against nation, and kingdom against kingdom. And there will be earthquakes in various places, and there will be famines and troubles. These are the beginnings of sorrows. But watch out for yourselves, for they will deliver you up to councils, and you will be beaten in the synagogues. You will be brought before rulers and kings for My sake, for a testimony to them. And the gospel must first be preached to all the nations. But when they arrest you and deliver you up, do not worry beforehand, or premeditate what you will speak. But whatever is given you in that hour, speak that; for it is not you who speak, but the Holy Spirit. Now brother will betray brother to death, and a father his child; and children will rise up against parents and cause them to be put to death. And you will be hated by all for My name's sake. But he who endures to the end shall be saved." Mark 13:5–13

1. What did Jesus warn against?

2. Explain in your own words the form and amount of deception.

3. Explain what Jesus instructed the disciples *not* to do.

4. Jesus described many signs that will precede the end of the age.

    a. Describe the signs.

    b. What did these signs indicate?

5. a. What did Jesus warn His disciples to do?

    b. Why? What would this ultimately accomplish?

6. Jesus predicted His disciples would be arrested and required to testify before the authorities.

    a. What two things did He command them not to do?

    b. How did He tell them to prepare for their trials?

7. Jesus' prophecy was multifaceted, describing the chaos prior to Jerusalem's fall (AD 66–70), the chaos all believers face, and the future tribulation period.

    a. Describe the lack of family loyalty during these times.

    b. Why will believers be hated?

    c. Explain the ultimate end for those who remain faithful to God.

LEARN ABOUT ...

4 Birth Pangs

Sorrows is translated *birth pangs* in the NIV. While the signs have always been evident, when they become more frequent and intense like childbirth, we know Christ's second coming is near: "Behold, He is coming with clouds, and every eye will see Him, even they who pierced Him" (Rev. 1:7).

5 Persecution

The councils were local Jewish courts that met in the synagogues. They punished lawbreakers by stripping them to the waist and beating them on the chest and back thirty-nine times.[3] History confirms that each of the disciples was persecuted for his allegiance to the gospel of Christ.

6 Fulfillment

Prophecy often has a dual fulfillment. Jesus' disciples were indeed subjected to the persecution He described. But those who proclaim their faith in Him during the tribulation period will also suffer similar persecution. God promises that His Spirit will speak in these circumstances; believers need not be anxious or plan what to say.

8 Ravenous Wolves

False prophets don't come with labels—instead they "come to you in sheep's clothing, but inwardly they are ravenous wolves" (Matt. 7:15). God's Word and His indwelling Holy Spirit enable us to recognize those on the wrong path who are determined to take us with them. The more familiar we are with the truth, the easier it is to recognize a lie.

---

9 To the End

Jesus said to "endure," which means to bear up under a load of misery. "To the end" means completely or to the limit. Those who persevere in faith regardless of circumstances will see the salvation of God. Those who are Christ's demonstrate their salvation by standing firm until the end.

LIVE OUT ...

8. Can you identify a false prophet? Match the Scriptures with the corresponding qualities *lacking* in a false prophet (because we will know them by what they are *not*).

    a. Godly characteristics   ___ Matthew 7:17–20

    b. Sound doctrine   ___ 2 John 1:9

    c. Good fruit   ___ Galatians 5:22–23

9. Jesus said that His coming would be preceded by increasing signs or sorrows. Do you think these signs are intensifying, or do you think things are as they always have been? Please elaborate.

10. a. In contrast to false christs, Jesus Christ is "the Alpha and the Omega, the Beginning and the End ... who is and who was and who is to come, the Almighty" (Rev. 1:8). One name Jesus identified with in Scripture was "I AM." Use the chart below to record the phrases describing Jesus.

SCRIPTURE	"I AM" ...
John 6:48	
John 8:12	
John 10:11	
John 11:25	
John 14:6	

    b. Which "I AM" do you particularly need Jesus to be for you today? Why?

· ∘ ● ∘ ·

"It's going to get worse before it gets better," said Richard Staar in 1986. An international studies director at the Hoover Institution of War, Revolution and Peace in Palo Alto, California, Staar went on to say, "There are more wars with more people killed all over the world than ten years ago."

Though it's been almost sixty years since the world's major powers last bombed and shelled each other, on any given day soldiers are firing in as many as thirty to forty nations. Wars of liberation. Territorial disputes. Wars over religious principles. The United States is currently engaged in what has been called The War on Terrorism. "One man's freedom fighter is another's terrorist," the saying goes, but the common denominator is death. In war, people die. The Center for Defense Information estimates the number killed since the early 1970s in the millions. While body counts vary and are hard to confirm, most participants in conflict agree peace is unlikely. The bottom line is that billions—yes, billions—of people live in lands enduring armed conflict. What's ahead? Staar concurs with Jesus: "Regional conflict will increase."[4]

When the world seems to be spinning into violence—terrorist attacks and armed conflict—we can take comfort in knowing that "God reigns over the nations; God sits on His holy throne" (Ps. 47:8). He is holy, His Word is true, and His promises are fulfilled. While others will come claiming to be Christ, we must keep our eyes looking to the great "I AM" revealed in the living Word—the Bible.

LISTEN TO …

I hope that the day is near at hand when the advent of the great God will appear, for all things everywhere are boiling, burning, moving, falling, sinking, groaning.

—*Martin Luther*

DAY 3

Coming Crisis

It happened again! A mountain in Mexico that had lain dormant for a very long time suddenly came alive. It erupted with so much power that it became the world's largest active volcano. The 4,000-foot El Chichon giant had been quiet for hundreds of years before its explosive reawakening. Prior to 1982 it was thought to be extinct. Consequently, the volcano was not being monitored, and the eruption was a total surprise. (However, with hindsight, local inhabitants had noticed increased earthquake activity for some months before the first eruption.) As a result, villages within a seven-kilometer radius were destroyed, and more than two thousand people were killed.[5]

It was a reminder of Mount St. Helens, which broke its long silence in 1980, when it transformed its majestic snow-covered peak and placid Spirit Lake into dust and vapor. In each case, the disruption and devastation were unexpected. People near the mountains lived in complacency, never anticipating such drastic changes.

Another crisis is coming that will take much of the world by surprise. However, if those on planet Earth notice the signs of the times, they will be prepared. Today's lesson teaches that if you're truly wise, you'll keep your eyes on Israel. Daniel and Jesus both prophesied about "the abomination of desolation" that would be seen in the temple. Biblical scholars say this foretold first Antiochus Epiphanes' sacrificing a pig in the temple in 168 BC and ultimately the Antichrist, who will set up an idol in the as-yet-to-be restored temple at Jerusalem. When this happens, the inhabitants of Judea are told to flee to the mountains.

LIFT UP ...

Thank You, Father, for being my strong tower and refuge in times of trouble. Amen.

LOOK AT ...

We've learned that false prophets, war, chaos, and persecution will abound in the latter days. Now we are hurtled further into the future to see a short period of intense suffering and persecution, especially for the Jewish people, preceding the second coming of Christ and the end of the age. In this portion of Scripture Jesus points to the midpoint of the tribulation period when a world dictator establishes himself as the object of worship (see 2 Thess. 2:3–4). This, of course, implies that the temple in Jerusalem will be rebuilt. We know that this has not yet occurred, but there are people who are busy making preparations to rebuild the temple. Jesus especially warned the people living in Judea to watch out for this world leader. Thankfully, Jesus prophesied many of these things ahead of time so that when they occur we will be ready. He does not tell us so we will be afraid but so we will be prepared.

READ MARK 13:14–23.

LEARN ABOUT ...

I Abomination

The "abomination of desolation" refers to someone or something that detracts from worship of the one true God, causing the temple to be abandoned and left desolate.[6] Daniel prophesied that "they shall take away the daily sacrifices, and place there the abomination of desolation" (Dan. 11:31).

"So when you see the 'abomination of desolation,' spoken of by Daniel the prophet, standing where it ought not" (let the reader understand), *"then let those who are in Judea flee to the mountains. Let him who is on the housetop not go down into the house, nor enter to take anything out of his house. And let him who is in the field not go back to get his clothes. But woe to those who are pregnant and to those who are nursing babies in those days! And pray that your flight may not be in winter. For in those days there will be tribulation, such as has not been since the beginning of the creation which God created until this time, nor ever shall be. And unless the Lord had shortened those days, no flesh would be saved; but for the elect's sake, whom He chose, He shortened the days. Then if anyone says to you, 'Look, here is the Christ!' or, 'Look, He is there!' do not believe it. For false christs and false prophets will rise and show signs and wonders to deceive, if possible, even the elect. But take heed; see, I have told you all things beforehand."* Mark 13:14–23

1. a. Describe the specific sign Jesus warned the Jews to watch for as He continued His warning about the future.

   b. What were they to do when they saw it?

Learn about ...

4 Tribulation

Tribulation means pressure, affliction, or distress. The tribulation period corresponds to Daniel's seventieth week (see Dan. 9:24–27) and will last seven years. At its midpoint, the Antichrist will declare himself worthy of worship in the temple and severely persecute the Jews and believers in Jesus Christ who refuse to acknowledge him.

---

5 Termination

Shortened means to abridge. God will terminate the great tribulation after a set number of days. "The elect" refers to Jews and Gentiles who believe and are converted during this time. "Man's days are determined; you have decreed the number of his months and have set limits he cannot exceed" (Job 14:5 NIV).

2. Read Matthew 24:15. Where, specifically, will the abomination of desolation stand?

3. The need to flee will be urgent. Summarize the specific admonitions Jesus gave.

   a. What should the people not do?

   b. Who will this be especially hard on?

   c. What should the people do?

4. Describe the severity of those days. What hint do you have that this prophecy has not yet been fulfilled?

5. a. Describe how God will show His mercy during the great tribulation.

   b. Why will He be merciful?

6. When people say Christ is here or there, they are not to be believed.

   a. How does news of these false messiahs spread?

   b. What will they do to convince the elect?

   c. How should those experiencing the tribulation respond?

LIVE OUT ...

7. During the tribulation, the Antichrist will stand in the temple and demand worship. True believers desire to worship the one true God. Why is God worthy of your worship?

8. a. Describe a time when you allowed someone or something to stand in God's place in your life and receive the worship only He deserves.

   b. Journal a prayer of confession and repentance for the sin of allowing abominable things on the altar of your heart.

9. Jesus commanded His followers to pray. God talks to us through His Holy Spirit and His Word, and we in turn speak to Him in trustful, believing prayer. Fill in the blanks below to discover ways to pray.

   1 Thessalonians 5:17   Pray _____.
   1 Timothy 2:8   Pray _____.
   James 5:16   Pray _____.

LEARN ABOUT ...

7 Devotion

The word *worship* is derived from an older word: *worthship*. It signifies the worthiness of the one receiving the special honor or devotion. Jesus is worth our praise and thanksgiving because He redeemed us and saved us from our sins: "All the earth shall worship You and sing praises to You" (Ps. 66:4).

8 Deception

False christs and false prophets will claim to speak in Christ's name in an attempt to lead the elect from their places of refuge. Satan will inspire counterfeit miracles in support of their claim to being the true Christ. Thankfully, God's Word and God's Spirit can help us recognize Satan's deception.

○ ○ ● ○ ○

"May it be Thy will that the temple be speedily rebuilt in our days." This plea to God, recited three times a day in Jewish prayers, expresses a yearning that makes Jerusalem's Temple Mount one of the most volatile thirty-five acres on earth.

Two talmudic schools located near the western (wailing) wall are teaching nearly two hundred students the elaborate details of Temple service. Other groups are researching the family lines of Jewish priests who may conduct sacrifices. There are conventions for those who believe themselves to be of priestly descent. Former Chief Rabbi Shlomo Goren, who heads another Temple Mount organization, believes his research has fixed the location of the ancient Holy of Holies so that Jews can enter the Mount without committing sacrilege. He insists, "I cannot leave this world without assuring that Jews will once again pray on the Mount."[7]

It's hard to imagine the events that will take place during the great tribulation. The good news is that you can view the events from a bird's-eye view—those who believe now will not walk through the great tribulation then.

What will you do with the information you have studied today? Will you tuck it away? Or will you share your knowledge and understanding of Scripture and tell someone about Jesus Christ? When we were in Israel, I (Penny) warned our unbelieving tour guide about the coming abomination of desolation on the Temple Mount. She had heard of Antiochus Epiphanes, but she had never heard Christ's prophecy that the Antichrist would again reinstate the abomination. I pray she comes to faith before the tribulation. If not, I know I have told her things beforehand so she can "take heed."

Listen to ...

When you from Sodom flee, the judgment to escape, Salvation will depend on never looking back.

—Angelus Silesius

DAY 4

Second Coming

On an expedition to the Antarctic, Sir Ernest Shackleton was forced to leave some of his men on Elephant Island. He intended to return but was unavoidably delayed. When he finally set out, the water had frozen, and he was cut off from those he had left behind. Three times he tried to reach them but was blocked by the unyielding frozen sea. Finally, he located a narrow channel through the ice. Guiding the vessel to the island, he was overjoyed to find his men alive and well.

His men had their belongings packed and were ready to get on board, so they soon set sail for home. When they were out of dangerous waters, Shackleton asked why the men could leave on a moment's notice. They told him that every morning, the leader rolled up his sleeping bag and shouted, "Get your things together, boys. The boss may come today."[8]

As believers we want to be ready when Christ comes. Better to be ready for the rapture than endure the tribulation. On God's divine timeline, the rapture will occur *prior* to the great tribulation when "the Lord Himself will descend from heaven with a shout.… Then we who are alive and remain shall be caught up together with them in the clouds to meet the Lord in the air" (1 Thess. 4:16–17). At His second coming, He *will* come to earth, along with the church, to battle the Antichrist and save Israel from destruction at the battle of Armageddon. If Christ called today, would you be ready to go?

LIFT UP …

Lord, I can't wait to see You face-to-face. Thank You for the hope that You are coming again. Without that hope, we would be the most miserable of all people. Amen.

LOOK AT …

Yesterday we read Jesus' detailed description of events leading up to His second coming. Today we see that Jesus, the Son of Man, will return in glory to stop the evil and save His people. It has been prophesied that there will be 144,000 Jews who come to saving faith during the tribulation (see Rev. 14:1). Many of these will be martyred by the world

LEARN ABOUT ...

2 Worship

Jesus' coming in the clouds
will bring one response
from all who see Him—
worship. "At the name of
Jesus every knee [will] bow,
of those in heaven, and of
those on earth, and of those
under the earth, and ...
every tongue [will] confess
that Jesus Christ is Lord,
to the glory of God the
Father" (Phil. 2:10–11).

3 Worthy

Jesus' favorite title for Himself
was the Son of Man. This
title essentially means
"the Man" and portrays
His humility: "Being in very
nature God, [He] did not
consider equality with God
something to be grasped
... [but] humbled himself
and became obedient to
death—even death on a
cross!" (Phil. 2:6, 8 NIV).

5 The Winds

God's angels will gather
unbelievers for judgment
and believers for glory.
From the four winds means
from all directions, north,
south, east, and west.
"At the Second Coming
of Christ no child of God
will be left unresurrected
or unrestored, but all will
share in the millennial
kingdom."[9]

leader known as the Antichrist. Many Christians believe that the church will have been raptured, or taken *off* the earth, before the tribulation. First Thessalonians 4:16–17 says that "the Lord Himself will descend from heaven with a shout, with the voice of an archangel, and with the trumpet of God. And the dead in Christ will rise first. Then we who are alive and remain shall be caught up together with them in the clouds to meet the Lord in the air." At the second coming, believers will come *with* Christ to the earth: "The armies in heaven, clothed in fine linen, white and clean, followed Him [Jesus] on white horses" (Rev. 19:14). Where will you be when Christ returns?

READ MARK 13:24–27.

"But in those days, after that tribulation, the sun will be darkened, and the moon will not give its light; the stars of heaven will fall, and the powers in the heavens will be shaken. Then they will see the Son of Man coming in the clouds with great power and glory. And then He will send His angels, and gather together His elect from the four winds, from the farthest part of earth to the farthest part of heaven." Mark 13:24–27

1. Describe how the heavens will be affected by the Son of Man's coming.

2. Explain what happens next and who will see it.

3. Why do you think Jesus called Himself "Son of Man" at this point in time? By what other names could He have appropriately self-identified?

4. Who will accompany Jesus, and what will they do?

5. To what lengths will Jesus go to gather His elect?

LIVE OUT ...

6. Jesus often referred to Himself as the Son of Man. He has over seven hundred other names in Scripture. Read the verses in the chart below, and record some of Jesus' other names.

SCRIPTURE	JESUS' NAMES
John 1:1	
John 1:14	
John 4:25–26	

7. a. Which of Jesus' names means the most to you and why?

   b. Journal a prayer of thanksgiving to the Son of Man. In your prayer use the name you chose and praise Him! "O LORD, our Lord, how excellent is Your name in all the earth!" (Ps. 8:9).

8. Read Acts 1:9, and compare Jesus' departure from earth with His return.

○ ○ ● ○ ○

Roy W. Gustafson once noted that in southern England there is a village with the curious name of Tiptoe. It seemed natural to call it by that name because years ago before paved streets and sidewalks were installed, the muddy condition of the lanes in that area often made it necessary for the people to walk on tiptoe. Gustafson said, "The child of God who walks the streets of this life faces a similar situation. He is to go forward on the tiptoe of expectancy, not only because of his evil surroundings, but also because he is waiting for Someone who is coming very soon!"[10]

Jesus described His second coming and detailed the supernatural events that will occur. He specifically answered the questions asked by

LEARN ABOUT ...

7 Wonderful

One of Jesus' names, Messiah, means "anointed one." In Greek it is *christos*, or Christ. It refers to Jesus' role as spiritual deliverer, the One who set all of God's children free from sin and death. Jesus said, "I, the Messiah, came to save the lost" (Matt. 18:11 TLB).

---

8 White Throne

When Jesus ascended, He was the suffering Savior. When He returns, He will be the Righteous Judge. At the white throne judgment, He will acknowledge tribulation survivors' decisions regarding faith in Him and send them to eternal separation or salvation. Believers will be judged for reward or lack of reward (see 1 Cor. 3:14–15).

the disciples in the gospels of Matthew, Mark, and Luke. The Epistles inspired by the Holy Spirit add insight. Have no doubt, He is coming and His timing is perfect. Let's keep "looking for the blessed hope and glorious appearing of our great God and Savior Jesus Christ" (Titus 2:13).

LISTEN TO ...

You may juggle human laws, you may fool with human courts, but there is a judgment to come, and from it there is no appeal.

—*Orin Philip Gifford*

DAY 5
Watch and Work

New Zealand is a cool place with nice scenery, great people, and a very tech-enabled society. And now it's even better as they have a fruit ripeness sensor that tells shoppers how ripe fruit is before they buy it. The RipeSense is a sticker on the package that uses the aroma of the enclosed fruit to determine the ripeness factor. How practical is that?[11]

Jesus offered the sight test concerning the end of times. He asked His disciples to look at the fig tree to see how the heavenly timeline develops. It seems that Jesus chose the tree carefully. Earlier in His ministry, He had cursed a fig tree for failing to bear fruit. Now He pointed to a fig tree ready to bloom.

The fruit of the fig was well-known to the listeners. It was (and is) one of the favorite foods in the East and was a considerable article of commerce. When fig trees failed to produce, it was a national calamity. The people believed figs' productiveness was a token of peace and symbolized God's divine favor. The fig tree differs from most other fruit trees in that its fruit is green and inconspicuously concealed among leaves until near the time of ripening. Symbolically, when the fig tree begins to bloom, Jesus will finally come to establish His perfect reign of peace, bestowing His divine favor on those who have believed.

LIFT UP ...

Father, I am so grateful for Your Word! Help me to keep it hidden my heart so I'll be ready to see You. Amen.

LOOK AT ...

Having answered the disciples' questions, Jesus turned His attention to the parable of the Fig Tree. The fig often symbolizes the Hebrew nation. By linking the parable of the Fig Tree with His discussion of the end times, Jesus linked Israel's fate with end-time events. He was clear that when the things He spoke of in previous verses began to happen in Israel, it would be wise to look for the coming of the Messiah. For a time, it was difficult for believers to understand these parables, because the state of Israel was disbanded and the

LEARN ABOUT ...

I Go Forth

Jesus used the fig tree to emphasize a point, comparing a tree found in nature with the events of nations. Some commentators believe the fig tree refers to the nation of Israel blossoming back to life; others believe it simply refers to world events coming to pass as Jesus predicted.

---

3 Generation

The word *generation* can mean those living at the same time as or descendents of a common ancestor. The generation alive following Christ's death saw the fulfillment of prophecy when Jerusalem was destroyed in AD 70. The generation alive when the unprecedented labor pains begin will see the second coming of Christ.

people were dispersed. However, in 1948 Israel was once again gathered together as a nation. These prophecies and parables prove that God's Word is true and His promises to His people are solid. These timeless stories help us to apply the truths of the prophecies spoken by Jesus.

READ MARK 23:28–37.

"Now learn this parable from the fig tree: When its branch has already become tender, and puts forth leaves, you know that summer is near. So you also, when you see these things happening, know that it is near—at the doors! Assuredly, I say to you, this generation will by no means pass away till all these things take place. Heaven and earth will pass away, but My words will by no means pass away. But of that day and hour no one knows, not even the angels in heaven, nor the Son, but only the Father. Take heed, watch and pray; for you do not know when the time is. It is like a man going to a far country, who left his house and gave authority to his servants, and to each his work, and commanded the doorkeeper to watch. Watch therefore, for you do not know when the master of the house is coming—in the evening, at midnight, at the crowing of the rooster, or in the morning—lest, coming suddenly, he find you sleeping. And what I say to you, I say to all: Watch!" Mark 13:28–37

1. a. What do we learn from the fig tree about the cycle of nature?

    b. What do you think this represents?

2. a. Based on everything we've learned this week, what do you think the phrase "it is near" refers to and why?

    b. How did Jesus reiterate the urgency?

3. a. How confident was Jesus that these events would take place?

    b. When would they occur?

4. a. Jesus' return indicates that some things will pass away and others will not. What will end?

   b. What will never end?

5. a. Regarding the day and hour when Jesus returns, who is the only one who knows when it will be?

   b. Why is that important?

   c. What admonitions did Jesus give in preparation for that day? Why?

6. Now we turn to another story about a man.

   a. Where was the man going?

   b. To whom did he give authority, and what did he expect?

   c. What did he command the doorkeeper to do?

   d. Who do you think the man, the servants, and the doorkeeper represent and why?

7. Summarize Jesus' distinct warning about being watchful.

LIVE OUT ...

8. Heaven and earth will pass away, but God's Word will endure forever. How often do you turn to His Word for guidance?

   ❏ Daily ❏ Weekly ❏ Monthly ❏ Yearly ❏ In crisis

LEARN ABOUT ...

4 God's Word

It is impossible for God's Word to be destroyed or altered. Jesus showed His reverence for Scripture by quoting the Old Testament sixty-four times. He said, "The Scripture cannot be broken" (John 10:35) and "It is easier for heaven and earth to pass away than for one tittle of the law to fail" (Luke 16:17).

5 Guard

Jesus warned believers to be on guard in two ways: watch and pray. *Watch* is a call to stay awake and be alert. *Pray* emphasizes the need for divine intervention. Paul told believers to "watch, stand fast in the faith, be brave, be strong" (1 Cor. 16:13).

8 Guidance

Since time began, the heavens have spoken of God's majesty. Everyone everywhere can gaze upward to see God's creative power: "The heavens declare the glory of God" (Ps.19:1). However, the best place to seek divine guidance is God's Word: "Your word is a lamp to my feet, and a light to my path" (Ps. 119:105).

9. a. The man called some to be servants and some to be doorkeepers. How has God encouraged you to be more of a servant as you've studied the parables?

   b. Now read 1 Timothy 6:20, and talk about how you can be the doorkeeper of your heart and home.

10. a. Jesus encouraged His followers to "Watch!" Fill in the following chart to discover what should accompany your watching.

SCRIPTURE	WATCH AND WHAT?
Habakkuk 1:5	
Luke 21:36	
Acts 20:31	
1 Corinthians 16:13	

   b. Journal about which of the Scriptures God used to nudge you to actively watch for His return. How will you obey?

o o ● o o

It's hard to believe we've already reached the end of our study in the parables. Our prayer is that they've drawn you closer to Jesus as you've studied the very stories He told His followers. How fitting that we end with the story of Christ's second coming.

A West African student wanted to know more about what Jesus says when He shouts for believers to join Him in the clouds. What does He yell out? So he asked his Bible college teacher in California. The teacher wanted to leave the question unanswered, to tell the student that we must not overinterpret the Bible or go past what Scripture has revealed. But the student persisted: "Paul says 'The Lord Himself will descend from heaven with a shout' (1 Thess. 4:16); I would like to know what that command will be." Gregory Fisher wrote this of the encounter:

My mind wandered to an encounter I had earlier in the day with a refugee from the Liberian civil war. The man, a high school principal, told me how he was apprehended by a two-man death squad. After several hours of terror, he narrowly escaped. After hiding in the bush for two days, he was able to find his family and flee to a neighboring country. The escape cost him dearly: two of his children lost their lives. I also saw flashbacks of the beggars that I pass each morning on the way to the office. Every day I see how poverty destroys dignity. I am haunted by the vacant eyes of people who have lost all hope. "Enough," I said. "He will shout 'Enough!' when He returns." A look of surprise crossed the face of the student. "What do you mean, enough?" "Enough. Enough sin. Enough evil. Enough suffering. Enough starvation. Enough terror. Enough death. Enough indignity. Enough lives trapped in hopelessness. Enough sickness and disease."[12]

Jesus has promised to come soon. And He always keeps His promises. As a student of His Word, you now are responsible to walk in obedience so you'll be ready for His coming. When Jesus finally declares that "enough is enough," will you be ready to meet Him in the air? We pray you'll be there.

LISTEN TO ...

He was God and man in one person, that God and man might be happy together again.

—*George Whitefield*

notes

Definitions are taken from Biblesoft PC Study Bible, Version 4.2b, © 1988–2004: *The New Unger's Bible Dictionary, Nelson's Bible Dictionary, Vine's Expository Dictionary of New Testament Words, Vine's Expository Dictionary of Biblical Words,* and *Strong's Greek/Hebrew Definitions.*

INTRODUCTION

1 G. Campbell Morgan, *The Parables and Metaphors of Our Lord* (Old Tappan, NJ: Revell, 1953) 17.

LESSON 1: ROOT DETERMINES FRUIT

1 Warren Wiersbe, *Windows on the Parables* (Wheaton, IL: Victor Books, 1979), 12.

2 "Encouragement," Index #1019, *Bible Illustrator for Windows* (Copyright © 2008 FindEx.com, Inc., and its licensors, used by permission), adapted.

3 "Buried Treasure," Index #1019, *Bible Illustrator for Windows* (Copyright © 2008 FindEx.com, Inc., and its licensors, used by permission), adapted.

4 Walt Meier, "Gry, Gry, Everywhere, and Not a Clue in Sight," http://www.word-detective.com/gry.html (accessed November 14, 2008).

5 "Death," Index #2158–2162, *Bible Illustrator for Windows* (Copyright © 2008 FindEx.com, Inc., and its licensors, used by permission), adapted.

6 "Prophecy," Index # 2889–2894, *Bible Illustrator for Windows* (Copyright © 2008 FindEx.com, Inc., and its licensors, used by permission), adapted.

7 *The New Unger's Bible Dictionary* (Chicago: Moody Press, 1988), adapted.

8 "Salvation: Only Through Christ," Index #3117, *Bible Illustrator for Windows* (Copyright © 2008 FindEx.com, Inc., and its licensors, used by permission), adapted.

9 "Wrong Choices," *Bible Illustrator for Windows* (Copyright © 2008 FindEx.com, Inc., and its licensors, used by permission), adapted.

10 "Fruitfulness," Index # 1336–1339, *Bible Illustrator for Windows,* version 3.0F (Parsons Technology, 1998), adapted.

LESSON 2: LOOKS CAN BE DECEIVING

1 James S. Hewett, *Illustrations Unlimited* (Wheaton, IL: Tyndale House Publishers, Inc., 1988), 288–289.

2 Simon J. Kistemaker, *The Parables: Understanding the Stories Jesus Told* (Grand Rapids: Baker Books, 2002), 238.

3 Author unknown, "American Notes Espionage," *Time*, March 3, 1986, www.time.com (accessed July 8, 2005).

4 James Montgomery Boice, *The Parables of Jesus* (Chicago: Moody Press, 1983), 22.

5 "Counterfeit: 'That's Not Jade!'" *Infosearch*, version 4.11d, www.infosearch.com (Arlington: The Computer Assistant, 1996), adapted.

6 John F. Walvoord and Roy B. Zuck, *The Bible Knowledge Commentary: New Testament* (Colorado Springs, CO: David C. Cook, 1984), 49.

7 Margena A. Christian, "When to Keep a Secret and When to Tell," December 22, 2003, findarticles.com (accessed July 17, 2005), adapted.

8 *Merriam-Webster's Collegiate Dictionary,* 11th ed., s.v. "Master."

9 "Counterfeit: Jewels of Glass," *Infosearch*, version 4.11d, www.infosearch.com (Arlington: The Computer Assistant, 1996), adapted.

10 Warren Wiersbe, *Be Loyal* (Colorado Springs, CO: David C. Cook, 1980), 84.

11 Penny Pierce Rose, *A Garden of Friends* (Ventura, CA: Regal/Gospel Light, 2005), 19, adapted.

12 Skip Heitzig, *History's Last Chapter* (Albuquerque: Connection Communications, 1998), 234.

LESSON 3: WHAT GOES AROUND COMES AROUND

1 Author unknown, "A Passing Phrase," January 1, 1998, www.hagshama.org.il/en/resources/view.asp?id=192, adapted.

2 "Counterfeit: Able to Forgive," *Infosearch*, version 4.11d, www.infosearch.com (Arlington: The Computer Assistant, 1996), adapted.

3 United States Attorney David E. Nahmias, Northern District of Georgia, "Crutchfield Sentenced to Life for Shooting Postal Worker," www.usdoj.gov/usao/gan/press (accessed January 5, 2006).

4 John MacArthur, *Matthew 16—23: The MacArthur New Testament Commentary* (Chicago: Moody Press, 1988), 147–148.

5 Robert J. Grossman, "The Five-Finger Bonus," October 2003, www.shrm.org (accessed September 10, 2005), used by permission.

6 "The Woodman and the Serpent," Aesop's Fables Online, www.aesopfables.com, adapted.

7 Chris Lutes, "What to Do When You're Angry," *Campus Life,* January 1991, 54, adapted.

8 R. C. Trench, *Notes on the Parables of Our Lord* (Grand Rapids: Baker, 1979), 58.

9 *Matthew Henry's Commentary*, in *PC Study Bible*, version 4.2b (Seattle: Biblesoft, 2004), adapted.

10 Author unknown, "Christians in Crisis," christiansincrisis.net (accessed September 10, 2005), adapted.

11 "Counterfeit: Turning the Other Cheek, " *Infosearch*, version 4.11d, www.infosearch.com (Arlington: The Computer Assistant, 1996), adapted.

12 Floyd H. Barackman, *Practical Christian Theology* (Grand Rapids: Kregel, 2002), 405.

13 Richard Anthony, comp., "Writings from Corrie ten Boom," http://www.ecclesia.org/truth/corrie.html, date unknown (accessed December 27, 2008).

14 C. Thomas Hilton, "Who Escapes Condemnation?" *Clergy Journal,* March 1988, 12–13.

LESSON 4: ALL'S FAIR IN GOD'S LOVE AND WORD

1 *Matthew Henry's Commentary on the Whole Bible: New Modern Edition*, Electronic Database (Peabody, MA: Hendrickson Publishers, Inc., 1991).

2 Ruth Harms Calkin, *Tell Me Again, Lord, I Forget* (Colorado Springs, CO: David C. Cook, 1974).

3 "Expectation Corner," Index #1188, *Bible Illustrator for Windows,* version 3.0F (Parsons Technology, 1998), adapted.

4 John MacArthur, *The MacArthur Study Bible* (Nashville: Word, 2005), 1429.

5 "Waiting for the Lord," Index #2693, *Bible Illustrator for Windows* (Copyright © 2008 FindEx.com, Inc., and its licensors, used by permission), adapted.

6 "Consistent," *Infosearch*, version 4.11d, www.infosearch.com (Arlington: The Computer Assistant, 1996), adapted.

7 "The Tate in Your Church," Index #726–761, *Bible Illustrator for Windows* (Copyright © 2008 FindEx.com, Inc., and its licensors, used by permission), adapted.

8 Spiros Zodhiates, *The Complete Word Study Dictionary: New Testament* (Chattanooga, TN: AMG Publishers, 1992), 379.

9 Ibid.

10 W. Y. Fullerton, "Charles Haddon Spurgeon: A Biography," 2001, spurgeon.org (accessed September 25, 2005).

11 "Providence United Methodist Church," 1999, http://homepages.rootsweb.ancestry.com/~jmack/photos/providen.htm (accessed July 18, 2008).

12 Simon J. Kistemaker, *The Parables: Understanding the Stories Jesus Told* (Grand Rapids: Baker Books, 1980), 76.

13 *Jamieson, Fausset, and Brown Commentary*, in *PC Study Bible*, version 4.2b (Seattle: Biblesoft, 2004), adapted.

LESSON 5: ACTIONS SPEAK LOUDER THAN WORDS

1 "New Coat," *Infosearch*, version 4.11d, www.infosearch.com (Arlington: The Computer Assistant, 1996), adapted.

2 *Matthew Henry's Commentary on the Whole Bible: New Modern Edition*, Electronic Database (Peabody, MA: Hendrickson Publishers, Inc., 1991).

3 "Love Tested," Index #2614–2619, *Bible Illustrator for Windows* (Copyright © 2008 FindEx.com, Inc., and its licensors, used by permission), adapted.

4 Simon J. Kistemaker, *The Parables: Understanding the Stories Jesus Told* (Grand Rapids: Baker Books, 1980), 84.

5 "Constitutional Hypocrisy," Index #3480–3484, *Bible Illustrator for Windows* (Copyright © 2008 FindEx.com, Inc., and its licensors, used by permission), adapted.

6 Dorothy L. Espelage, *Bullying in Early Adolescence: The Role of the Peer Group*, ERIC Digests, www.ericdigests.org/2003-4/bullying.html (accessed September 28, 2005).

7 Ibid.

8 "Rejection: The Despised Benefactor," *Infosearch*, version 4.11d, www.infosearch.com (Arlington: The Computer Assistant, 1996), adapted.

9 Author unknown, "Crop Rotation," www.wikipedia.org (accessed September 29, 2005).

10 *Nelson's Illustrated Bible Dictionary*, in *PC Study Bible*, version 4.2b (Seattle: Biblesoft, 2004), adapted.

11 John MacArthur, *The MacArthur Study Bible* (Nashville: Word**,** 2006), 1555.

12 Leonard B. Hertz, "Grafting and Budding Fruit Trees," 1993, www.umn.edu (accessed September 29, 2005).

LESSON 6: ALWAYS BE PREPARED

1 "Commentary," *Today in the Word*, April 1989, www.sermonillustrations.com, 27 (accessed October 9, 2005).

2 Stone Phillips, "Can Humility, Faith Be Good for Business?" February 28, 2004, www.msnbc.msn.com (accessed October 9, 2005), adapted, used by permission.

3 "Hypocrisy: Counting the Change," *Infosearch*, version 4.11d, www.infosearch.com (Arlington: The Computer Assistant, 1996), adapted.

4 Herbert Lockyer, *All the Parables of the Bible*, (Grand Rapids: Zondervan, 1963), 237–238, adapted.

5 "Don't Blow Yourself Out," Index #2173, *Bible Illustrator for Windows* (Copyright © 2008 FindEx.com, Inc., and its licensors, used by permission), adapted.

6 Herbert Lockyer, *All the Parables of the Bible*, (Grand Rapids: Zondervan, 1963), 238, adapted.

7 Skip Heitzig, Tape #2405 (Albuquerque: Connection Communications).

8 "Watch and Wait," Index #1348, *Bible Illustrator for Windows*, version 3.0F (Parson Technology, 1998), adapted.

9 "Second Coming of Christ," Index #1344–1350, *Bible Illustrator for Windows*, version 3.0F (Parsons Technology, 1998), adapted.

10 John F. Walvoord and Roy B. Zuck, *The Bible Knowledge Commentary: New Testament*, (Colorado Springs, CO: David C. Cook, 1984), 80.

11 Spiros Zodhiates, *The Complete Word Study Dictionary: New Testament* (Chattanooga, TN: AMG Publishers, 1992), 510.

12 "Second Coming: What Would He Find?" Infosearch, version 4.11d, www.infosearch. com (Arlington: The Computer Assistant, 1996), adapted.

LESSON 7: USE IT OR LOSE IT

1 "The Miser," Aesop's Fables Online, www.aesopfables.com, adapted.

2 Herbert Lockyer, *All the Parables of the Bible* (Grand Rapids: Zondervan, 1963), 242.

3 U.S. Census Bureau, 2000 Census, Table DP-3. Profile of Selected Economic Characteristics: Male Worker Full Time Year Round, Table DP-3, p. 3, http://censtats. census.gov/data/US/01000.pdf (accessed December 28, 2008).

4 Edwin W. Kopf, "Florence Nightingale as Statistician," *Publications of the American Statistical Association* (American Statistical Association, 1918), 388–404.

5 "God Did It All," Index #3897, (Copyright © 2008 FindEx.com, Inc., and its licensors, used by permission), adapted.

6 Alexandra Marks, "How One Airline Flew Back into the Black," *Christian Science Monitor*, July 25, 2005, http://www.csmonitor.com/2005/0725/ p01s03-usec.html (accessed October 18, 2005).

7 "Redemption," Index #2979, *Bible Illustrator for Windows* (Copyright © 2008 FindEx. com, Inc., and its licensors, used by permission), adapted.

8 "Reward: Not Cash and Carry," *Infosearch*, version 4.11d, www.infosearch.com (Arlington: The Computer Assistant, 1996), adapted.

9 "Home," Index #1670, *Bible Illustrator for Windows*, version 3.0F (Parsons Technology, 1998), adapted.

10 "Greed," Index #2131–2133, *Bible Illustrator for Windows*, version 3.0F (Parsons Technology, 1998), adapted.

11 *Matthew Henry Commentary*, in *PC Study Bible*, version 4.2b (Seattle: Biblesoft, 2004).

12 *QuickVerse SermonBuilder*, *The Quotable Spurgeon*, version 4.0 (Copyright © 2005 FindEx. com, Inc., and its licensors, used by permission).

13 Ken Botton, "Are We Burning or Are We Just Bushed?" *Interest*, March 1995, 2.

14 *Nelson's Illustrated Bible Dictionary,* in *PC Study Bible,* version 4.2b (Seattle: Biblesoft, 2004), adapted.

15 "Faithfulness: The Harvest Is Sure," *Infosearch,* version 4.11d, www.infosearch.com (Arlington: The Computer Assistant, 1996), adapted.

LESSON 8: THE BEST THINGS IN LIFE AREN'T THINGS

1 "Cheerful Giving," *Infosearch,* version 4.11d, www.infosearch.com (Arlington: The Computer Assistant, 1996), adapted.

2 "Counterfeit: For Want of Things," *Infosearch,* version 4.11d, www.infosearch.com (Arlington: The Computer Assistant, 1996), adapted.

3 James S. Hewett, *Illustrations Unlimited* (Wheaton, IL: Tyndale, 1988), 372, adapted.

4 "Selfishness," Index #3222–3223, *Bible Illustrator for Windows,* version 3.0F (Parsons Technology, 1998), adapted.

5 Author unknown, "The Skylark's Bargain," July 30, 1997, www.dailywisdom/archives/old/1997/07/dw-07-30-97.html (accessed October 29, 2005).

6 Author unknown, "A Spotty Scorecard," December 16, 2004, www.unicef.org.

7 "Contentment," *Bible Illustrator for Windows,* version 3.0F (Parsons Technology, 1998), adapted.

8 *The Wycliffe Bible Commentary,* Electronic Database (Chicago: Moody Press, 1962).

9 *National & International Religious Report* 8, no. 10 (May 2, 1994): 8.

10 Author unknown, "John Wanamaker," http://www.pbs.org/wgbh/theymadeamerica/whomade/wanamaker_hi.html.

11 Author unknown, "Death of Soul-winning Merchant, John Wanamaker," June 2007, http://chi.gospelcom.net/DAILYF/2002/12/daily-12-12-2002.shtml.

12 "Can't Take It with You," *Bible Illustrator for Windows,* version 3.0F (Parsons Technology, 1998), adapted.

LESSON 9: THERE'S NO PLACE LIKE HOME

1 James Hewett, *Bible Illustrator for Windows,* version 3.0F (Parsons Technology, 1998), adapted.

2 Herbert Lockyer, *All the Parables of the Bible* (Grand Rapids: Zondervan, 1963), 284.

3 Skip Heitzig, Tape #2481 (Albuquerque: Connection Communications).

4 Thomas Spurgeon, "Compared to a Flock," Index #746-748, *Bible Illustrator for Windows,* version 3.0F (Parsons Technology, 1998), adapted.

5 John MacArthur, *Grace to You Newsletter,* April 15, 1993, www.christianglobe.com (accessed November 2, 2005).

6 Herbert Lockyer, *All the Parables of the Bible* (Grand Rapids: Zondervan, 1963), 282.

7 Simon J. Kistemaker, *The Parables: Understanding the Stories Jesus Told* (Grand Rapids: Baker, 1980), 178.

8 Herbert Lockyer, *All the Parables of the Bible* (Grand Rapids: Zondervan, 1963), 286.

9 Kenneth W. Osbeck, *101 Hymn Stories* (Grand Rapids: Kregel Publications), 52.

10 Doug Kutilek, "As I See It," February 2000, http://www.kjvonly.org/aisi/aisi_archives.htm (accessed November 3, 2005).

11 C. S. Lewis, "Surprised By Joy," *The Essential C. S. Lewis*, ed. Lyle W. Dorsett (New York: Collier Books, 1988), 50.

12 Simon J. Kistemaker, *The Parables: Understanding the Stories Jesus Told* (Grand Rapids, Baker Books, 1980), 180.

13 "The Walk of Love," Index #1643–1657, *Bible Illustrator for Windows,* version 3.0F (Parsons Technology, 1998), adapted.

14 "Not Everyone Was Festive," Index #1643–1657, *Bible Illustrator for Windows,* version 3.0F (Parsons Technology, 1998), adapted.

15 "Jealousy: Fable of the Jealous Eagle," *Infosearch*, version 4.11d, www.infosearch.com (Arlington: The Computer Assistant, 1996), adapted.

LESSON 10: GOOD THINGS COME TO THOSE WHO WAIT

1 Shirley O. Corriher, "Choosing Fruit That's Truly Ripe," *Fine Cooking* 28: 22–23, The Taunton Press, http://www.taunton.com/finecooking/articles/choosing-ripe-fruit.aspx (accessed December 30, 2008).

2 Skip Heitzig, Tape #2446 (Albuquerque: Connection Communications).

3 John MacArthur, *The MacArthur Study Bible* (Nashville: Thomas Nelson, 2005), 1491.

4 "Topic: War, Warfare," Sermons.org, October 15, 2008, http://www.sermons.org/war.html.

5 Author unknown, "El Chichon," geocities.com, May 30, 1998, http://www.geocities.com/RainForest/Canopy/5236/el_chichon.htm (accessed October 9, 2005).

6 John F. Walvoord and Roy B. Zuck, *The Bible Knowledge Commentary: New Testament* (Colorado Springs, CO: David C. Cook, 1984), 169.

7 "Second Coming of Christ," Index #1344–1350, *Bible Illustrator for Windows* (Copyright © 2008 FindEx.com, Inc., and its licensors, used by permission), adapted.

8 "Waiting: The Boss Might Come," *Infosearch*, version 4.11d, www.infosearch.com (Arlington: The Computer Assistant, 1996), adapted.

9 John F. Walvoord, *Every Prophecy of the Bible* (Colorado Springs, CO: David C. Cook, 1999), 390.

10 "Waiting: Tiptoe Expectancy," *Infosearch*, version 4.11d, www.infosearch.com (Arlington: The Computer Assistant, 1996), adapted.

11 RipeSense, November 6, 2008, http://www.ripesense.com.

12 Gregory Fisher, "The Loud Command: Enough!" elbourne.org, http://elbourne.org/sermons/index.mv?illustration+4887 (accessed November 10, 2005).

About the Authors

Lenya Heitzig is an award-winning author and sought-after speaker at conferences and retreats worldwide. She is the coauthor of the first two books in the Fresh Life Series: *Live Fearlessly: A Study in the Book of Joshua* and *Live Intimately: Lessons from the Upper Room.* Serving as the director of Women at Calvary, one of the core ministries at Calvary Albuquerque, she delights in seeing God's Word do His work in the lives of women. Her husband, Skip Heitzig, is the senior pastor of the fourteen-thousand-member congregation that has been ranked one of the fastest-growing churches in America. She received the Gold Medallion Award for coauthoring *Pathway to God's Treasure: Ephesians,* which also includes *Pathway to God's Plan: Esther* and *Pathway to Living Faith: James* in this same series. She also contributed a number of devotionals to *The New Women's Devotional Bible,* which was a finalist in the 2007 Christian Book Awards. Her most recent book, *Holy Moments,* published by Regal, enlightens the reader to see God's hand of providence move miraculously in daily life. Lenya loves jogging with her dog, Winston, as well as sampling pastries wherever she goes, fulfilling her motto "Run so you can eat!" She lives in Albuquerque, New Mexico, with her husband Skip. She has a son, Nathan, and a daughter-in-law, Janaé, who serve the high school group at Calvary Albuquerque.

Penny Rose is the Gold Medallion Award–winning coauthor of *Pathway to God's Treasure: Ephesians,* as well as *Pathway to God's Plan: Esther* and *Pathway to Living Faith: James* published by Tyndale House. She also coauthored *Live Intimately: Lessons from the Upper Room* and *Live Fearlessly: A Study in the Book of Joshua,* the first two books in the Fresh Life Series. She contributed to Zondervan's *True Identity: The Bible for Women* and was the general editor and a devotional writer for its *New Women's Devotional Bible,* a finalist for the 2007 Christian Book Award. She wrote *A Garden of Friends* published by Regal as an ode to biblical friendship. A longtime member of the Women at Calvary Steering Committee, Penny thrives on teaching at conferences and retreats nationwide. Penny lives in Albuquerque, New Mexico, with her husband, Kerry, a pastor at Calvary Albuquerque. They have two daughters, Erin and Ryan, and one son, Kristian. She loves to spend time with family and friends, read, travel, and take naps.

Live Relationally: Lessons from the Women of Genesis   ISBN: 978-1-4347-6748-6
Live Deeply: A Study in the Parables of Jesus   ISBN: 978-1-4347-9986-9
Live Intimately: Lessons from the Upper Room   ISBN: 978-1-4347-6790-5
Live Fearlessly: A Study in the Book of Joshua   ISBN: 978-1-4347-9941-8

To learn more visit our Web site or
a Christian bookstore near you.

800.323.7543   •   DavidCCook.com